Killing Ground on
OKINAWA

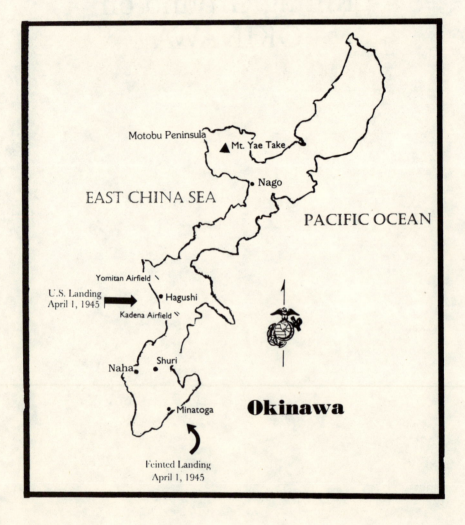

Motobu Peninsula

▲ Mt. Yae Take

EAST CHINA SEA

• Nago

PACIFIC OCEAN

Yomitan Airfield

U.S. Landing
April 1, 1945 ➡️ • Hagushi

Kadena Airfield

• Shuri

Naha •

• Minatoga

Okinawa

Feinted Landing
April 1, 1945

Killing Ground on

OKINAWA

The Battle for Sugar Loaf Hill

James H. Hallas

PRAEGER

Westport, Connecticut
London

This book is for Stovall, Courtney, Little Bit Davis, Ruess, Fincke, Harry, Pinner, Tucker, Zilch, Dean, Dancause, English, Bartelme, Stoney Craig, Perrault, Baranek, Nealon, Munier, Costa, Whitman, Kowalski, McDonough, Roden, Possessky, Howard, Myers, Shumann, Woodhouse, Harwick, Siroky, Goff, Conti, Klusmeier, Albano, Irish George Murphy, Wilmot, Mullooly, Outen, Cullen, Doyle, Allen, Gaillard, Wallace, McKee, Coomer, Donnell, Zuk and all the others who didn't come home . . . and for all their buddies who left a part of themselves with them. *Semper Fidelis*.

In thy faint slumbers I by thee have watch'd
And heard thee murmur tales of iron wars . . .
                    —Shakespeare, *Henry IV*

Contents

Photo essay follows p. 94

Maps

Preface

To thousands of combat veterans, Okinawa will be forever remembered as a series of hellish terrain features with names ranging from the wonderfully exotic to the grotesquely incongruous: Kakazu Ridge, Shuri, Wana Draw, Dakeshi Ridge, The Chocolate Drop, Love Hill. . . .

For the 6th Marine Division, it was Sugar Loaf Hill.

Over a period of seven days in 1945, from 12 to 18 May, the 6th Marine Division suffered over 2,000 casualties as it struggled to seize this nondescript hill on the western flank of the Japanese Shuri Line. Students of the battle credit the Marines with at least 11 assaults on the hill before it was finally captured. Losses were horrendous. Companies became platoons. Platoons became squads. Squads disappeared in the maelstrom of Sugar Loaf. At the end of the campaign for Okinawa, one gunnery sergeant in the 22d Marines checked his unit roster and found that his company, including replacements, had lost over 500 men—twice its normal complement. Put more directly, the company had been wiped out twice over.

Such losses made Okinawa the bloodiest land battle of the Pacific war. U.S. ground forces lost 7,613 killed or missing, 31,312 wounded, and 26,211 "other" casualties during the 82-day campaign. Naval forces lost another 4,320 killed and 7,312 wounded in their attempt to provide supply and gun support for the land operation. 6th Marine Division casualties totaled 8,227 killed or wounded. In the division's three infantry regiments, two out of every three men fell.

There is no question Sugar Loaf was critical in the overall context of the campaign; so too were the actions of the 1st Marine Division at Wana Draw, the 7th Infantry Division at the Rocky Crags, the 96th Infantry Division at Conical Hill and the 77th at Ishimmi Ridge. Though it may not have been clear to the riflemen with their faces buried in the dirt, none of these actions took place in a vacuum.

Sugar Loaf's unique significance was its position anchoring the western end of General Mitsuru Ushijima's Shuri Defense Line. A breakthrough at Sugar Loaf toward the Okinawan capital of Naha would uncover the Japanese flank and potentially force a withdrawal or collapse. All too aware of that threat, the Japanese reacted with great ferocity to any effort to occupy Sugar Loaf and its supporting hills.

The U.S. casualty list testifies to the enemy's success. That same list summons up one of the great nagging questions of the Okinawan campaign: why did General Simon Bolivar Buckner, the American ground force commander, refuse to approve an amphibious landing *behind* the Japanese defense line? Such a landing was urged on more than one occasion by a number of ranking officers, both Army and Marine, but was repeatedly denied. Buckner's critics argue that such a landing would have substantially reduced U.S. casualties and hastened the conquest of the island. Opponents say such an end run was simply not feasible. It is an argument which continues to this day.

A note is in order here on unit organization. The 6th Marine Division landed on Okinawa with 23,832 men. Among its components were three infantry regiments—the 4th Marines, 22d Marines and 29th Marines—each numbering 3,412 officers and men[1]—an artillery regiment, a tank battalion and various engineers, military police, transportation and support troops. Each infantry regiment was composed of three battalions (996 men), which, in turn, were made up of three rifle companies (242 men), along with headquarters personnel. Each rifle company was composed of three rifle platoons of 42 men each, a machine gun platoon and a 60 mm mortar section. Each platoon consisted of three 13–man rifle squads, plus platoon headquarters.

For the sake of clarity, I have at times resorted to a commonly accepted shorthand for unit designations. In this "shorthand," a unit such as G Company, 2d Battalion, 22d Marines would be referred to as G/2/22. Similarly, the 1st Battalion, 22d Marines, would be referred to simply as 1/22.

Combat as a rule is confusing, chaotic. The battle for Sugar Loaf was no exception. Eyewitness accounts of incidents vary, sometimes dramatically. Some fictions have become "fact" through repetition over the years. In many cases officers became casualties before they could set down an official record of events. In later years, memory fails or becomes selective. I have tried to reconcile these discrepancies as best I could in light of the available information. Any errors are mine alone.

In the course of my research, I have consulted unit histories, personal narratives, unit journals and special action reports and combat footage of the battle. But the heart of the book springs from the interviews so generously provided by nearly 100 veterans of Sugar Loaf. I would like to express special gratitude to Owen Stebbins, who took a great interest in this project and provided far more help and encouragement than I could reasonably have expected. Thanks also to Bill Pierce, another true believer, the 6th Marines Division Association public relations chief, historian, archivist and keeper of the flame, who never asked, "What do you want?" but always, "What do you need?"

I have become acquainted with many Marines in the course of researching this book. Like men in general, they vary much—the long, the short and the tall, the quiet and the boisterous, those whole and the wounded of body or spirit. They count among their number self-made millionaires, former salesmen, two Marine generals, a doctor, farmers, truck drivers, a teacher, a pharmacist, a state Supreme Court justice, two ministers, an aerospace engineer and at least one ex-convict.

Despite their varied paths in life, all have one thing in common: they are extraordinarily proud to have served as Marines. Their one request, 50 years after Sugar Loaf, is very simple, as expressed by the Sugar Loaf veteran who, half in tears at the memory of buddies long dead, choked out at the end of our interview: "Be careful and try to tell it like it is . . . as much as you can find out. So the world can know."

I have tried, in my small way, to do justice to the indomitable spirit of the Sugar Loaf Marines. This is their story.

NOTE

1. Totals include naval personnel, primarily corpsmen: 11 officers and 134 enlisted per regiment, 2 officers and 40 corpsmen per battalion, along with assorted other assignments.

Chapter 1

The Reason Why

17 April 1945.

The grimy brown army truck wheezed along the narrow Okinawan road. In the back of the truck, open to the elements and the red dust billowing from the road, lay its cargo . . . dead men, unseeing and uncaring, each neatly packaged like a bundle of wrinkled green laundry.

Corpses were no novelty on Okinawa. Over the past two weeks thousands of men had been killed in the fighting on land and off shore. These particular unfortunates, each wrapped in a dark-green flashproof mattress cover, were sailors from the destroyer USS *Laffey*. The day before, standing picket duty for the invasion fleet off Okinawa, the *Laffey* had been attacked by a swarm of kamikazes. Blasted by bombs and struck by six kamikazes, the battered destroyer had miraculously survived the 79–minute battle, shooting down nine of the enemy aircraft.

The cost (and there was always a cost) was 31 dead or missing and 72 wounded. Now *Laffey*'s dead were on their way to the 6th Marine Division Cemetery, located on the island's western shore, overlooking the transport anchorage. In the front seat of the truck sat the living: the driver, an army corporal, accompanied by two naval officers, one of them a chaplain. As the truck pulled up to the cemetery, the corporal marveled at the scene before them. "Did you ever see so many stiffs? Just look. Don't even have time to cover 'em up," he blurted.

He was right. Lying on the red Okinawan clay were four long columns of shrouded dead. Hundreds of them. The burial detail, directed to stay 100 graves ahead was more than that number behind.

The *Laffey*'s dead were aligned with the fourth column. Empty sake bottles containing each man's identification was tucked inside his battle dress. "God is our refuge and strength," intoned the chaplain. "Though the earth be removed and though the mountains be carried into the midst of the sea . . . each to earth, ashes to ashes, dust to dust." In the near distance, the boom of artillery served as a reminder that the killing—on land and on sea—had only begun.

From the standpoint of plans and operations, the road to the 6th Marine Division Cemetery had begun seven months before.

Up until mid-1944, U.S. planners had expected to seize Formosa as a prelude to any invasion of the Japanese home islands. But at a three-day conference with the Joint Chiefs of Staff in late September 1944, Central Pacific Commander Admiral Chester Nimitz and others had argued forcefully for abandonment of the Formosa operation. Such an operation was unrealistic in terms of Pacific Theater resources, he argued. It was also unnecessary.

Instead of Formosa, Nimitz suggested allowing Southwest Pacific Commander General Douglas MacArthur to proceed with the liberation of Luzon and the Philippine Islands capital of Manila. His own Central Pacific forces would seize Okinawa in the Ryukyus and Iwo Jima in the Bonins, cutting Japan off from her oil supply lines and paving the way for an invasion of the enemy home islands.

After much discussion, the Joint Chiefs of Staff approved Nimitz's proposal. Central Pacific forces would take responsibility for the Iwo Jima and Okinawa operations. MacArthur would take responsibility for the seizure of Leyte, Luzon and the rest of the Philippines. Tentative invasion dates were 20 December 1944 for Luzon; 20 January 1945 for Iwo Jima; and 1 March 1945 for Okinawa. Delays in shipping subsequently forced changes in that timetable, with the Okinawa assault rescheduled for 1 April 1945.

Code named *Iceberg,* the invasion would ultimately involve about 548,000 men and nearly 1,500 ships. The initial assault force would number some 182,000 men—75,000 more than had hit the beaches in Normandy on D-Day the year before. Fifth Fleet Commander Admiral R. A. Spruance was designated as implementing commander of the operation under the strategic direction of Admiral Nimitz. Vice Admiral Richmond Kelly Turner, Commander Amphibian Forces Pacific Fleet, received command of the Joint Expeditionary Force. General Simon Bolivar Buckner, commanding the Tenth Army, was assigned to command the expeditionary troops for the amphibious phase of the operation.

Major components of the amphibious forces were III Amphibious Corps (IIIAC), commanded by Major General Roy S. Geiger as the landing force of the Northern Attack Force; and XXIV Corps under Major General John R. Hodge as the landing force of the Southern Attack Force. IIIAC consisted of the 1st Marine Division (Major General Pedro A. del Valle) and the 6th Marine Division (Major General Lemuel C. Shepherd, Jr.). XXIV Corps would consist of the 96th Infantry Division (Major General James Bradley) and the 7th Infantry Division (Major General Archibald V. Arnold).

The 77th Infantry Division (Major General Andrew D. Bruce) and the 2d Marine Division (Major General Thomas E. Watson) were assigned as the Landing Forces of the Western Islands Attack Group and the Demonstration Group, respectively. The 27th Infantry Division (Major General George W. Griner, Jr.) made up Buckner's floating reserve. The 81st Infantry Division (Major General Paul Mueller) was designated area reserve under Admiral Nimitz.

Few of those scores of thousands of men bound for Okinawa had ever heard of the place, first visited by Americans in 1853 when Commodore Matthew Perry negotiated establishment of a small base to provision U.S. ships. Located in the middle of the Ryukyu chain, Okinawa lay only 350 nautical miles from the Japanese home island of Kyushu, 330 miles from Formosa, and 450 miles from Shanghai. The largest island in the chain— which itself formed a barrier to the Japanese home islands—its location, anchorages, and airfields made it the ideal staging area for an invasion of Japan.

Okinawa is barely a third the size of Rhode Island. Sixty miles long, the island is 18 miles across at its widest point where the Motobu Peninsula extends into the East China Sea. Just below is the Ishikawa Isthmus, only two miles across, the narrowest part of the island. In 1944 the Ishikawa Isthmus was more than just a narrow land bridge; it divided Okinawa into two very different regions for military planners to deal with. To the north lay two thirds of the island's land mass, mountainous and heavily wooded with sheer coastal cliffs, all sparsely populated. In sharp contrast, the southern part of the island—except for a narrow rugged section just below the isthmus—was rolling and lightly wooded. Though broken by steep scarps and ravines, the hills rarely exceeded 500 feet in height. Heavily cultivated—the principal crops being sweet potatoes, sugar cane, and rice—the southern area was home to two thirds of the island's population.

It was also the site of Naha, the Okinawan capital, the main commercial center and chief port.

At the time of the U.S. invasion, Okinawa had a population of almost half a million, primarily farmers. The Japanese, who annexed the Ryukyus in 1879, considered Okinawa part of the homeland, and it was represented in the Diet as one of the country's 47 prefectures. Despite that standing—and the fact that thousands of Okinawans had been absorbed into the army—most mainland Japanese did not consider the Okinawans their social equals.

In ancient times, the Ryukyus had been a dependency of China and that influence remained evident. The language, though related to Japanese, is different enough to stand as a separate tongue, and the Okinawans themselves are shorter and fuller-faced than the Japanese. Their religion was a form of Chinese ancestor worship, and lyre-shaped tombs containing the ashes of their dead dotted the hillsides. Both Japanese and American troops would find they made handy pillboxes and shelters.

As late as 1939, the sole Japanese defense installations on Okinawa consisted of a small naval station at Naha and a navy airfield just to the south. A few hundred artillerymen arrived in 1941. Along with some lightly armed guard companies, and a few assorted naval and airfield maintenance personnel, they constituted the entire garrison for some three years.

But in the spring of 1944, as U.S. forces drove ever closer to the Japanese homeland, Okinawa took on a new importance and Imperial General Headquarters created the 32d Army with headquarters on Okinawa to defend the Ryukyus. By June 1944, as U.S. forces were seizing Japanese-held Saipan and preparing to invade Guam, reinforcements—ground, naval, and air—began to converge on Okinawa in significant numbers.

One of those units, the Japanese 44th Independent Mixed Brigade, lost over 5,000 men—all but about 600 of its complement—when its transport, the *Toyama Maru* was sunk by the submarine USS *Sturgeon* on 29 June. Imperial General Headquarters hastily sent the 15th Independent Infantry Regiment to Naha by air transport. By sea, came the 9th, 24th and 62d Infantry Divisions, though the 9th was later sent to Formosa. The 24th Division, brought in from Manchuria in August, consisted of 14,000 men, including several thousand Okinawan conscripts. The 62d Division, which arrived in June, numbered 12,000 troops, mostly infantry, and had fought against the Chinese in April and June in Northern Honan Province.

To head the newly strengthened 32d Army, in August 1944 Tokyo appointed 57-year-old Lieutenant General Mitsuru Ushijima. Quiet and reserved, almost fatherly, Ushijima had been an infantry unit commander during the campaign in Burma and was much respected by his subordinates. Prior to being named to lead the 32d Army, he had been serving as commandant of the Japanese Military Academy at Zama.

Ushijima's chief of staff and second in command was Lieutenant General Isamu Cho, an aggressive, short-tempered firebrand. Cho, a lover of strong drink and pretty women, was rash where Ushijima was controlled, fractious where Ushijima was serene, a strident jingoist where Ushijima was apolitical.

The third factor in the command equation was the Senior Operations officer, Colonel Hiromichi Yahara. Nicknamed "Sobersides," Yahara, 42, was intellectual and rational, more Western in outlook. A fine tactician, he considered war a science. He had graduated from the Military Academy's Class of 1923, attended the Japanese War College, spent nearly a year in the United States and served as a staff officer in China, Thailand, Malaya and Burma. He knew his business and much of the grief the Americans would later endure was of his engineering.

The assignment of Ushijima and Cho to the Okinawan command reflected the Japanese conviction—bolstered by the fall of Saipan in July—that U.S. forces planned to invade either Formosa, the Ryukyus, or the Bonins by the spring of 1945. Part of that prediction became reality when Iwo Jima, in the Bonins, was invaded that February. By the time of the American landing on Okinawa, six weeks later, Ushijima had about 100,000 troops at hand. These included 67,000 men in regular army units of the 32d Army (the 24th and 62d Divisions and the reconstituted 44th Independent Mixed Brigade); 9,000 men in the Naval Base Force; and about 24,000 Okinawan Home Guard fighters called *Boeitai.*

Despite the size of that garrison, there was little hope Ushijima would be able to crush an invasion, particularly after the departure of the crack 9th Division for Formosa in December. His force was essentially part of a delaying action. His men's lives would buy time for the defense of home islands, in the process inflicting as much punishment as possible on the Americans. The ground action would also tether U.S. naval forces to nearby waters where they could be destroyed by Japanese suicide planes, the soon-to-be notorious kamikazes. Isolated from naval support, the ground attack would bog down, creating stalemate and disrupting the planned invasion of Japan.

This concept of attrition would also be carried out on a lower tactical level. The Japanese had learned some hard lessons about American firepower over the past two and a half years, and Ushijima intended to spend his soldiers frugally. The ability of dug-in Japanese to inflict heavy casualties on attacking U.S. forces had already been demonstrated on Peleliu and at Iwo Jima. Ushijima would not attempt to defeat the Americans on the beaches where U.S. naval gunfire reigned supreme. Instead, strong defensive positions would be established inland.

U.S. operations on northern Okinawa would be generally uncontested. Ushijima would reserve his main strength for battle in the south. There he would rely on three successive defense lines beginning at the outer defense shell anchored by Kakazu Ridge and a number of other ridges about three and a half miles north of Shuri Castle, the ancient capital of Okinawa. The 32d Army's main defense zone was established in the hills and ridges running across the island like a wall just north of Naha on the west coast, through Shuri and on to Yonabaru on the east coast. The third line ran east from the town of Itoman to Gushichan, through the Yuza-Dake and Yaeju-Dake.

In an effort to buck up his troops for their coming trial, Ushijima's staff devised a resolute battle slogan:

> One Plane for One Warship.
> One Boat for One Ship.
> One Man for Ten of the Enemy
> or One Tank.

As anticipated by General Ushijima, U.S. planners decided to land across the Hagushi beaches on Okinawa's western coast, just below the Ishikawa Isthmus, less than ten miles north of Naha. III Amphibious Corps (IIIAC), made up of the 1st and 6th Marine Divisions, would land on the left. The 7th and 96th Infantry Divisions, under the XXIV Army Corps, would land on the right. The operation was to proceed in three phases. The first would involve the seizure of southern Okinawa and development of staging areas. Under phase 2, Ie Shima and the remainder of Okinawa would be captured. Under phase 3, the new positions were to be exploited and other islands in the Ryukyus would be captured.

Love Day, as the assault date was optimistically code named, was Easter Sunday, 1 April 1945. Seas were calm, skies clearing and temperatures a mild 75 degrees. Under the massed fire from 10 battleships, 9 cruisers, 23 destroyers and assorted other vessels, four U.S. divisions swept ashore, virtually unopposed. More than 16,000 combat troops were ashore in the first hour. By 1,000 hours, only 90 minutes after H-Hour, 6th Division Marines had occupied Yontan Airfield and some of the leathernecks were already indulging in a crap game. Army patrols from the 7th Infantry

Division had reached Kadena Airfield, also undefended; the 1st Marine Division and 96th Infantry Division were also virtually unopposed. "We were on Okinawa an hour and a half after H-Hour, without being shot at and hadn't even gotten our feet wet," reported the GI's favorite correspondent, Ernie Pyle, newly arrived from Europe to cover the Pacific War.

Tenth Army casualties for the assault totaled only 28 dead, 104 wounded, and 27 missing—less than any other major landing except Guadalcanal. By nightfall, the assault divisions held a beachhead over eight miles long and nearly three miles deep. This extraordinary good fortune continued over the next several days. The island was cut in half on L (Love Day) plus 1; by 3 April, the assault divisions began their pushes to the north and south. Most resistance was offered by local defense units and was easily brushed aside. There was little evidence of regular army forces. Gains were particularly impressive to the north where IIIAC was operating. The 1st Marine Division advanced so rapidly that by 3 April, it was 8 to 13 days ahead of the *Iceberg* timetable. Similarly, the 6th Marine Division was 12 days ahead of schedule.

Ground force commander Lieutenant General Simon Bolivar Buckner decided to slip the leash on his Marines. In response to the light resistance facing the Marine divisions, he notified IIIAC commander, General Roy Geiger, "All restrictions removed on your advance northwards." The push was not a complete walk-over; the worst fighting occurred around 1,500–foot Mount Yae Take on the Motobu Peninsula where the 6th Marine Division ran into the so-called "Udo Force," about 1,500 Japanese infantry stiffened with light and medium artillery. The Yae Take position was broken on 16 April, and organized Japanese resistance on Motobu had ended by 20 April at a cost of 207 Marines killed, 757 wounded, and 6 missing. The Marines counted over 2,000 Japanese dead.

Progress was also encouraging to the south where XXIV Corps was advancing ahead of schedule. The L plus 10 objective line had been seized by 4 April and the optimists began to think casualties would be much less than anticipated. On 8 April, Vice Admiral Turner sent Nimitz a lighthearted radio message: "I may be crazy, but it looks like the Japs have quit the war, at least in this sector." Nimitz's reply was brief, but spoke volumes: "Delete all after 'crazy.' "

His response was prophetic. The following day, elements of the 96th Infantry Division ran into the hard shell of General Ushijima's defenses at Kakazu Ridge, a rough coral hogback 4,000 yards north of 32d Army Headquarters at Shuri. Dug into caves and tunnels, Japanese from Colonel Munetatsu Hara's 13th Independent Infantry Battalion threw back an assault by two U.S. battalions. The 96th Division's 383d Regimental Combat Team suffered 326 casualties, including 23 killed and 47 missing. The 1st Battalion was so badly shot up trying to take the ridge as to be considered ineffective.

Kakazu Ridge was the start of the real grind for Okinawa. From 9–12 April, the 96th Division Deadeyes beat themselves against the enemy ridges. The 7th Division advanced to Ouki and was promptly driven out. Casualties in both divisions totaled 2,880, with 451 dead. A general assault by the 96th, 7th, and 27th Infantry Divisions on 19 April failed dismally. In the fighting around Kakazu Ridge, the 27th Division lost 22 of 30 tanks.

The next two weeks saw U.S. forces spinning their wheels against the Japanese defenses. Successes were dearly won. On 23 April the 96th Division finally succeeded in clearing most of Nishibaru and Tanabaru Ridges—at a cost of 99 killed, 19 missing, and 660 wounded. Meanwhile, on 20 April, the 27th Division ran into a Japanese defense point nicknamed Item Pocket. The GIs battled for the pocket for five days before taking possession, then spent another three days digging out enemy diehards. Casualties were heavy and at one point two companies fled in panic after being surrounded and cut off. But progress was made. Their outer defense ring penetrated in a number of places, on 23 April the Japanese rapidly and successfully withdrew some two miles to their next defense position, the Shuri-Yonabaru-Naha Line where they regrouped and prepared for the next onslaught.

Ushijima's command post was established in a vast tunnel 150 feet beneath Shuri Castle, built in the 16th century and once home to Okinawa's kings. The defense line extended across the six-mile width of the island, the Asa Kawa on west, the Shuri Heights in the center and the hills of Yonabaru on the eastern coast. Tunnels and caves contained extensive firing ports and quarters for troops. One veteran later described the fortifications, deeply dug into the limestone and coral heights, as "like ships inside hills."

Virtually impervious to U.S. artillery and naval gunfire, the positions were designed to be mutually supporting, with interlocking bands of fire. There was no shortage of weaponry. One sector less than half a mile square contained 16 light mortars, 83 light machine guns, 41 heavy machine guns, 7 antitank guns, 6 field pieces, 2 mortars, and 2 howitzers. Both reverse and forward slopes were fortified. Artillery was placed in caves, often on tracks so it could be rolled outside, fired, and then rolled back inside to avoid retaliatory fire.

Ushijima lectured his troops: "You cannot regard the enemy on a par with you. You must realize that material power usually overcomes spiritual power in the present war. The enemy is clearly our superior in machines. Do not depend on your spirits overcoming this enemy. Devise combat methods based on mathematical precision: then think about your spiritual power."

Sailors remained under almost constant kamikaze attack. Losses were heavy. As early as 19 March, the aircraft carrier *Franklin* had been devastated by kamikazes, with 724 of her crew killed. The carrier *Wasp* had lost 101 men killed and 269 wounded that same day. Since the landing on 1

April, the list of damaged or sunken ships and killed and wounded sailors had grown with frightful speed: the transport *Dickerson*, sunk; destroyer *Bush*, sunk; destroyer *Colhoun*, sunk; minelayer *Emmons*, sunk; LST 447, sunk; battleship *Tennessee*, damaged. The list went on and on. All told, over 60 vessels had been sunk or badly damaged by air attacks between 1 and 22 April. Naval casualties totaled over 1,100 dead and nearly 2,000 wounded in those attacks alone.

Deeply disturbed by those losses, Admiral Nimitz flew from Guam to Okinawa to confer with General Buckner on 23 April. Some naval—and Marine—officers felt Buckner was proceeding too slowly, too conservatively and with a decided lack of imagination. Now Nimitz said the operation ashore must be speeded up so the supporting fleet could be released.

A big, ruddy-faced Kentuckian, the 58-year-old Buckner was respected for his long experience as a student and teacher in staff schools, his ability and his grasp of tactics. He was not known as a man who liked to take risks; his instinct was to grind forward with the relentless use of superior firepower. A graduate of West Point, class of 1908, he had been promoted to brigadier general in 1940 and to lieutenant general two years before the invasion of Okinawa. Soldiering ran in his family; his father had been a Confederate general in the Civil War and later served as governor of Kentucky. Buckner himself had served as commandant of West Point, where he earned a reputation for punctiliousness. In 1943 he led the successful American campaign in the Aleutians. No shrinking violet, he responded to Nimitz's implied criticism with the retort that the ground campaign was an Army affair—the insinuation being that he could handle it quite well without interference from Nimitz.

The normally affable admiral turned a cold eye on the ground commander. "I'm losing a ship and a half a day," he returned. "So if this line isn't moving within five days, we'll get someone here to move it so we can all get out from under these damn air attacks."

In fact, as both Nimitz and Buckner knew, a possible solution—an amphibious assault on the enemy rear—had already been suggested and now continued to be touted as an alternative to a purely frontal assault. Marine Corps Commandant A. A. Vandegrift suggested using the 2d Marine Division, now waiting on Saipan in IIIAC reserve after feinting a landing at Okinawa's southeastern coast on Love Day. Vandegrift felt the division could be landed in the Nakagusuku Bay area behind the Shuri Line—or, barring that, even deeper behind Japanese lines at Minatoga. IIIAC Commander Geiger agreed.

Nimitz's deputy chief of staff, Admiral Forrest Sherman, said it would take too long to load out the division from Saipan. Vandegrift disagreed. He had recently visited the 2d Marine Division on Saipan. The division could be underway in six hours, he assured Sherman. Sherman was not persuaded, "nor did Buckner seem impressed," recalled Vandegrift.

This was not the first time Buckner had received suggestions for a more daring solution to his tactical problem. Seeing no percentage in decimating units in frontal attacks against the dug-in Japanese, several officers had suggested an amphibious end run around the Shuri Line. General Andrew D. Bruce, commander of the 77th Infantry Division, had proposed such a landing even before his division sailed from Leyte. The 77th had participated in a spectacularly successful amphibious landing behind Japanese lines at Ormoc on Leyte and Bruce was eager to repeat the performance.

As the 77th Division concluded seizure of the small island of Ie Shima off the Okinawan coast toward the end of April, Bruce pressed his recommendation to land the 77th Division on the southeast coast of Okinawa just north of Minatoga. Those beaches had been the alternative landing sites for the original invasion. Bruce thought it would be necessary to link up with American forces to the north within ten days to be successful.

General Lemuel Shepherd, commanding the 6th Marine Division, had also suggested such a landing using Marines. A simple diversionary landing by the 2d Marine Division on the southeastern coast of Nagusuku Bay would be sufficient, he felt. "You don't have to go far, just go in there and establish a beachhead," he advised Buckner. "This will necessitate the Japanese to withdraw forces from their main line to resist this landing on the other side." It would be enough to break the impasse, he said.

"Well, it's a big operation," replied Buckner. "We don't have the ammunition."

Shepherd said the 2d Marine Division had organic support to sustain itself for at least 30 days. "They can do it. I know they can do it," he promised.

In each instance, Buckner demurred. He said his supply system would break down if he implemented a second front. Kamikazes had destroyed two ammunition supply ships, creating a shortage which would seriously affect a second front. He said he needed to retain the 2d Marine Division for further landings in July on Kikai, north of Okinawa. He also observed that Minatoga was dominated by steep cliffs which would allow the Japanese artillery to massacre any attempted landing over the beaches below. Tenth Army intelligence had reported that Japanese reserves were still stationed in the south—both the 24th Division and 44th IMB were still positioned where they could quickly combat any landing. It would be "another Anzio but worse," Buckner declared.

Another consideration was that by late April, when the 77th Infantry Division became available, the other three army divisions in the line—the 7th, 27th and 96th—were suffering from high casualties and fatigue.[1] There were so many combat fatigue cases that Tenth Army had reserved one entire field hospital for GIs suffering from psychoneurosis. Buckner felt that an influx of fresh troops, massed artillery, naval gunfire and flamethrower tanks would be enough to finally break the Japanese defense line, without resorting to an amphibious assault. Nimitz listened carefully to the argument and ruled in favor of Buckner's tactics "provided they produced early results."[2]

By opting for conservative frontal tactics, Buckner was doing exactly what Ushijima had hoped he would do. There was no chance for surprise— the Japanese were dug in and waiting. There was no easy flank to turn—the enemy line stretched from coast to coast. Nor were the Japanese oblivious to the threat of an amphibious end run. In their defense planning, Ushijima's staff had anticipated an amphibious assault either on the southern coast or the Chinen Peninsula to the east. To guard against that threat, Ushijima had retained the 44th IMB and the 24th Division in those areas. Now, ironically, even as Buckner fretted about "another Anzio," Ushijima had decided there would be no amphibious landing. By 22 April, both the 24th Division and the 44th IMB were moving north to bolster the Shuri Line.

The move did not go unnoticed. About 26–28 April, Colonel John W. Guerard, G-3 for XXIV Corps noticed that 24th Division troops had been identified on the front line during the past few days of fighting. This seemed to indicate that the 24th had been moved up to replace Japanese casualties. With the Japanese stripping their defenses in the south to man the Shuri Line, Guerard believed a landing to the south was now feasible. He recommended landing the Marines on the Minatoga beaches. His opinion was seconded by corps commander General Hodge who went to Tenth Army headquarters to urge his view. Buckner again refused, citing logistical considerations.

Interviewing Colonel Yahara after the war, U.S. interrogators were told, "Until the end of April, enough troops were left in the south to deal a severe blow to any landing. Hope of defending the southern coast was given up [by early May] . . . The absence of a landing puzzled the 32d Army staff, particularly after the beginning of May when it became impossible to put up more than a token resistance in the south." U.S. Army historians later noted that "The prevailing opinion [among the Japanese] was that the Tenth

Army wished to obtain as cheap a victory as possible by wearing down the Shuri Line rather than committing elements to a possibly hazardous landing in the south in the interests of bringing the operation to a speedier end."

It is one of those dark quirks of history that Buckner had discarded the suggestion of an amphibious assault on the Japanese rear just when the prospects for such an assault were rapidly improving. Had Buckner been able to foresee the results of his decision, he might have been more receptive to the alternatives. In fact, his frontal assault against the Shuri Line with an attempted double envelopment would prove anything but cheap. Later, his conservatism would be decried in U.S. newspapers as a "fiasco" and "a worse example of military incompetency than Pearl Harbor." But that would be after much more dying.

For his renewed push against the Shuri Line, Buckner decided to use the Marines of IIIAC, now relatively unoccupied since seizing northern Okinawa well ahead of schedule—accomplishing phase 2 of the operation before XXIV Corps was able to complete phase 1. On 28 April, Buckner informed IIIAC that the 1st Marine Division would relieve the 27th Infantry Division on the western flank in two days. The 6th Marine Division would follow as IIIAC took responsibility for that end of the line on 7 May.

Ushijima chose this moment to make a rare mistake. Urged on by Cho, on 29 April he agreed to a massive counterattack. Only Colonel Yahara raised a dissenting voice. "To take the offensive with inferior forces against overwhelming superior enemy forces is reckless and will lead to early defeat," he argued. The Americans were taking heavy losses and the Japanese defense still had major elements left intact to prolong the battle, buy time and inflicting still more losses on the invaders, he pointed out.

The attack, spearheaded by the 24th Division, on 4 May was a disaster. Emerging into the open, Ushijima's men were slaughtered by superior American firepower. XXIV Corps later counted 6,237 Japanese corpses in front of its lines. U.S. losses totaled about 700 dead and wounded. It was later estimated that the failure of the attack may have shortened the fighting on Okinawa by as much as two weeks. Buckner may have found this development encouraging, but it was not a mistake Ushijima intended to repeat. With tears in his eyes, he summoned Colonel Yahara to his quarters and told him he would abide by his advice in the future. Yahara's recommendation was brutally simple: Japanese soldiers would stay in their holes and kill as many Americans as they could before they were themselves killed.

With Buckner determined to hammer directly at the Shuri Line, the 6th Marine Division's bloody collision with Sugar Loaf was now mere days away.

NOTES

1. By the end of the month, the 96th Division had suffered nearly 3,500 casualties. On 20 April alone, the 27th Division lost 506 men, the greatest single day's loss for an army division on Okinawa.

2. Admiral Nimitz may have been reluctant to take stronger action because of the great controversy that had arisen on Saipan the previous summer when Marine Corps General Holland M. Smith relieved the commander of the 27th Infantry Division, Ralph Smith, of his command. The furor over that incident had left commanders wary of pushing too hard in disputes involving the different services. 1st Marine Division commander Major General Pedro del Valle later said he felt the secondary landing should have been made. On the other hand, not all agreed with Vandegrift and Shepherd. IIIAC Marine Chief of Staff Merwin M. Silverthorne, who witnessed the various discussions, later said he felt the logistical problems posed by a second landing "would have been out of proportion to the tactical advantage gained." Some naval officers also doubted the navy could provide sufficient cover for a second landing.

Chapter 2

The Marines Head South

The men of the 6th Marine Division were not happy to learn they would be heading south to "rescue the army." Having seized the bulk of Okinawa—436 square miles of it—in 20 days, the leathernecks felt they had done their share.

The division had settled down quite comfortably at Nago. "To us, Okinawa was over with," observed Private First Class Bill Pierce, assigned to Weapons Company, 29th Marines. During the fighting on northern Okinawa, the division had lost 236 killed, 1,601 wounded, and 7 missing. Now the men cleaned their weapons, took photographs, slept, played ball and generally wound down. One regiment even set up its own private bordello where the going rate was three yen—about 30 cents. The first indication that all was not well came with the issue of steaks, the traditional preassault meal. When fresh eggs were served for breakfast, the men were sure they were headed back into combat. The orders came only hours later.

There was no doubt in anyone's mind that the "Striking Sixth" was up to the job. Organized on Guadalcanal in September 1944, the 6th Marine Division was the youngest of the Marine divisions, but it had a character all its own. One observer, General O. P. Smith, Marine liaison officer to Tenth Army, considered the 6th to be "more flashy" than the 1st Marine Division which was "more of a plugging division than the 6th Division." To Smith's mind, the 6th Marine Division was "a little more cocky than the 1st Marine Division." In a word, the division had "style."

As many as half of the men in the division's three infantry regiments—the 4th, 22d and 29th Marines—were veterans of previous Pacific battles.

The rest ranged from older draftees to eager young teenagers. Commanding this assortment of old hands and green youngsters was Major General Lemuel C. Shepherd, Jr., who was considered one of the fair-haired officers of the Marine Corps. A graduate of Virginia Military Institute, Shepherd knew the terrors of combat firsthand. Wounded three times fighting with the Marine Brigade in France during World War I, he had earned the Navy Cross, second only to the Medal of Honor. As a company commander at Belleau Wood, he had been shot in the neck, but remained in command until incapacitated by a wound in the leg.

Despite his distinguished combat career, Shepherd was known as "a schools man." He had commanded the Marine Corps Schools, where he enhanced his reputation as a teacher of tactics. More recently, he had served as assistant commander of the 1st Marine Division during the 1943 landing on Cape Gloucester, and he had led the 1st Provisional Brigade on Guam before being named to command the 6th Marine Division.

It was a very good division. Veteran combat correspondent Robert Sherrod observed, "Shepherd had chosen his staff carefully, and he had built up one of the best I saw in the war against Japan." Shepherd shared that high opinion of his division. Years later he remarked, "When we went into Okinawa, the 6th Marine Division was the best trained organization the Marine Corps ever had, in my opinion."

Of the division's three infantry regiments, the 4th Marines had the most tradition. The original 4th Marine Regiment had been lost in the Philippines at the beginning of the war; the regiment had subsequently been reconstituted around the former Marine Raider Battalions. A proud elite, the Raiders had seen much fighting at Tulagai, Guadalcanal, Bougainville and New Georgia before being formed into the 4th Marines on Guadalcanal. The regiment was commanded by one of Annapolis's great athletes, 41-year-old Colonel Alan Shapley and, according to one estimate, included in its ranks two complete All-American football teams.

The 22d Marines had been formed as an independent regiment in early 1942 and about a third of its personnel had served in Iceland. The regiment had been in reserve for the attack on Kwajalein. In February 1944 it seized Japanese-held Eniwetok in the Marshall Islands where it lost 184 killed and 540 wounded. In late March, the 22d Marines and the 4th Marines were formed into the 1st Marine Provisional Brigade, which saw heavy fighting in the recapture of Guam. The regimental commander was Colonel Merlin F. Schneider, a Naval Academy graduate of 1923. Now in his 40s, Schneider had seen wide service in Haiti and China before the war; he had joined the 22d Marines upon its organization in 1942 as commander of the 3d Battalion, later becoming regimental executive officer, and in March of 1944, regimental commander. He had been overseas almost since the outbreak of the war, serving on Wallis Island, the Solomons, Kwajalein, Eniwetok and on Guam, where he won the Navy Cross.

The third infantry regiment in the division, the 29th Marines, was the last infantry regiment formed by the Marine Corps during the war, being activated in May 1944 at Camp Lejeune, North Carolina. It included many veterans of the 2d Marine Division, which had fought at Guadalcanal and Tarawa. Its 1st Battalion had also participated in the fighting on Saipan where it suffered over 50 percent casualties during 24 days of fighting. Its original commander had been relieved on northern Okinawa for not pushing hard enough for Shepherd's liking. The regiment was now commanded by Colonel William J. Whaling, a combat veteran of World War I, who had fought on Guadalcanal and commanded a regiment at Cape Gloucester.

The division's ranks included men of all types and backgrounds, from high-school dropouts to college graduates, from Depression-era dead-end kids to wealthy heirs, from bright-eyed young volunteers to skeptical draftees. Large numbers were still in their teens; few of the others were past their early 20s. "They called you 'Pops' if you were 26 or 27," recalled Private First Class Floyd Enman.

Sergeant William Manchester later observed that most of the Marines he knew had enlisted fully recognizing that the Corps was the most dangerous branch of service. "I remember them as bright, physically strong and inspired by an idealism and love of country they would have been too embarrassed to acknowledge," he remarked. A great number of junior officers had been college football stars, two of the best known being "Irish" George Murphy of Notre Dame and Rade (Mike) Enich of the University of Iowa. Others had come out of the V–12 college officers training program. A special few had been commissioned from the ranks, having demonstrated their ability on the battlefield.

As for the enlisted men, their roads to the Marine Corps were almost as varied as the men themselves. Sixteen-year-old Ronald Manson was setting pins in a California bowling alley when he got tired of listening to one of his fellow workers sound off about their patriotic duties. They hitchhiked to San Francisco to the Marine Corps recruiting office and the 120-pound Manson passed everything but the weight requirement. "I told them I was 17 and the guy told me to go out and drink a lot of milk and all the bananas I could and come back at two o'clock with a certificate from my parents," he recalled. "The consent cost me a jug of wine. I had some wino sign the consent. And I bought about two quarts of milk and a bag full of bananas, ate that and went back to the recruiting station, squatted, took a piss, raised my right hand and I was on a train and gone. But the guy who talked me into going? He flunked out of recruit depot."

Paolo DeMeis, a tough Italian kid from Brooklyn, was also under age. "I'd gotten in trouble with the law," he recalled. "I had an assault and battery rap against me. I had a couple of raps against me already for running numbers and horses. They gave me 90 days to find government employment or get in the service or you're going to college. And 'college' at that time was Elmira Prison." DeMeis went to join the Navy or the Coast Guard, but the lines were too long. Somebody told him, "There's no lines over there at Whitehall Street." Whitehall Street turned out to be the location of the Marine recruiting station. And so, largely because the lines were short, DeMeis ended up in the Marines.

Many others chose the Marines because of the organization's reputation as tough fighters. "I'd been out of high school a little while," recalled D. C. Rigby, a youngster from Texas. "I'd been working around the area and it come time to go in and I went in. I figured if I was going to have to get in, I might as well get right in the middle of it."

Still others came in as a result of the draft. Landon Oakes reported for the draft in Richmond, Virginia. "Then I wound up on the Navy side; they called for volunteers [for the Marine Corps] and I stepped forward." Sometimes this method of obtaining recruits wasn't quite so polite. "*They* enlisted *me*," observed Leon Paice of his entry into the Marine Corps at the induction center in Utah. "They said, 'You, you, you and you, you're going into the Marine Corps.' "

Each man had his own story, but the end result was the same. All were now members of the same family, the United States Marine Corps and the 6th Marine Division.

Packed into trucks, the Marines headed south on 2 May, led by the engineers and elements of the 6th Service Battalion. The 29th and 15th Regiments followed on 3 May, with the 4th, 22d, and other units following on successive days. They were to be replaced by the 27th Infantry Division.

"It was still kind of a joke," observed Private First Class W. R. Lightfoot. "We heard the Army was having trouble . . . we figured we could handle it—kick a little ass and that would be it." The Marines were especially annoyed that the Army unit coming out of the line to replace them in the north was the 27th Infantry Division. The 27th was notorious among Marine outfits throughout the Pacific as a mediocre outfit. On Saipan the preceding summer, the 27th's commander had been relieved when his division failed to keep up with the Marines in the operation. "We hated the 27th from Saipan and now this," noted Bill Pierce. "Us relieving them? We were really teed off."

Some of the Marines expressed their contempt as the trucks carrying the GIs rumbled by heading north. "Whenever we stopped, they would receive rocks, C ration cans, bullets, anything we could throw at them," recalled Pierce. "They cringed in their trucks from the bombardments."

The antipathy of the Marines for GIs was rooted in more than interservice swagger. There were real differences in the way Marines and army troops operated. The Marines were trained as assault troops; their mission in the Pacific war was to hit a beach, secure it, and let other forces handle the mop-up. As assault troops, they tended to travel lighter and do with less. With their vulnerable ships at stake during amphibious assaults, they had been drilled to keep moving, to always press the attack, to accept high casualties but never failure.

Army forces were more inclined to take things slowly and let the weight of their firepower clear the way. "It's always been a controversy, I guess," reflected a former Marine private first class 50 years later. "They'd take three weeks to take a hill and we'd take it in two. Now, we'd lose a lot of men, but the Army would, too. And who wants to go through all that laying in the mud and stuff? You know, if you're going to get killed . . . well, hell, let's do it now."

Hard feelings aside, as the army troops now came back to the rear, at least some of the Marines observed they had taken quite a beating. "I would say they just had a dumbfounded look on their faces," observed Ralph Miller, a corpsman with the 29th Marines. "They had those curtains pulled down in most of the trucks," noted Private First Class Warren "Ike" Wanamaker. "They weren't looking at anybody. They were in bad shape."

Just how bad was recorded by General O. P. Smith at Tenth Army Headquarters. "They were a mess," he recalled of the 27th Division, his contempt only thinly veiled. "The 1st [Marine] Division went down and found that they hadn't buried their dead—the dead were lying around—and they complained to the Army. The Army made the 27th Division send back working parties to bury their own dead."

By 6 May, the entire 6th Marine Division was quartered around Chibana less than ten miles north of the front lines. The next day the 22d Regiment moved to the high bluff overlooking the Asa Kawa (Asa River) and relieved the 7th Regiment of the 1st Marine Division. The 29th Marines moved in on 9 May, establishing a defensive position covering the beaches along the western flank of Machinato Airfield. The 1st Marine Division contracted its lines to the eastward.

Eighteen-year-old Private Ken Long, a Depression-era farmboy from Minnesota, carried all the gear typical of a newcomer to the line: He wore one pair of skivvies (Marine green), one pair of socks (Marine green), one set of dog tags and chain, one pair of leggings, one pair of boots, one pair of fatigues (Marine green with emblem on the jacket pocket), one web belt, one helmet liner (fiber), one helmet (steel), one waterproof wristwatch (a gift from his brother). In his pockets he carried a small Bible he had received in a packet from the Salvation Army on the train from Camp Lejeune, some atabrine and halogen tablets, a handkerchief, and toilet paper. The rest of his load consisted of an M1 rifle complete with cleaning tools and "lubriplate" in the stock; one cartridge belt with ten clips of ammunition; one canteen complete with cover and cup, one first aid kit; one bayonet and sheath; one K-Bar knife; one pack containing a bedroll with shelter half and blanket, one poncho, three pairs of socks, two pairs of fatigues, mess kit, three sets of skivvies, one carton of cigarettes and one packet of matches wrapped in wax paper. Like most of the other men, he had left his gas mask on the beach. His one nonregulation item, glued to the inside of his helmet liner, was a picture of movie star Jane Russell lounging provocatively on a haystack with a piece of hay in her mouth.

More experienced Marines soon squared him away. "Two suggestions they gave me were: Instead of wearing dog tags around the neck (where they sometimes clank at night) lace one in each boot, laced through the bottom portion of the shoelace," he recalled. "The second was to put a sock around the canteen cup to prevent any noise when the canteen was removed or reinserted. My mess kit was also discarded at this time and only a fork was kept."

As his outfit neared the southern lines less than ten miles below the original landing beaches, Sergeant William Manchester became aware of "a grumbling on the horizon, which turned into a thumping, then a drumming, then a rumbling, and then an enormous thudding." It was the artillery pounding away incessantly on an army front not much longer than the distance between Arlington National Cemetery and the Washington Navy Yard.

On 8 May a newspaper correspondent approached Corporal Walt Rutkowski. "Hear that? The European war is over," he said, referring to news of the German surrender. "That's good," replied Rutkowski wistfully. "I wish it was this one." He wasn't alone. Over the past few days the men of the 1st Marine Division had begun to learn why the GIs had been having so many problems in the south. The reverse slope defense mounted by the Japanese was highly effective. The leathernecks would take the forward slope and then lose half their riflemen trying to stay there as the enemy emerged from protected positions on the reverse slope.[1] Tanks provided some help, but were often savaged by mines or the Japanese 47 mm gun which fired a 3.6-pound armor-piercing projectile and had a muzzle velocity of 2,700 feet per second. On 4 and 5 May, the 1st Marine Division lost 649 men killed, wounded or missing. On 6 May alone, enemy antitank guns knocked out three Shermans.

Coming in on the right of III Amphibious Corps (IIIAC), the 6th Division Marines quickly realized they were not going to escape unbloodied. Across the Asa Kawa, the enemy-held ground rose gently to the horizon, 2,000 yards away. The whole area was primarily a large drainage basin for the Asa River. From time to time enemy soldiers could be seen scooting in and out of caves on the other side of the river. Though the Marines had yet to determine the enemy order of battle, the IIIAC was faced by the 44th IMB with the 15th IMR as a nucleus, the 3d Battalion of the 2d Infantry Unit and various attached troops—about 5,500 men in all. The 15th IMR had been newly raised in Narashino, Chiba-ken, an area on Tokyo Bay where the main industry was fishing. The 2d Infantry Unit was formed around survivors of the original 44th IMB, nearly wiped out in a submarine attack in June while en route to Okinawa. The original unit had been raised that spring on Kyushu. Replacements had been obtained from Kyushu, rounded out with conscripted Okinawans.

Over the coming days, these units would resist the 6th Marine Division's attack toward Naha, a mile and a half to the south. Major General Shepherd did not anticipate a cake walk. In a training order to be read twice by every platoon leader to his men, Shepherd showed considerable respect for the enemy, pointing out that the battle in southern Okinawa "is different from anything this Division has encountered in the operation thus far." He noted the following in part:

a. The enemy has a great deal of artillery and is using it far more intelligently than in any operation to date.

b. The enemy has plenty of ammunition and isn't afraid to use it if he sees a target.

c. The enemy has excellent observation and takes every opportunity to watch what our troops are doing.

d. The enemy has sown antitank and antipersonnel mines in every conceivable locality.

e. The enemy is aggressive and is willing to counterattack by every available means, land or water.

f. The enemy has a strong defense line; one which cannot be breached by simple frontal attack without heavy losses.

He reminded the men to take every advantage of cover and concealment and to use maneuver. "Don't try to outslug the Jap;—outflank him," he advised all unit commanders, from battalion down to the squad level. He added, "Keep driving—Your enemy can't think as fast as you can and he is no match for a determined aggressive Marine who has confidence in himself and his weapon."

Miles to the south, a Japanese editor was also pondering the future. "The Sixth Marine Division is a fresh unit," he wrote for his newspaper. "Among the badly mauled enemy it is a tiger's cub and their morale is high . . . If we deal the Sixth Division a mortal blow, we probably will be able to control the enemy's destiny."

That time was fast approaching. With naval losses mounting, Buckner was under heavy pressure to get the ground attack moving. He and his staff had scheduled an army-wide attack on 11 May in hopes of cracking the Shuri Line. According to Buckner's plan, the Tenth Army would attack with two corps abreast: the IIIAC on the right and XXIV Corps on the left. The scheme of maneuver called for an envelopment of Shuri by the Marine divisions on the west and the Army divisions on the east, while strong pressure was maintained in the center. From left to right, the divisions were the 7th, 96th and 77th Infantry Divisions of XXIV Corps and the 1st and 6th Marine Divisions of IIIAC.

Shepherd had specifically requested that his division be assigned the western flank of the assault. Part of the reason was his confidence in his operations officer, Lieutenant Colonel Victor H. Krulak. Krulak was a naval gunfire expert and Shepherd felt naval gunfire would be of great assistance in an attack up the coast.

There were other advantages as well. Discussing the matter with IIIAC Commander General Roy Geiger, Shepherd offered, "Let me take the zone of action along the west coast. We'll push right on down until we out-flank Shuri Castle." Geiger agreed, but when the corps order arrived, it tied the 6th Marine Division to the advance to the 1st Marine Division on the left. Shepherd approached Geiger again. "General, I want to make my main effort along the coast so that I can get around behind Shuri Castle," he protested, showing his plan on the map.

Geiger turned to his operations officer. "Why didn't you write the order so that Shepherd could carry out his plan?" he asked. The operations officer

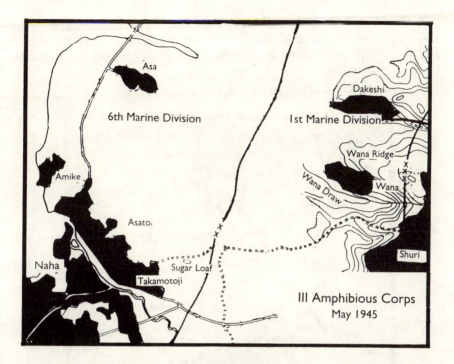

Asa

Dakeshi

6th Marine Division

1st Marine Division

Wana Ridge

Amike

Wana Draw

Wana

Asato

Naha

Sugar Loaf

Shuri

Takamotoji

III Amphibious Corps
May 1945

argued that the 6th Marine Division should remain tied to the advance of the 1st Marine Division on the left. "General, if you let me push down the coast, I can flank the Shuri position and get into the southern end of the island," promised Shepherd. Geiger agreed and told his operations officer to change the order accordingly.

Shepherd was not the only officer to see potential opportunity on the coast. Tenth Army staff also believed the Japanese positions were weaker on the right and that the Marine divisions could hope for a quick break-through on that flank. However, they were too cautious to stake everything on this hope. The Tenth Army plan would keep intense pressure along the whole Shuri Line and exploit a breakthrough wherever the Japanese finally cracked, be it on the flanks or elsewhere.

Buckner sounded a hopeful note. "It will be a continuation of the type of attack we have been employing to date," he explained. "When we cannot take strong points, we will pinch them off and leave them for the reserves to reduce. We have ample firepower and we also have enough fresh troops so that we can always have one division resting." One thing was already painfully clear: the original timetable which called for all of Okinawa to be in American hands by 10 May had been fond fantasy.

9 May. Platoon Leader Paul Dunfey led his 45-man platoon, part of K Company, 22d Marines, toward the Asa Kawa, the sluggish tidal river which meandered into the East China Sea about ten miles south of the invasion beaches.

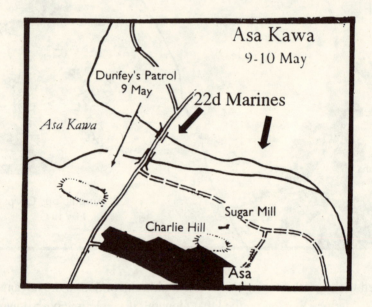

Dunfey, a 26-year-old from Lowell, Massachusetts, had worked variously as a draftsman, salesman, sheet metal worker and in the family restaurant before joining the Marines five days after Pearl Harbor. Now he was one little cog moving toward the army-wide assault Buckner had ordered for 11 May. In the 6th Marine Division zone of operation, this would entail crossing the Asa Kawa, carving out a bridgehead, then advancing over relatively open ground toward Naha. Dunfey's platoon, stiffened with 17 Weapons Company men, was assigned to reconnoiter the other side of the river before the division launched its attack. As a crossing point, Dunfey picked a spot about midway between the mouth of the river and a knocked out road bridge a short distance inland. The Marines waded across the brackish river at low tide, hoisted themselves over a seawall and edged cautiously toward a low ridge to their front.

Among the men in the patrol was Sergeant Ray "Doc" Gillespie, a veteran of the fighting on Guam and the Marshall Islands, where he had been wounded. Approaching the bottom of the ridge, Gillespie saw a large cave opening. Dimly visible inside were narrow gauge railroad tracks and a couple of cross passageways further back. At least three other cave mouths were visible higher up the slope.

The Marines left an explosive charge in the cave and had started up the slope when they began to come under fire from the front. Suddenly the enemy seemed to be everywhere. The Marines could hear excited Japanese voices just below their position. Enemy troops were also visible on the right, while others seemed to be moving toward them from the front. Working along the ridge line, Gillespie came upon Corporal Frank Coomer peering over the top of the ridge. "Doc," said Coomer excitedly, "I just got one!" Gillespie was crawling over Coomer's outstretched legs when he heard a sickening thud. A bullet had smashed through Coomer's helmet, killing him. Within moments, Private First Class William Donnell was also shot in the head and killed.

Gillespie found Dunfey. Japanese were coming in on both flanks, he reported, and, judging from the noise, there seemed to be more Japanese behind the ridge. Any doubts Dunfey might have had vanished as a Japanese mortar round hit behind them. "Get the men down and let's get the hell out of here," said Dunfey.

As the Marines scrambled off the hill, Coomer's teenaged buddy—nicknamed "Squeaky" in honor of his still-changing voice—yelled at Gillespie, "I'm not leaving Coomer's body here." Most of the other Marines had already started for the river. Gillespie and three others lingered to help Squeaky carry Coomer, even though Gillespie realized it wasn't the smartest thing to do. They made it back to the sea wall and left Coomer on the mud flat before wading back across the river.

Some hours later, Lieutenant Dunfey found himself at 6th Marine Division headquarters, a large underground bunker which had once served as a Japanese command post. This was no low-level debriefing. The more than three dozen officers included division commander Lemuel Shepherd and Tenth Army commander Simon Buckner. Dunfey had been shot at before. He had participated in the Marshall Islands campaign and the fighting on Guam. But he had never encountered the type of defensive positions he had just seen south of the Asa Kawa. Caves and gun emplacements dotted the hills. Some of the larger caves apparently concealed artillery. Others had openings on the front and rear slopes.

Dunfey answered questions about what he had seen on the patrol across the Asa Kawa and was finally dismissed. But feeling that he hadn't been able to convey the true nature of the Japanese defenses, he asked to add something. "Dismissed!" snapped a staff officer. But another officer called Dunfey back and the young lieutenant spoke his piece, adding his doubts about the wisdom of a direct assault on such well integrated defenses. He could not know, of course, that General Buckner's strictures left the 6th Marine Division with little alternative.

None of the handful of reconnaissance patrols mounted across the river returned with particularly encouraging news. They indicated that the road bridge across the river was badly damaged—probably by preinvasion air attacks—and was impassable by men or vehicles. At high tide, the river was only about four feet deep in the shallowest places, but the bottom was a gelatinous muck, not firm enough to bear the weight of tanks. If necessary, the assault troops could wade across, but tanks and trucks would have to await construction of bridges. As a result of this information, a company of engineers was placed in direct support of each regiment going into the attack; construction of a footbridge was also ordered.

The initial crossing would be made by the 2d and 3d Battalions of Colonel Merlin Schneider's 22d Marines. The 2d Battalion on the left would maintain contact with the 1st Marine Division. The 3d Battalion would attack along the seacoast. The 1st Battalion would maintain contact between the other two and occupy the first high ground south of the river. The assault would jump off a little before dawn. Not everyone was enthusiastic about the timing. Captain Owen Stebbins, commanding G Company, observed, "The older combat veterans, used to attacking in the day and shooting whatever moved at night, were dubious of the idea."

Toward evening, enemy artillery hit Marine lines along the northern bank of the Asa Kawa. The shelling was from big guns—about 150 mm, which threw 80–pound projectiles—and more accurate than anything Marine veterans of other campaigns had experienced before. Under cover of darkness the Marine engineers moved down along the base of the coral cliffs along the north bank of the Asa Kawa and began putting together a footbridge. Bomb disposal squads were also active, clearing routes through Japanese minefields on the assault route. Waiting on the cliffs above, Marines of the 22d Regiment were ready to cover this activity with fire on the opposite shore. The noise of the engineering work was plainly audible to them but there was no reaction from the Japanese.

Not until 0230 when the footbridge was complete did the Japanese react. Machine-gun and rifle fire streaked redly across the river as the engineers ran for cover. The first infantry units started across the bridge at 0330. The general attack was to begin at dawn after the Marines formed on the southern bank. In the meantime, the Marines had been instructed to move quietly, hold their fire and refrain from smoking.

The 2d Battalion, on the left, waded through thigh-deep water. The 3d Battalion used the newly constructed bridge. Japanese flares sporadically lighted the sky. Corporal Charles Trofka, walking across the footbridge with K Company, was startled to see a Japanese officer, replete with sword, wading along the river edge not more than a few yards away. Trofka wanted very badly to shoot this bold intruder, but obeyed the order against firing. He kept moving across the bridge and left the inquisitive Japanese behind.

Also among the 3d Battalion Marines heading down toward the foggy river bottom was Private First Class Charles Pugh, a 32-year-old former railroad brakeman from Mississippi. Pugh, the oldest man in his company, had been inspired to join the Marine Corps by an uncle who had served in the Marine Brigade at Belleau Wood during World War I. Neither the fact that that war had cost his uncle a lung, nor the protestations of his weeping wife and the recent arrival of a baby boy had deterred him. As he trudged toward the river, Pugh saw that engineers with mine detectors had swept the road and drawn big rings around the mines they had located. The rings were visible in the pale moonlight as the Marines edged their way down to the one-plank footbridge across the Asa Kawa.

Each assault battalion managed to push two companies across the fog-bound river before dawn. Pugh's outfit had just crossed to the southern bank when they heard an explosion behind them. A two-man Japanese suicide team had rushed the bridge with satchel charges of TNT. The resulting blast destroyed the span and the two Japanese. The destruction of the bridge forced the rest of the 3d Battalion to get their feet wet using the same crossing as the 2d Battalion.

At daybreak the Marines attacked south toward a series of terraces and smallish hills. The Japanese reaction was fierce. Mortars and small arms fire flayed at the Marines. Pugh found himself near a low rock wall. The men had to jump up one at a time and cross an open area to reach the shelter of a ditch. When it came his time to go, Pugh noticed a Marine lying in the ditch. As he looked at him, a mortar shell splinter hit the man in the small of the back under his pack and laid him open as if with an ax. In the early morning chill, steam rose from the ghastly wound, reminding Pugh of the deer and hogs he had seen butchered on cool days back home. Jumping into the ditch, Pugh saw that the dead Marine was a teenaged replacement. The youngster had been in tears much of the night before, afraid he was going to be killed. His fears had come all too true.

Stiffened by air support from dive bombers and fire from self-propelled guns and 37 mms on the northern bank, the Marines made slow progress. In the center, the 1st Battalion had made its way across the Asa Kawa by

0600 and pushed its way about 150 yards to the high ground south of a bombed-out sugar mill where the attack bogged down. The 3d Battalion's assault had also bogged down on the right as the Marines came under fire from a rocky point jutting into the sea on the right and from emplacements in a 30–foot embankment to the left. "The situation is bad," reported battalion commander Lieutenant Colonel Malcolm O. Donohoo. "We're getting hit, but we are across and we are going to stay."

In the assault as part of 2/22 was Captain Owen T. Stebbins's G Company. Stebbins, an easy-going Californian who had played football for Fresno State College, was no novice to combat. A graduate of Officers Candidate School, he had fought on the Marshall Islands and been shot in the leg on Guam. He was, recalled one of his men, a fair-minded man, "a gentle soul, a scholar and born leader of men. I never ever heard him even use the word 'shit.' "

G Company had waded the Asa Kawa before dawn with 7 officers and 189 enlisted. The company had been lucky in the fighting on northern Okinawa, losing only 22 men—none killed. That was about to change. As the 2d Platoon approached several small huts near a grove of trees, they ran into intense fire from rifles and nambu machine guns. Many of the Japanese had built lidded fighting holes called "spider holes" and were very difficult to locate. "These spider holes were shallow, individual holes with a round cover, usually made of woven boughs or reeds," observed G Company demolitions man, Cliff Mezo. "They were usually covered with more local vegetation for camouflage."

Mezo found himself in an area choked with weeds and five-foot-tall undergrowth. The Marines could see only a few feet in the brush and were taking casualties. The corpsman was having a hard time locating the wounded. An automatic weapon chattered abruptly, cutting down Private Ernest Outen and wounding several others. One man said he saw the muzzle flash of the enemy weapon located in a bunker. "Others in the platoon were pointing too," recalled Mezo, "and I asked them to fire machine-gun tracers to indicate the target."

Lugging a bazooka, Mezo crawled closer to a bunker, afraid the mass of willow-like undergrowth would deflect the rocket. Finally satisfied, he fired two rockets that hit the bunker. Both failed to explode. The effort only drew enemy attention to him and Mezo began to come under fire from other, unseen automatic weapons.

The fighting lasted most of the morning as the Marines resorted to flamethrowers and rifle grenades. The first grenades—the rounded type— failed to work on the dug-in Japanese. The Marines obtained some of the pointed type of rifle grenades, which seemed to have better detonation. Finally overrunning the position, they found a nambu machine gun protected by spider holes, now littered with the bodies of defenders. Other dead Japanese lay in a ditch where the flanking squad had caught them as they tried to finally get away. "The battalion was fighting through a classic rear guard action, where nambu [machine] guns protected by riflemen would put up determined fire fights long enough to cause casualties and delay, and then either slip away finally or fight to the death," noted Captain Stebbins.

Despite that coolly professional assessment, Stebbins was frankly taken aback at the scope of the Japanese defenses. The day before, Marine patrols had gone beyond these positions and returned without discovering them— the Japanese letting the patrols through to avoid revealing their defense works. The enemy positions were so superbly camouflaged that some of the G Company men were hit from only five yards away.

On G Company's right, Corporal Bob Hodges received a firsthand lesson on the enemy's skillful use of camouflage. Hodges, a demolitions expert, had been assigned to the 1st Platoon earlier that morning to seal off cave openings behind the assault so the Marines would not have to worry about being gunned down from behind as they advanced. As Hodges searched for openings, he walked right up to a concealed nambu emplacement and was shot down before he even realized what was happening. Now his buddies could see him lying motionless only 20 feet from the enemy emplacement.

Miraculously, the 20-year-old Georgian was alive. Hit in the thigh, he had fallen with his left leg useless. A second burst hit him in the ribs as he rolled into a slight depression in the ground. He stayed there, not moving, as the machine gun, concealed in the vegetation just beyond him, continued to fire on the 1st Platoon.

Unable to determine if Hodges was dead or merely shamming, the Marines held up the attack, fired carefully and watched him, hesitating to use the heavier weapons that might obliterate him along with the Japanese. Navy corpsman George Spillman attempted to get out to Hodges under the cover of the platoon's fire, but was hit and killed. Finally, the platoon called in mortars and knocked out the Japanese position. Hodges, protected by the depression he had rolled into, survived the ordeal.

G Company covered only a few hundred yards during the day. The cost was 29 men and 1 officer killed or wounded—the officer being Lieutenant Joe Carrigan, who was evacuated dazed and with shrapnel wounds to his face from a close miss from an enemy mortar round. The men considered the losses heavy . . . they would come to change that view.

In the center of the regiment's push, the 1st Battalion had come under fire from a mound of decayed coral limestone. "Most of the damned fire is coming from that knob up there," observed Charlie Company commander Captain Warren F. Lloyd. "Probably have to take it before we get anywhere near Naha. It won't be a picnic." Lloyd was right. Soon to be dubbed "Charlie Hill" in honor of C Company's efforts, the hill stood about 300 yards inland, halfway between the Asa and Asato rivers.[2] The Marines would find out the hard way that the Japanese had tunneled into the hill like gophers—and they intended to stay.

Naha soon seemed like a pipe dream, as C Company measured its gains in feet. Enemy fire pounded in whenever a group larger than a squad tried to push forward. One squad lost four men as it attempted to maneuver toward the enemy positions. Two scouts sent out to protect the rear were shot through the head. Later, 20 or 30 Japanese soldiers materialized behind boulders and rocks on the crest of the hill and began firing on the Marines at short range. Commanding the 2d Platoon, Lieutenant Wallace G. Loftis got his men into a defiladed spot, but was unable to move up or down. A runner he sent out to inform Captain Lloyd of his predicament was shot as he emerged into the open. Loftis finally got his men out, but not without casualties. Loftis himself was knocked to the ground during a mortar barrage. When the young North Carolinian got to his feet and felt himself over, he found a jagged piece of steel had ripped his pack from his back.

Possibly among the least surprised at the stiff Japanese resistance was Lieutenant Paul Dunfey, who had conducted the platoon reconnaissance across the river the day before. Now as Dunfey tried to advance through the small ditch in front of the seawall, a bullet hit his belt buckle, driving fragments of bullet and buckle into his abdomen, severing his bowel. A corpsman made it up to him and gave some treatment, but there was too much incoming fire to get the wounded officer out. Crawling over a litter of grenades dropped by the men in front of him, Private First Class Charles Pugh came across Dunfey lying in the ditch, gasping and unable to move. "The heat of the day caused the gases in his intestines to come through one of those holes and it was on top of his stomach and looked like a big balloon lying on his stomach," recalled Pugh. As Pugh crawled on by, Dunfey, still the Marine officer, cautioned, "Keep your head down."

Sergeant Ray Gillespie and a few men had made it to the ridge where Corporal Coomer had been killed the day before. They tried to knock out a couple of Japanese machine guns, but the effort failed as one of the Browning Automatic Rifle (BAR) men was picked off by a sniper; another Marine was shot twice in the leg. The survivors headed back for the seawall.

Several more men were wounded on the way, including the Marine who had been shot in the leg earlier; this time a bullet hammered into the back of his neck, exiting through his upper teeth and carrying his upper lip away.

Gillespie's turn came when he paused to snatch up a discarded BAR. The extra load threw him off stride and a Japanese machine gunner caught up with him just yards from the seawall ditch. The burst ripped open his side and sent him tumbling into a small shell hole. Gillespie could feel warm wet blood seeping out on his abdomen. Dirt splattered on him as the enemy machine gunner tried to finish him off. Just beyond his face, a pair of Marine boondockers stuck out from behind a knoll. The owner was moaning. "Who are you?" asked Gillespie. "Flynn," came the reply. He had been hit in the shoulder, he told Gillespie. Gillespie figured his own problems were larger than that. "You son of a bitch, stop moaning and move your fucking ass forward!" he blurted. Flynn made it into the seawall ditch and Gillespie got into the shelter of the tiny knoll, but found he could go no further. A corpsman finally pulled him into the ditch. Gillespie's intestines were sticking out; word had been passed that he was dying. One by one, his buddies crept up to say goodbye. One man awkwardly kissed him on the cheek. Another took his hand and said, "Take care of yourself you son-of-a-bitch." Despite their fears, Gillespie was still alive and conscious as he was evacuated out through the ditch and back across the river later that day.

Also evacuated, hours after he was hit, was Lieutenant Dunfey. Dragging a stretcher, a corporal crawled 100 yards to get to him. By then, the 3d Battalion was attempting to regroup. Pinned down in the ditch all day long, the K Company Marines finally got some relief when a couple of armored amtracs churned up to the seawall and drove the Japanese to the cover of their caves. Lieutenant Reginald Fincke emerged on the tidal flat to see two men trying to hold a bloated corpse out of the mud. The dead man was Corporal Frank Coomer, left there the day before. One of the Marines was Coomer's buddy, Squeaky. "I just want to get him to a safe dry place," Squeaky said to the other man. Fincke could see what was happening. He approached Squeaky and offered to help. "I know just the place," he said gently. "You and I will put him up on the seawall next to the bridge. That way the Japs won't see him and our people will pick him up. He'll be taken care of soon."

Ray Gillespie somehow survived the move back to an aid station and then a second move even further back where the wounded were being sorted for transport either to a hospital ship or to field hospitals. Gillespie found himself moved to a third line of stretchers. Still somewhat alert, he noticed a doctor talking to two chaplains. The doctor pointed toward the line of stretchers Gillespie was in. The chaplains walked over to the first stretcher to Gillespie's right. They were giving last rites.

Tears of resignation were welling up in Gillespie's eyes when he heard someone say, "Gillespie, is that you?" Incredibly, it was the same corpsman who had treated him when he was wounded in the Marshall Islands the year before. The corpsman looked at Gillespie's wound, then went and corralled a doctor who also examined the wound. They filled out a tag and the doctor yelled, "Get this man to the Army Field Hospital 76."

Transported to the field hospital, Gillespie found the facility overwhelmed with wounded men. Deep in a morphine-induced fog, he was awakened by someone shaking him. It was his friend, the corpsman. "Hold on, you're fourth in line," urged the corpsman. Gillespie hung on. He survived the operation and eleven days later he was evacuated by air to Guam.[3]

By day's end, the Marines had seized a bridgehead 1,400 yards wide and 400 yards deep. Casualties in some units were heavy. By noon, casualties in 3/22 were estimated at 15 killed and 55 wounded. K Company alone had lost four officers, including Dunfey. The survivors faced an unknown number of enemy troops. Their own supporting weapons remained on the north side of the Asa Kawa.

That night, hoping to get things moving, General Shepherd ordered construction of a Bailey bridge over the river so tank support could be pushed across for the next day's attack. The Japanese laid artillery fire on the bridge site as the engineers began work at 2200. The intermittent shelling delayed completion of the bridge by six hours—it was 1103 before the first Marine tanks rumbled across. "We'll do it again whenever you need us," a little red-haired engineer called to the tankers as they jockeyed forward. "Blast them all to hell!"

Clinging to the other shore, the Marines heard the tanks coming across. "You don't know how good those tanks looked when they came across that day," said Private First Class Charles Pugh. The tanks homed in on the enemy caves and tombs, blowing in the entrances while Marine riflemen gunned down any survivors who scuttled forth.

Even with the arrival of tanks, Charlie Hill continued to be a problem. During the morning Major Thomas J. Myers's 1st Battalion had stalled in front of the hill. In the early afternoon, Myers called for naval gunfire support. The USS *Indianapolis*, flagship of the fleet, stood in near the mouth of the Asa Kawa, registered on the hilltop and put down a succession of almost perfect 8–inch concentrations on the position. The ground shuddered and great lumps of coral tumbled down the hillside. The dust was still hanging in the air when Myers's battalion pushed forward. Incredibly, fire continued to come from a camouflaged pillbox and from slits in the face of the hill. Studying the hill through high powered glasses from a nearby ridge, an observer later said he could see Japanese gather at the mouths of caves to shoot at the Marines; one of the enemy soldiers even seemed to turn and grin at the others before turning back again to fire his rifle at the Marines.

Creeping up the hillside, Charlie Company Marines managed to knock out the pillbox and one platoon of C Company crawled past. Scuttling through tunnels inside the hill, the Japanese reoccupied their original positions and cut off the platoon. Company commander Lloyd, with a squad led by Sergeant Joe Passanante rushed one of the tombs occupied by enemy infantry. In five minutes half the squad was down. The rest took cover.

From lower on the slope, Platoon Sergeant Sam Howard shouted up to Lloyd, "Any wounded up there?" Lloyd said some of the Marines had been hit, but it would be nearly impossible to try to recover them under the Japanese guns. "I'm going!" replied Howard. He ran forward and had almost reached the wounded Marines when a Japanese machine gunner killed him.

The C Company survivors slowly pulled back about 400 yards as tanks clanked forward to fire point-blank into the tombs rimming the edge of the hill. Enemy observers retaliated by directing heavy artillery fire on the tank/infantry teams, breaking up their coordination. The withdrawal and preparatory fire by the tanks took over an hour. Finally, at 1615 the remnants of C Company got up and went for the hill again—and this time they made it to the top. Tired and shaken, they dug in. Japanese counterattacks began at midnight under cover of a heavy mortar barrage. The attacks continued throughout the night, but Charlie Company kept its grip on the hill.

With daylight, tanks again came forward, firing directly into the tombs and pillboxes. Four flamethrower tanks sprayed the most persistent areas of resistance and by nightfall the hill was secure. When Lloyd got around to taking a head count, he found C Company had lost 35 killed and 68 wounded out of its original complement of 256. Examination of Charlie Hill showed the reason. The limestone knob had been fortified over three levels with tunnels and corridors leading into rooms and defense positions. Bunks stood against the walls. Bandages, shattered bottles of medicine, and surgical instruments littered the rank-smelling chambers. One chamber contained a Japanese automobile. Also found were 7 knee mortars, 13 nambu machine guns, two 20 mm guns, two 47 mm guns, 1 heavy field piece mounted on railroad tracks, dozens of mines, hand grenades, 17 small ammo dumps, three large ammo dumps and hundreds of dynamite satchel charges.

Dead enemy soldiers lay scattered about in heaps. Near them were knapsacks taken from Americans in the fighting further north. They were now filled with Japanese socks, charms, picture postcards and underwear. Many of the uniforms were brand new. There was also evidence the Japanese had not been having things all their own way. A freshly sealed chamber—apparently a mass grave—was found. In front of the wall were a hundred or so metal identification tags, medals, and a few swords, rifles and flags.

Lloyd, a small man with a hairline moustache, could not contain his pride over C Company's effort in seizing the hill. "And most of them are just kids," he remarked. "Oughta be in high school some place." Lloyd himself was an ancient 24.

The 22d Marines had made respectable gains over the past two days—better than any other U.S. outfit battering the Shuri Line along its 12–mile length. They could have crossed the Asato Gawa into Naha, but that would have accomplished little militarily. Instead, the plan for 12 May called for the attack to push south and east toward the 1,000–yard-wide corridor between Naha and Shuri. Ultimately, it was intended to cross the upper reaches of the Asato, push toward Kokuba, advance up the Kokuba River Valley toward Yonabaru on the east coast and encircle the Shuri bastion.

Between the Marines and this goal, lying between the Shuri Heights and the Asato estuary, were three small hills, part of an area defended by Colonel Seiko Mita's 15th Independent Infantry Regiment and attached units—numbering about 2,000 men in all. History would come to know this deadly triad as Sugar Loaf, Half Moon, and the Horseshoe.

NOTES

1. For the sake of consistency, hills will be referred to from the defenders'—that is to say, the Japanese—perspective. The "forward slope" will refer to the slope facing the Marines. "Reverse slope" will refer to the side of the hill facing away from the Marines.

2. Not to be confused with the Charlie Hill and Charlie Ridge further south toward Sugar Loaf.

3. Recalled Gillespie, "While on leave from the hospital [in San Francisco] in August 1945, I was at the Trianon Ballroom and felt very awkward and out of place. I saw a girl I knew from high school, she was with two other girls. I spoke and said, "Hello." She looked at me and said, "You look like hell." They turned and left me standing. I left, walked towards downtown, then to the Cherry Street Bridge. I smoked a cigarette or two and then I wept."

Chapter 3

George Company Meets Sugar Loaf

The morning of 12 May started out badly for George Company, one of nine rifle companies in the 22d Marines. Rations, ammunition, and water had just been distributed at early light when a flurry of mortar shells suddenly slammed into the company. A direct hit on the command post took out three runners. Two other men were wounded. The losses brought the company down to 6 officers and 151 men, well below its authorized strength of 7 officers and 236 enlisted.

Captain Owen Stebbins was still reforming platoons and seeing to the evacuation of casualties when the 0730 jump-off time arrived. Stebbins got a semblance of an attack underway by sending out his scouts on schedule. As it turned out, the main attack was delayed anyway, because the tank support had not made its way forward. The tanks finally arrived at about 0807 and George Company jumped off to the attack.

The companies had developed an administrative system similar to that used by battalions. They kept a command post (CP) well behind the lines where the executive officer would gather his headquarters, handle reserves and pass requests to the rear by phone. The captain would be forward of the CP, controlling the two assault platoons, connected by wire or radio to the rear echelon. While on the move, the company commanders were at the mercy of the portable SCR 300 hand-held radios, which had an annoying habit of cutting out behind hills and failing altogether in bad weather.

On the left, 1st Lieutenant Frank Gunter's Easy Company was covering the regiment's exposed flank. Gunter's Marines soon began to take heavy enfilade fire from the Shuri Heights, which overlooked the 2d Battalion from the left and left rear. "We weren't in direct assault contact with the enemy and yet we're getting casualties far beyond what we should be getting," observed Lieutenant John Fitzgerald, executive officer of Easy Company. "That's what killed us." There were few Japanese to be seen. "You could pick them up once in a while in the glasses," said Fitzgerald. "They were almost shapeless forms. Masters of camouflage."

A sergeant came back to the company CP and asked for a tank to deal with a Japanese heavy machine gun. The gun was well dug in and "raising all kinds of hell," recalled Lieutenant Richard "Heavy" Pfuhl, a former enlisted man who had received a battlefield commission. Pfuhl called battalion and soon a tank lurched into view. Pfuhl and the sergeant accompanied the tank to the front line, about 60 yards forward of the CP. The tank remained in defilade while Pfuhl and the sergeant moved up to get a fix on the enemy gun. The sergeant pointed left just as an unfriendly machine gun opened up from the right. The sergeant caught three slugs, flush in the neck, side, and leg. Pfuhl felt a burning sensation as he was hit in the right thigh, lower testicle, and left buttocks by a single bullet. He pulled the sergeant to cover and saw him onto an ambulance jeep before letting a corpsman look at his own injury. "I felt kinda silly on my hands and knees with my skivvies at half mast and a corpsman digging a spent slug out of my big behind," he wrote later. "A little sulpha and I'm as good as new. I bring the tank to the targets and the Sherman works them over until they are quiet."

Pfuhl's small success aside, there wasn't much E Company could do about the fire except try to struggle forward. Their advance soon slowed. Things were better on the right where the George Company Marines pushed forward rapidly against fairly light resistance. Captain Mike Ahearn's F Company followed in reserve. Further toward the coast, the advance was going even better, due in large part to the greater distance from enemy observation and fire from the Shuri massif. The 1st Battalion seized the high ground north of the Asato Gawa (Asato River) by 1400. On the division right, 3/22 reached the commanding ground at 0920 and sent patrols through the suburbs of Naha. The patrols found the bridge over the river demolished and the river bottom muddy and unfordable. Both battalions dug in for the night with their lines on the northern edge of the Naha suburbs.

The division left continued to lag behind. Toward late morning the 3d Battalion of the 29th Marines moved up to help cover the growing gap between Company E and the 1st Marine Division to the left rear. As the units tied in, 2d Battalion commander Lieutenant Colonel Horatio C. Woodhouse assigned G Company a new objective. Taking his three company commanders to a road junction he pointed out a draw or corridor leading to an oddly shaped mound of dirt rising from the flat terrain. "We'll attack that prominent hill," he told them.

"The objective located in Target Area (TA) 7672G was a stark hill, barren except for a few scrubby trees," recalled Captain Stebbins. "It looked no more ominous to us than other draws, ravines, or steep inclines faced in previous combat actions." As far as Stebbins was concerned, this "very unprepossessing hill" looked much less formidable than Charlie Hill, seized by C Company the day before.

If there was anything odd about the hill—which was only about 50 feet high and some 300 yards long—it was the shape. "I guess the best way to describe it was if you took a watermelon and cut it in half," recalled a Sugar Loaf survivor. "And the upper half would be similar to the type of hill it was. It came up steep on all sides . . . it really wasn't all that high."

Woodhouse was no fool. Physically a small, very slender man, he bore little resemblance to the stereotypical Marine, but he was very intelligent, sharp and a fine tactician, well-liked by his officers. He also happened to be a cousin of General Shepherd—they shared the same middle name, "Cornick," and both were graduates of Virginia Military Institute—but Woodhouse's record spoke for itself. He had taken command of the battalion on Guam after the original commanding officer was injured. "He turned that battalion around in 12 hours," recalled a company officer. "He squared us away and we knew we had a winner with him right away." Woodhouse's adept handling of the battalion on northern Okinawa caused it to be referred to in some quarters as the "Lucky 2d." That luck was about to end.

Company G's attack toward the hill would now turn left—south or southeast—taking it away from the southerly direction of the 6th Marine Division main push and exposing the company to enemy fire from the south. In selecting the draw as an assault corridor, the tactically astute Woodhouse had given Stebbins perhaps the only avenue of attack that would offer some protection against converging cross fire.

Little was known about the objective hill. Aerial photographs of 10 May had revealed trenches on TA 7672G. The following day it was noted as a strong point. The division periodic report noted that a captured enemy document indicated the high ground in the area was defended by "a network of small group positions organized for AT [antitank]."

"We didn't think we were going to have too tough a time," recalled Stebbins. The plan was for an attack "against a routine strong point." The Marine infantry would be supported by a platoon of tanks.

The G Company scouts moved out as the tank engines revved and backfired, ready to move up the draw. Lieutenant Robert Nealon's 2d

Platoon worked along a slight rise to the left of the draw. Moving out on a slightly higher ridge to the right, Lieutenant Ed Ruess's 1st Platoon could see the ruins of Naha to the south and across the Asato River. F Company, still in reserve, was mopping up caves, huts and other areas that might harbor snipers. E Company remained on the battalion flank. Both Easy and Fox continued to catch machine-gun and mortar fire from the Shuri Heights.

Initially, the draw provided G Company with some protection from the fire from the flanks, but as the Marines emerged into the open terrain leading up to the objective, the 1st and 2d Platoons came under heavy fire from the hill to their front. The Marines kept pushing. Captain Stebbins had been moving along the draw between the two platoons, two runner-messengers with him forming his observation post (OP). With him was the 3d Platoon under Platoon Sergeant Ed DeMar and the tanks. The Marines stayed some distance from the Shermans, but kept a watchful eye for Japanese satchel attacks on the armor.

The danger was very real. As he followed along, Cliff Mezo saw a big Marine sergeant, a Thompson submachine gun in hand, jump out of the turret hatch of one of the tanks. The sergeant rushed over to a hole in the ground, shoved the muzzle inside and emptied the clip in one sustained burst. As he passed by, Mezo looked down and saw a freshly killed Japanese curled up in the hole. The "spider hole" lid lay nearby. The enemy soldier had been trying to attach a magnetic mine to the sergeant's tank when he was spotted and chased down.

The M4A3 Shermans had not proceeded far up the draw when artillery fire began to fall among them. Moments later, the artillery fire was joined by high-velocity 47 mm antitank fire. One of the tanks on the right stopped in a cloud of smoke—whether it had been hit or was the victim of a near miss, Stebbins was unable to determine. Then a second tank was stopped. Another shell made a direct hit on two Marines advancing behind a tank. The explosion dismembered the two men. The tanks held up as the troops moved on past. "The Japs seemed to have every inch of the terrain zeroed in," noted Cliff Mezo. "The tanks began to take cover behind outcroppings of rock that were 7 to 10 feet high. They would move out to fire on a specific target, then move back to positions behind cover again."

The tank support had little effect on the volume of automatic weapons fire building against the advancing Marine riflemen. Unseen Japanese pounded the Marines, who were all too visible as they struggled forward. Particular trouble was suffered from the so-called "knee mortars," actually a hand-held grenade launcher which fired a projectile about the size of a beer can. The launcher could fire the Japanese Model 91 grenade 175 yards or the Model 89 shell 770 yards—and the enemy used the weapons lavishly and with deadly accuracy. They paid particular attention to the machine-gun squads in the Marine assault platoons. With very little cover on the approach, those machine-gun squads that survived were the crews who set up to give fire support, fired briefly and then moved quickly to a new spot before they could be targeted by the Japanese mortars.

Stebbins carried a hand-held SCR 300 radio to keep in touch with his CP, where the company exec, 1st Lieutenant Dale Bair of Pocatello, Idaho, was coordinating the battalion mortars and artillery support for the infantry assault. Concerned about holding the ridge on his exposed right flank, Stebbins tried to contact Bair, only to find that the walkie-talkie had gone dead. A stolid, serious hulk of a man, Bair stood 6 feet 2 inches tall and weighed in at over 200 pounds. He had won the Silver Star in the Marshall Islands operation; a fellow officer described him as "fearless." Now Bair did just the right thing and kept the fire support going against the rear slope of the hill in an effort to suppress some of the mortar fire directed against the attacking Marines.

Some moments before, Stebbins had sent a runner to Lieutenant Ruess in the 1st Platoon, directing him to pull over to the inner slope of the ridge line. Stebbins hoped this would limit his casualties until he could call the tanks forward to get the attack moving again.

Now Stebbins saw Ruess running toward him through the enemy gunfire, sprinting a few steps, then hitting the deck and scrambling to his feet for another dash.

Ruess dashed up and told Stebbins he could hold where he was despite the cross fire. However, he had about five men who had gotten partially onto the oddly shaped hill to their front and were now trapped. Some of them were wounded. Stebbins could see the men lying on the lower slopes of the hill. The Japanese were beginning to roll grenades down on the injured Marines. Ruess asked for help from the tanks to get his platoon onto the hill.

"Yes, I'll get them," Stebbins replied, figuring the tanks could at least lay in smoke shells and enough covering fire so Ruess's platoon could move onto the hill and bring out their wounded. Stebbins had great respect for Ruess, who was "everything you'd want in a Marine." A husky, rugged, former football player, Ruess was highly aggressive—some thought impetuous, maybe too much so. "You're not running for a touchdown commanding a platoon in combat," observed one of Ruess's friends. "You've got 50 men and you want to protect and lead." As they hunkered down talking things over, Stebbins noticed that Ruess had a dirty bandage around his hand. He later learned Ruess had been wounded in the hand a day or so earlier and not bothered to mention it. It was typical of the lieutenant. "He probably told the corpsman, 'I'll kill ya if you tell anybody,' " Stebbins observed years later.

As Ruess headed back to his platoon, Stebbins stood up to survey the ground one last time before going back for the tanks. Concerned about drawing attention in the open terrain, he had been running a lean OP, with only a runner-messenger besides himself. Despite that precaution, some sharp-eyed Japanese had picked him out as a person of importance. As he got up, the ground around his feet erupted with Japanese machine-gun fire. Hit high in the legs, Stebbins went down. His runner vanished. Stebbins thought the man "ran away to escape the fire," but the youngster was long past running. Killed outright by the same burst that wounded Stebbins, he had rolled out of sight into a ditch.

With no help at hand, no radio and no runner, Stebbins began crawling along a shallow drainage ditch leading some 300–400 yards back toward the company CP. His main thought was to get back and let the CP know that his assault platoons desperately needed tank support—with that in mind, his tortoise-like progress seemed painfully inadequate.

Unaware that Stebbins had been shot, Ed Ruess had returned to his platoon. Private First Class Wendell Majors saw the burly lieutenant trying to push the attack along. "Hey guys, get over here!" yelled Ruess. "They're coming out of their holes! Let's get 'em!"

Ruess had an unnerving way of locating enemy machine guns. He would jump out and jump back, making a target of himself until the gun opened fire. Other Marines would then locate the source of the machine-gun fire. It had worked before, but now Ruess tried the trick once too often. "Watch my tracer," he said, trying to designate a target. He fired and immediately drew automatic weapons fire, some of it kicking up dirt right around him. "He started skipping back and to his left, now firing from the hip instead of the shoulder," observed Cliff Mezo.

The Japanese firing stopped, and Ruess went back to his original position and began to fire again. The Japanese opened up and this time Ruess went down, hit hard. "He had three gunshot wounds in the lower abdomen and seemed in extreme pain," recalled Mezo. "His face began to turn ashen and I didn't feel he would suffer long." Mezo was right. Ruess was tough, but he had been hit too hard; he survived the evacuation from Sugar Loaf only to die of his wounds a couple of days later.

Meanwhile, an alert tank commander spotted Stebbins crabbing his way along the drainage ditch and radioed for stretcher bearers. As Stebbins was being bandaged, Colonel Woodhouse came over with a concerned look. Stebbins briefed him on the situation and the need for tanks to help get the attack moving. As they talked, a young G Company Marine, Wendell Majors, arrived from the line with a message about the situation up front. Lying there with his legs all shot up, Stebbins, typically, had concern only for the youngster. "What, they sent you back alone!" he exclaimed. Fifty years later, Majors marvelled, "Here I had not been touched, and he was so shot up there and was more concerned about me than about himself."

Stebbins and the colonel said their goodbyes and Woodhouse headed off to get Lieutenant Dale Bair and the tank CO to coordinate another attack that afternoon. It was still felt that G Company could move with help from the tanks.[1]

Platoon Sergeant Ed DeMar was reorganizing the remnants of his platoon when Bair arrived and told him Stebbins had been machine gunned in both legs. Ruess was dead, he added.

DeMar, 26, was one of the outfit's few prewar regulars. The Brooklyn-born noncom had enlisted in the Marine Corps a year and a half before Pearl Harbor and spent two years on security duty in Panama before ending up with the 6th Division. To the 18- and 19-year-olds in his platoon, he was an old man: they called him "Mommy," in recognition of his mother-hen attitude toward them. DeMar had inherited 3d Platoon two days earlier when the lieutenant in command was wounded by mortar fire. Now Bair told him that Ruess's platoon had only 19 men left. "The others are just as badly off," he added. "DeMar, how many men do you have left?"

"Twenty-eight," said DeMar.

"We've got to take that hill," said Bair. "No one knows what we'll find up there, but we've got to go up. Easy Company is pinned down and taking a lot of killed and wounded. Can't do a thing. It's up to us." He told DeMar the attack would jump off at 1600, supported by tanks. The plan was simple. DeMar and his men would move forward on the left, while Bair took the 1st Platoon forward on the right. The tanks would move out at the same time. The 2d Platoon already formed a base of fire. A machine-gun section would provide fire support on each flank.

The tanks were waiting in a hollow where they remained out of sight of the Japanese gunners on the hill. Bair and DeMar talked the plan over with the officer in charge of the four Shermans: Circle 1, Circle 2, Circle 3, and Square 1. The tanker wanted some assurance that the Marine infantry wouldn't leave him "high and dry." Without sharp-eyed riflemen keeping guard, his Shermans would be sitting ducks for enemy foot soldiers with satchel charges or antitank grenades. DeMar told him not to worry. "We'll stick to you like flies on shit," he promised. "Don't worry about a thing there."

Returning to his platoon, he briefed his squad leaders, then waited for his watch to wind down to 1600. He was worried about his men. His radio had been knocked out, so communications were going to be problematical, especially with the intense Japanese fire on the flanks. Just to the south, the objective hill rose out of the ground, "just another lump, a brownish incline with a little knoll on top" from what he could see.

And then it was time. The four tanks lumbered up on line and the Marines deployed and started forward at Bair's signal. DeMar had a moment to wish he were someplace else and then he was shepherding his platoon toward the hill.

The enemy fire, already intense, became unbelievable. Small arms and automatic weapons fire came not only from the hill directly ahead, but from two other hills, one to the left and one to the right and slightly behind the objective. Some of his men were already down. Private First Class Jack Houston suddenly saw a Japanese running toward a tank with a satchel charge. At the same time, the gunner in another tank spotted the attacker and vaporized him. Houston "fired at patches of bushes that didn't seem normal, but I couldn't see any Japs though we were getting casualties in the platoon."

On the left flank, the Circle 1 tank shuddered and stopped as it ran over a land mine. Then the Sherman on the right took a hit. Moments later, Square 1 bogged down in a shell hole. The tank commander, Platoon Sergeant George F. Beranek, left the safety of the Sherman to hook up a towing cable. Captain Phil Morell pulled up behind and was watching through his tank commander's periscope when a bullet hit Beranek in the throat, "and he gushed blood as if from a garden hose . . . [it] squirted up all over my tank and everything else."

With no cover, the Marines kept going. Advancing with the demolitions team, Joseph Campanella saw one man hit by enemy fire as he reached the top of the hill. The Marine started to run "and it seemed he ran about 20 feet before he fell dead," recalled Campanella. Captain Phil Morell realized the Japanese were firing from apertures in the face of the hill. "If you were not in their path, you could stand up and be safe—but if you went 10 or 12 feet either way and got in their path of fire, boy you were a dead duck," he observed.

"Men were going down everywhere," recalled DeMar. On his left was his squad leader, Sergeant Richard M. Rupe. To his right was Private First Class Julian "Red Dog" Porter and his BAR (Browing Automatic Rifle) man, Private First Class James "Little Bit" Davis. Suddenly Porter sagged, shot in the head. DeMar saw Private Martin Tucker, a youngster he had known in Panama before the war. The boy wore thick glasses and DeMar had never been able to figure out how he had talked his way into the Marine Corps. Now Tucker lay dead next to his machine gun.

As they approached the crest of the hill, DeMar saw Lieutenant Bair signaling to him. Though immobilized, the Circle 1 tank had its guns in action and was interfering with the attack's left flank. As DeMar started for the tank, he saw Bair lurch as he was hit in the upper part of his left leg. Then DeMar himself was hit by shrapnel in the left thigh. His leg buckled and he fell down. Seeing what was happening, Sergeant Rupe made it to the tank and banged on the turret with his rifle butt, yelling for the tankers to hold their fire.

Phil Morell got out of his tank to consult with the infantry. Outside was total chaos. An amtrac came up with reinforcements and a bullet zipped through the direct vision slot and hit the driver in the middle of his forehead. "The support troops came pouring out a ramp in the rear and were cut down by direct fire," observed Morell. He saw his radio liaison man come running out the rear with his radio on his back; the man suddenly tripped and did a complete somersault. "It probably saved his life as he landed flat on the ground and crawled out of the field of fire," said Morell.

Inside his Sherman, Sergeant Gerald Bunting could see wounded and dead Marines strewn around his disabled tank. A couple of amtracs pulled up to help but were knocked out almost immediately. Some of the wounded were screaming for a corpsman. The tankers emerged from the escape hatch, Bunting toting a light machine gun and several belts of ammunition. Working the gun, he gave covering fire as his crew, the wounded, and other survivors attempted to find cover.

Dragging his numb and useless leg, DeMar crawled up the hill where he saw an incredible sight. Lieutenant Bair was to his right front standing with a light machine gun he had picked up by Tucker's body. Cradling the gun in his arms, the ammunition belt over his shoulder, he fired burst after burst at the Japanese. A bullet struck him in the left arm, but Bair continued to fire, so the surviving Marines could crawl to cover.

Others were past crawling. To his right, DeMar could hear Little Bit Davis screaming, "Mother! Mother! Dad! Dad! Please help me!" Davis was a big youngster and tough enough, but he was only 18 and he had obviously been wounded very badly. Concerned that the noise would draw Japanese to them, DeMar grunted at him to pipe down. Davis eventually stopped screaming. DeMar tried not to think too hard about why.

Among those pinned down in front of Sugar Loaf was Private First Class James Chaisson. Nearby huddled a sergeant, "a big rugged guy . . . crying like a baby." Chaisson went over to the Marine and chided him, "Listen, you're a damned leader. You're not supposed to be over here crying." The man seemed to pull himself together, but Chaisson soon had other concerns of his own.

Bair had been trying to get in touch with Lieutenant Colonel Woodhouse at the 2d Battalion CP, but without success. The CP was in among some big rocks not far behind them, but the radioman couldn't seem to get through, probably because of the terrain. Bair told Chaisson to go back and ask Woodhouse for support on the right side where the assault was taking a lot of fire. Chaisson replied, "Yes, sir!" and took off.

Wading through what appeared to be a drainage ditch running north and south, Chaisson dodged sniper fire from four or five farm houses off to the flank and finally made it back to the battalion CP. Woodhouse had watched him making his way in. "Looked like you were taking a hell of a long time getting here," he told Chaisson unsympathetically.

"Hell, yeah," said Chaisson, not standing on formalities. "There's snipers in those damn houses."

"Dammit, I told them to burn the houses as they went up," said Woodhouse. "When you go back I want you to take a couple of the flamethrowers and burn those houses."

Oh, Jesus, thought Chaisson, sincerely hoping he wouldn't be able to find a flamethrower. Forlorn hope. Two flamethrower men were sitting right there with full tanks, "doing nothing, waiting to burn the whole place down," recalled Chaisson disgustedly.

Woodhouse asked Chaisson about the situation up front. "How many men you got?"

"I don't know, there's 12 to 16 left," said Chaisson. He told the colonel that Bair needed support on the right.

"Well, you tell Dale to bring 'em on back and we're going to send some people up on the right to give you some cover," directed Woodhouse.

Chaisson said there were men pinned down and crying for help. He also complained about the air support. U.S. Corsairs could not seem to separate friend from foe on the forward line. "They're gonna kill us up there!" he told Woodhouse.

"Well, ya'll pull back and we'll see what we can do," said Woodhouse. "It'll be dark pretty soon." He also told Chaisson to take some panels back to mark the Marine position for air support.

On the way out with the flamethrower operators, Chaisson saw one of his buddies, W. M. Daniel. "Hey, Daniel, we need some cover for these flamethrowers," he said.

"Go to hell, I've got nothin' but a 16–gauge shotgun," returned Daniel. He told Chaisson he'd originally been assigned to CP guard and the scatter gun was all he had for a weapon.

"Well listen, you're coming with me, aren't you?" said Chaisson.

"Oh yeah, hell, I'll go with you," sighed Daniel.

Firing his Thompson submachine gun and with Daniel blasting away with his 16–gauge shotgun, Chaisson's little assault team moved up and set fire to the three houses. The minute the houses went up in flames, the snipers stopped, probably burnt to a crisp, assumed Chaisson. A Navy awards board later gave him credit for 12 enemy dead.

Chaisson hadn't forgotten about the air panel he was carrying. Back at the hill, he got to the top of an Okinawan burial tomb and started to unroll the colored cloth panel to mark the U.S. position for friendly planes. "And a damn Nip stood up and looped a hand grenade right over my head," he recalled. The grenade went over Chaisson's head and landed in the little patio area at the entrance of the tomb where three or four Marines were crouching. The explosion killed one Marine and broke another one's leg. The spray of shrapnel also hit Chaisson in the leg and back.

Still mobile, he made his way down the slope and found Bair in a shell hole by the base of the hill. Also in the hole was Private First Class Richard W. Bartelme. He was leaning over, and Chaisson saw he was "dead as a mackerel" with a bullet hole in his head. Bair was also pretty well shot up with a bullet hole in the arm, a bullet furrow across his chest and a nasty hit high up between his legs. Bair had been too busy to have the wounds tended to. The sight upset Chaisson. The big Idahoan was his friend and Chaisson didn't want to see him die. "Dale," he said, "will you sit your ass down so we can get to the holes in your legs."

Bair obligingly sat down and Chaisson started to take his pants off so he could get to the wounds. "Go to hell!" protested Bair. "You're not taking my damn pants off!" Exasperated, Chaisson took his K-bar out and cut off the legs of Bair's pants right up to the crotch. The lieutenant had been hit "right below where it missed the essential parts, but he had some holes in the sides of his leg." Chaisson and the corpsman doused the holes with sulfa powder, applied some bandages, and doctored him up.

Amid all the confusion, Chaisson could hear some Marines crying for help. Four machine gunners had been trapped by enemy fire and were screaming, "Hey, help us! We're pinned down! Heeeelp!" At least one had been badly wounded and appeared to be dying, they called.

By Marine Corps standards, Chaisson, at age 34, was not just old, he was ancient. He'd given up a comfortable deferment because "I got sick of being a damn civilian." His age had made him something of a father figure to both officers and men. Now his age and special relationship to the younger Marines made him feel he had to do something to help the stranded machine gunners.

Mulling it over, he suddenly noticed the indentations made in the ground by the tank treads. The tracks were several inches deep. Jeez, he thought to himself. I can hold on to the back of a damn tank and lay down and I can be pulled out there . . . no Nip can get to me until I get out to the machine gunners. He broached his plan to a nearby Marine.[2] "How about getting on the other side? Let's get out there and get those machine gunners."

"Okay," said the other man without hesitation.

They told the tank driver what they wanted to do, then hung on to the underside of the tank as it rumbled out to where the machine gunners were pinned down. Dropping off, each of them grabbed a wounded man and started back. The trip up had been made under cover; the trip back with the wounded was a different story; now, completely exposed to enemy fire, Chaisson and the other Marine crabbed along with the wounded men, using the track indentations for cover. The two remaining wounded Marines managed to follow the tank out by themselves.

By now, some of the men, realizing the situation was hopeless, had begun dismantling the M1s of dead Marines and scattering the parts around. Still up on the crest, DeMar tried to press himself into the ground. His rifle had jammed from dirt. He'd thrown a couple of grenades over the crest, but now he noticed there didn't seem to be any other Marines around except for dead and wounded. He looked at his watch. It was 1645. Trying to stay calm, he decided to wait where he was. His leg was numb and he knew he had lost a lot of blood, but soon it would be dark. Darkness would give him concealment and maybe he could crawl off the hill before the Japanese found him. He was still waiting when someone spoke to him from behind. The unseen samaritan asked if he had been hit bad. "We asked for smoke up here to get you guys out. Can you crawl?"

"Can I crawl?" replied a greatly relieved DeMar, face still pressed in the dirt. "If I had to, I'd crawl to the States."

Soon afterward the tanks put 140 smoke shells down on the hill and DeMar started down. Someone came up behind and cut off his pack so he could make better progress. DeMar squeezed into a little ditch and kept

crawling until he came up against the corpse of one of his men, Private First
Class "Stoney" Craig. Stoney had taken a bullet through the head. DeMar
tried to drag the body along with him, but the unseen samaritan behind him
urged him on. There was no time to worry about the dead. DeMar finally
made it down the slope where he found Lieutenant Bair, half standing, half
sitting, still holding the machine gun. A few other Marines were also there,
along with one of the tanks.

Gerald Bunting tried to keep the enemy down. "I remember, as I was
standing there firing the machine gun, trying to cover my crew and the few
Marines that was left, I was wondering how we were going to get out,"
Bunting wrote later. He spotted the one remaining tank to his right and told
his crew to make a run for it. Not seeing any more live Marines in the
immediate area, he threw the machine gun and made a dive for the tank.

Also heading back was Jack Houston. He and several other Marines were
creeping back along the trails made by the tank treads in the soft ground.
"The Japs were firing at us, but couldn't depress their weapons enough to
quite hit us," he noted. "But they shot the packs off the backs of some of
the men. We couldn't raise up to take off our packs, so someone in the rear
yelled for everyone to cut the pack off the man in front of him. We did that
and strangely enough, it worked. We then were able to get to better cover
behind the tank."

The wounded were being loaded on the tank. One of them was Little Bit
Davis, who had been pulled out by Jim Chaisson and now lay dying on the
tank's front plate. Another was DeMar. Corporal Howard Perrault, driver
of one of the knocked out tanks, wrapped his battle dressing around
DeMar's thigh. It was Perrault, DeMar learned, who had crept up on the hill
to get him out. As the tankers lifted DeMar onto the tank behind the turret,
Perrault was shot in the leg. He was lifted up and placed next to DeMar.
DeMar leaned toward him to ask where he'd been hit when a burst of enemy
automatic weapons fire ripped through the expeditionary can hanging
inches from his head. Another round hit Perrault in the neck, spattering
DeMar with blood.

Phil Morell had been in contact with Colonel Woodhouse previously and
Woodhouse had told him to re-group and withdraw to a low hill area a few
hundred yards back. Morell had relayed that order to "someone in the
infantry" and they began to move back, using the surviving tank for cover.
"But they were firing down and the shells were ricocheting off the ground
and hitting guys in the feet and ankles," recalled Morell.

DeMar was almost falling off the tank and Bunting pushed him back.
"We're getting the hell out of here," he replied. "Get your ass closer to the

turret and hang on the rail." DeMar did as he was told. He gripped the rail and held Perrault as the tank started back. "You could hear bullets thudding into the body of the man lying next to [DeMar] on top of the tank," said Houston, one of the Marines using the tank as a shield. "[DeMar] was so exposed I can't imagine how he ever survived the fire pouring against the tank."

"The tank gave us some protection from the fire until we got back to a knoll that was our company CP, but during the withdrawal there was a space of 40 to 60 yards that was open to heavy fire," noted Houston. "Of our group around the tank, one was killed and four wounded as we came back. I found the butt plate of my rifle was shattered by a bullet, and bullet holes through my dungaree trousers and jacket sleeves."

Morell suddenly heard a blast of machine-gun fire from directly behind him. "Oh, shit, they are behind us!" he thought, assuming the guns were Japanese. But when he looked, he found they were Marine guns from the 2d Battalion.

Back on his feet and still cradling the light machine gun, Lieutenant Bair put down covering fire as they backed away. With his sawed off trousers, "it looked like he was in a bathing suit," observed Chaisson. Chaisson himself was laying down fire with his tommy gun and the other Marines were firing when they could. Just before they got behind the rocks where the CP was located, Bair got hit yet again, this time through the buttocks. "Down he went," recalled Chaisson. "He just couldn't take any more." And then, incredibly, Bair started to get up again, struggling to pick up the machine gun.

"For Christ sakes, leave the damn machine gun, Dale," shouted Chaisson. "Get the hell behind the rocks!"

Wounded four times, Bair docilely did as he was told. He left the machine gun on the ground and sought cover behind the rocks.

No sooner had Bair found cover than the youngster standing next to Chaisson crumpled with a rifle bullet through the guts. Chaisson put him on his shoulder and carried him back to the rocks, though he didn't hold out much hope that the man would survive.

Pulling back with the others, Cliff Mezo was nervous about being so close to the tank because he knew they drew fire. The Sherman had rotated the turret to the rear and was putting machine-gun fire on the hill. Seeing a big rock outcropping just ahead and to the left, Mezo yelled, "Come on," and ran for cover. But no one followed. He stopped a few feet from the outcropping, turned and yelled again, "Come on!" An instant later something slammed into his chest. It felt like he'd been hit with a sledgehammer.

He fell down and tried to catch his breath. The next thing he knew, he was behind the rock and someone was dressing a wound in his chest.

Captain Phil Morell made it back to a low ridge and found himself talking to Lieutenant Colonel Woodhouse about what had happened. One of his radio liaison men, a boy named John Penn, came up with a message from the tank battalion commander. For some reason Morell couldn't comprehend, Penn was shouting at the top of his lungs. One of the battalion communications people said, "Look, Skipper," and pointed to the back of Penn's head. Morell looked and saw a piece of shrapnel about an inch and a half long sticking out of Penn's skull just behind his ear.

Meanwhile, the tank had brought Ed DeMar and the other wounded to the Fox Company CP. A lieutenant came over to help him off the tank. DeMar told him to get Davis and Perrault off first. The lieutenant came back too quickly. "Sarge," he said, "they're both dead," and helped DeMar off the tank. A Fox Company sergeant asked DeMar how things were going. "Pretty rough on that goddamn hill," replied DeMar.

Huddled in the cover of the rocks at the company CP, Jim Chaisson was hurting. His leg was bandaged, his back was peppered with little shrapnel holes. Still, he considered himself lucky. "I didn't have my guts blown out like a lot of them did," he observed darkly. Other Marines, many of them wounded, were still pinned down out to the front—a few trying to survive by playing dead. Lieutenant Nealon came over to Chaisson and said, "Chaisson, you want to try it again and see if you can go and get those fellas out there? They're pinned down."

Stiff from his wounds, Chaisson looked at him and said, "Yeah, I'll go."

"No, don't send Chaisson," someone else pitched in. "He's been up there enough."

Chaisson decided to take their word for it. "I was so damn tired, I could hardly speak," he recalled. Seeing an amtrac coming up for the wounded, he threw his pack in it and then stopped to confer with Nealon. "And I missed the damn amtrac," he remembered. "The amtrac took off with my pack. So I said, Oh Jesus. All my good souvenirs were in my pack. All gone. And my clothes. So I felt kind of bad. And I was hurt and I was tired and I was bleeding here and there." Casting around, Chaisson saw a truck parked off to the side. He crawled underneath and promptly fell asleep.

Cliff Mezo was luckier. He was put on a stretcher in a jeep rigged as an ambulance. It was getting dark by then and the road back was rough. The driver apologized whenever he hit a hole. Later Mezo found himself in a field hospital. He was stripped and placed on a table where a doctor was going to cut and clean around his wound. Mezo heard someone say they were going to burn his clothes and managed to warn them about the blasting caps in a special pocket in his trousers. Then the doctor gave him a shot and he went out.

Ed DeMar was put on a truck at the battalion aid station. The battalion surgeon handed him a bottle of whiskey. DeMar figured he was supposed to take a sip or two and then give it back. The truck pulled out with DeMar still in firm possession of the bottle. When he got to regiment, the chaplain came over and asked DeMar's religion. "Protestant," said DeMar. The chaplain looked at DeMar's dungarees and exclaimed, "Good grief, Sergeant, is that all your blood?"

"No, sir," said DeMar. "Some of it is, but most of it belonged to a tanker who had just tried to pick me up when he took a fatal round in the neck."

The chaplain reached down in his bag and broke out a bottle of brandy. "Here, Sergeant, take a couple of tumblers of this. It'll make you feel better."

DeMar obliged.

At 1000 that evening, Lieutenant Colonel Woodhouse sent a series of grim and dispassionate notes to regiment:

Got as far as 7672 George [later named "Sugar Loaf Hill"]. Took hill but casualties were so heavy that George could not hold it.

Estimate about 75 men left in George Company including Headquarters platoon.

7672 George is tunneled and caved. Lost three tanks in that area. All wounded were evacuated. 3–4 dead were left behind.

The 2d Battalion's failure to seize Sugar Loaf on 12 May came as a surprise not only to the Marines who participated in the effort, but to those who had ordered it. As far as the 6th Division was concerned, the unprepossessing hill wasn't even a major objective; it was just another piece of ground needed to amass fire support against a higher hill called Kokuba about a mile farther south on the other side of the Asato Gawa.

What made Sugar Loaf such a stunner was its seeming insignificance. There had been no fears expressed that Captain Stebbins's G Company would not be able to handle the objective. "It wasn't a mountain," recalled a veteran of the fighting. "It wasn't even a hill. It was a piece of shit."

This "piece of shit" had just stopped the attack of a Marine rifle company supported by tanks. The tanks alone had expended 852 rounds of 75 mm, 140 two-inch smoke rounds and 86,250 rounds of .30 caliber. Three tanks had been abandoned out beyond Marine lines. It was clear to Lieutenant Colonel Woodhouse that the hill would have to be softened up by air strikes and artillery before his Marines tried again.

The enemy units facing the 6th Marine Division appeared to be elements of the newly arrived 44th Independent Mixed Brigade. As early as 11 May the 6th Division reported taking a diary from a dead Japanese corporal. The title page bore the notation 15th IMR and gave the commanding officer's name as "Mita." Identifications from other enemy dead indicted the presence of the 3d Battalion, 2d Infantry Unit of the 44th IMB, "and probably a battalion of the 44th IMB." Also identified was the 81st Field Antiaircraft Battalion (with six 75 mm guns) and the 103d Machine Cannon Battalion, armed with 20 mm guns. The 44th IMB had a total strength of 4,485, which included the 2d Infantry Unit (2,046), 15th IMR (1,885) and attached artillery and engineers. As the Marines of the 6th Tank Battalion could testify, there were also antitank units in the area, but these had yet to be identified.

The enemy troops appeared to be in peak condition. "A considerable number of enemy dead examined were wearing clean clothing, new shoes, and gave no indication of having been in caves or trenches for any length of time," observed a division intelligence evaluation. "It was also noted that these fresh and well-supplied troops clung savagely to their pockets of resistance until destroyed at close quarters by advancing troops." Enemy morale was described as "extremely high."

As darkness fell, Marines continued to straggle back through the lines. Some of them had feigned death to avoid attention from the Japanese. Other Marines, truly dead, would lie out in the open, exposed to the elements, for days before they could be retrieved. G Company had taken a terrible beating. Ed DeMar's 3d Platoon alone had lost five killed and ten wounded—a casualty rate of 50 percent. The other rifle platoons had also been hit hard, as had the attached machine gun sections. Both the 1st and 3rd Platoons were without platoon leaders and platoon sergeants. "We'd been shot up so bad that the 3d Platoon no longer existed, and our squads and fire teams were gone because the company was short of people," observed Jack Houston.

All told, G Company had lost four more officers, Platoon Sergeant Ed DeMar and 81 enlisted—more men than the company had left. Among the dead was Corpsman Carmine Villano, killed when he dashed out to save a wounded Marine. Lieutenant Hugh T. "Hymie" Crane, G Company's third company commander in one day, walked the lines, tying everybody in. The survivors were exhausted and in a state of shock. Digging in for the night, G Company machine gunner Corporal Dan Dereschuk was "boned out exhausted." The last thing he remembered was trying to build a parapet for cover in front of his gun. When he awoke the next morning, he still had his entrenching tool in one hand and a piece of rock in the other.

Some replacements were also received. A number of these arrived at Headquarters Company, 22d Marines, the night of 12 May where they came under the wing of Private First Class D. C. Rigby. Rigby was struck by how painfully young and naive the replacements were. They were kids, maybe 17 or 18 years old and they didn't know much of anything. Rigby heard two of them get into an argument over how much windage to put on their rifles. "You won't need any windage on it," he informed them grimly. "You'll be so close, just point it and pull the trigger." The two youngsters just looked at him. "They didn't know hardly what to say," recalled Rigby.

Jim Chaisson, wounded during the G Company assault on 12 May finally found his way to a hospital, but not before one last stroke of good fortune. Waking up, stiff and sore, under a truck the morning of the 13th, he hitched a ride to the rear on an amtrac, still distressed over the disappearance of his pack and souvenirs. But on the way back to the hospital, he saw a field with about four numbered amtracs parked there. "Goddamn!" he exclaimed. "There's number 21. That's where my pack is!"

Chaisson asked the driver to stop, jumped out, and went over to the number 21 amtrac to find three or four Marines sitting around. They had opened his pack and were dividing up his souvenirs. "Fellas, that's my pack," said Chaisson, presumably something of an apparition all covered with blood and bandages. "You'd better let me have it."

"You know," he recalled in some surprise years later, "they put everything back and handed it to me."

Guam, May 12—(Associated Press)—Four attacking American divisions and bitterly resisting Japanese were locked in close quarter combat today along the entire Okinawa island front where both sides frequently charged with fixed bayonets.

Perhaps 50,000 to 100,000 Japanese and Americans were involved in fighting over ridges and ravines. . . . "You won't see spectacular advances because this isn't that kind of fighting," said Lieutenant General Simon Bolivar Buckner, Jr. as his Tenth Army opened its greatest assault yesterday while Japanese suicide planes attacked shipping off-shore. "But you will see many Japs killed and you will see them gradually rolled back."

NOTES

1. Stebbins's left leg healed quickly and cleanly. The right leg was another story, having a big hole in the thigh. The injury was first thought to have been caused by a "dum-dum" bullet, but later was figured to be from a ricochet which tumbled end over end through Stebbins's leg.

2. Later Chaisson could remember only that the man was from Bend, Oregon.

Chapter 4

The Push Continues

It would be four more days before the Marines fully understood the significance of the hill complex that had decimated G Company, 22d.

The irregularly rectangular lump of a hill—soon to be dubbed "Sugar Loaf"—looked almost innocuous under the shadow of the Shuri hill mass to the east. Before the war, Okinawans had called the height Kerama-chiiji or "Kerama Top" because from its top one could see all the way to the Kerama Islands, 15 miles to the west. The Japanese referred to it simply as Hill 51.2. Only 50 to 60 feet tall and about 300 yards long, there was hardly room for a crowded company on top. But the hill, a pile of reddish dirt and boulders, had an importance belied by its appearance. Heavily fortified with caves and tunnels, it formed one element of a triangular system of defenses which anchored the western end of the General Ushijima's Shuri Defense Line.

About a quarter of a mile southeast of Sugar Loaf lay another hill, soon to be titled "Half Moon" by virtue of its shape. A narrow-gauge railway ran south through the valley between the two hills, winding gradually down to Naha. A Marine who dug in next to the track was startled to see that the steel was boldly stamped, "Tennessee 1914." Less than 200 yards to the south of Sugar Loaf lay still another hill, soon to be known as "the Horseshoe."[1]

From a defensive standpoint, the three hills formed a spearhead aimed at the advancing 6th Marine Division, with Half Moon and the Horseshoe serving as the base and Sugar Loaf as the point. Each supported the other, making any assault—as G Company discovered to its sorrow—a very costly enterprise. It was not a large area—Major Phillips D. Carleton observed, "the whole battlefield and its approaches could be put inside a thousand yard square"—but the Japanese had turned that square into a killing zone, what 6th Marine Division historians later called "an almost classic study in static defense."

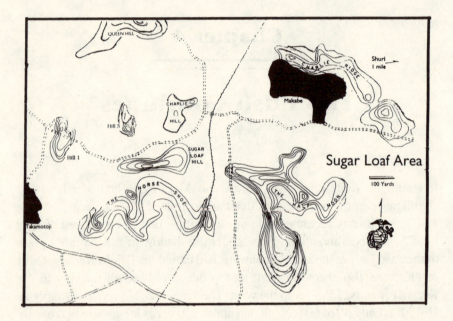

A deep depression in the Horseshoe gave the Japanese protected mortar positions, immune to anything short of a close in attack with aimed rifle fire and grenades. Tunnels and galleries riddled the hill system, allowing the covered movement of supplies and troops. Later in the campaign, the Marines would capture enemy sketch maps of defense positions on Sugar Loaf and Half Moon. The maps indicated the Japanese were holding each hill in less than company strength. Those numbers were misleading in that plenty of reserves were available should any part of the defense be threatened. The garrisons were also heavily armed. The sketch maps indicated the presence of at least 45 mortars and 29 grenade dischargers.

The terrain heavily favored the defenders. There was no cover on the bare approaches for an attacker. All they could do was approach as close as possible in the best defilade they could find, then break forward in a sudden assault. Marines assaulting any one part of the system were in full view and exposed to fire from the other two.

The entire area was also open to fire from machine guns, mortars and artillery emplaced on the Shuri Hill mass just to the east and northeast. Behind Sugar Loaf and its supporting hills lay a broad corridor which led into the Shuri fortress area. But so long as the Japanese retained possession of the three hills, they had little to fear from any flanking movement from the west. "For strategic location and tactical strength it is hard to conceive of a more powerful location than the Sugar Loaf terrain offered," concluded the 6th Marine Division Special Action Report.

Enemy artillery pounded the Marines. As the division history later admitted, "[The enemy] used their artillery with an accuracy and coordination beyond anything yet encountered in the Pacific." Watching from the Shuri Heights, the Japanese could see every move the 6th made. "They could put them shells in a milk bottle," a Marine observed in undisguised awe. It was later estimated that weapons zeroed in from other locations—unseen and unreachable—caused between 50 and 75 percent of the American casualties around Sugar Loaf. The Japanese had plenty of artillery, thanks to shipments originally bound for the Philippines but stranded on Okinawa by U.S. submarine attacks. The 44th Independent Mixed Brigade alone had at least eight 100 mm howitzers and four mountain guns. These weapons were supported by artillery and mortars of adjacent units.

In quieter times, Naha had been the site of a Japanese artillery school. During the months of preparation before the actual invasion, the Japanese had reportedly used Hill 51.2 [Sugar Loaf] for artillery spotting. The whole area was reported to have been an artillery training ground. Some Marines noticed red stakes on the battlefield—speculation was that they were Japanese aiming stakes. Artillery fire was so precise, the gunners did not even need to use registration rounds.

"My God, we were getting battery fire!" recalled Captain Marvin "Stormy" Sexton, still taken aback 50 years later. It was the first time Sexton—a former Marine Raider and combat officer of wide experience—had ever been subjected to massed Japanese battery fire. "I was told afterwards by a number of people that the Japanese were laying down school problems that they had mapped out in that very area on paper during their artillery training," he remembered.

On the morning of 13 May, the 6th Marine Division attack was scheduled to jump off at 0730. The jump-off was delayed until 1115 because supplies and rocket trucks were late in getting to the front lines over the rough terrain.

Despite the beating taken by G/2/22 on 12 May, the division apparently failed to recognize how fiercely the Japanese were prepared to contest the Marine advance. The division periodic report for 13 May noted, "The enemy has lost possession of the important tactical terrain between Naha and the Asa Kawa, and by the end of the period, no heavily organized enemy defenses had been noted to the Division's front."

Shepherd decided to make the main effort on the left where 2/22 and 3/29 [battalions] worked toward the high ground overlooking the upper reaches of the Asato River. Noted the 22d Marines special action report, "Without stating so, this order meant that 2/22 must attack one thousand yards and make the Regimental main effort in that the 1/22 and the 3/22 on the coast had already reached their portion of the phase line which overlooked Naha." Artillery fire from the division guns and naval gunfire from ships offshore—including one battleship, four cruisers, and three destroyers—attempted to soften up the resistance. Supporting aircraft flew many sorties to deliver rockets and hundreds of 100–pound and 500–pound bombs against enemy positions. Despite that pounding, Japanese opposition was strong from the start.

Among those moving up with 3/29 was Lieutenant Perry Zemlicka's G Company platoon. Coming up on a ridge line known as Queen Hill less than 200 yards north of Sugar Loaf, "Zem," as he was nicknamed, saw a line of dead Marines by the base of the slope, where they had apparently been gunned down by an automatic weapon.[2] As he surveyed the situation, blond-headed Private First Class Gilbert Costa started up the slope. Zemlicka called to him and as Costa turned, a nambu opened up from a cave behind them and hit the boy right in the chest.

Costa fell close to some foxholes dug by the Marines that had passed through earlier. Zemlicka ran up the slope, jumped in one of the holes and tried to pull Costa in. Platoon Sergeant George C. Munier, an old salt who had fought on Guadalcanal back in 1942, also scrambled up the slope. Munier got hold of Costa's legs and started to push him into the hole with Zemlicka. It was the last thing he ever did. Watching from the cover of some holes just down the slope, the other Marines saw a bullet hit Munier square in the head, practically between the eyes. "He never knew what hit him," recalled a witness.

Zemlicka was again reaching out for Costa when something hit him a terrific blow to the side of the head. A sniper had shot him through the ear, the slug coming out the back of his neck. Zemlicka fell back in the hole, out of sight from the Marines on the slope below.

One of those Marines was Private First Class H. Ross Wilkerson, known to his buddies as "Tennessee." Wilkerson and two other Marines had taken cover in a shell hole as the nambu raked the slope. "Any time anybody'd move, they'd shoot," he recalled. "They had us all pinned down." After a while the corpsman, a man by the name of Newell, jumped in the hole with them. He said Costa was dead, so was Munier. Some of the others had been hit. "What about Zem?" inquired Wilkerson.

"Well, Zem got hit," said Newell. "He got hit in the head. I ran up there and put a wound pack on him and did the best I could for him, but he's probably dead by now."

It was about two hours later by Wilkerson's reckoning—about 1400— when he heard a voice up on the hilltop calling, "Tennessee! Tennessee!"

"Yeah!" Wilkerson shouted back. "Is that you, Zem?"

"Yeah," came the reply.

"You want me to come get you?" shouted Wilkerson.

"No," replied Zemlicka. "Just keep talking. I'm coming to you."

Suddenly Zemlicka jumped up, clutched his head, and "just wobbled" down the hill toward Wilkerson's hole. As Wilkerson reached up and pulled him in, the nambu opened up, but Zemlicka's move had caught them by surprise and they missed.

Down in the shell hole, Wilkerson was looking at Zemlicka in horror. The lieutenant's head had swelled like a watermelon. One of his eyeballs had been pushed nearly out of the socket. As Zemlicka pulled his helmet off, the wound started bleeding again, the blood running down his chest. "Zem, you all right?" asked Wilkerson, knowing full well he wasn't anywhere near all right.

"Yeah, I'm gonna be okay," said Zemlicka. "We just got to get out of here though."

Talking it over, Wilkerson and Zemlicka decided the only way anybody was going to get out of there was with the help of a tank. Leaving his rifle, but taking Zemlicka's .45, Wilkerson crawled out of the hole toward the rear to find a tank. He got back to the company command post (CP) and told them what the situation was and got on the field phone. It wasn't more than four or five minutes before a tank came clanking up. Using the tank as a shield, Wilkerson and a couple of other Marines helped Zemlicka walk back as nambu bullets ricocheted off the armor on the other side. Finally out of the line of fire, they lifted the lieutenant onto the tank, tied him down, and the tank took him out[3].

Tank and infantry teams of 2/22 were also subjected to murderous fire from the hill complex to the front and flanks. Due to G Company's heavy losses the day before, the burden fell on E and F Companies.

By late afternoon, E Company had reached a small knob north of Sugar Loaf, but was forced to give ground in the face of enemy fire. F Company, which waited all morning for 3/29 to come abreast before it attacked toward an adjacent knob, was also stalled and finally driven back by enemy fire.

The battalion special action report noted that some Marines made it as far as Sugar Loaf, but "were driven off because of insufficient troops."

Lieutenant Joe Bystry's F Company platoon was savaged by enemy mortars. Nothing seemed to be going on, when all of a sudden, 18 or 20 mortar shells slammed in. It looked just like "somebody throwing a handful of stones up in the air," noted Bystry. That one volley cost his platoon three dead and eight wounded. Bystry couldn't understand why the Japanese didn't follow up with more shells. "They would have got us all," he said.

"The policy was to pick up the wounded and the rifles and get out of there," recalled Bystry. "Leave the dead. So my sergeant and I started going around and looking . . . 'This one, he's dead. He's dead.' And we came to Caldwell. I knew Caldwell because he was the only other Connecticut guy there. We came to Caldwell and the sergeant said, 'I think he's dead.' And I said, 'No, I don't think so.' I've got to admit, Caldwell looked bad. But I said, 'No, take him back.' So they carried him back."

Bystry was talking with his company commanding officer (CO) when one of his men came over and said, "Caldwell's okay! Come over here!" Recalled Bystry, "They had to pry his teeth open with a bayonet because he was foaming at the mouth, he couldn't breathe. And they pried his teeth open, he started breathing and they took him back to the hospital." Caldwell suffered 43 puncture wounds from mortar shell fragments, the worst of which almost took off his foot, but he survived. Later he told Bystry he had been able to hear them discussing whether or not he was alive, but had been unable to speak.

Also wounded during the afternoon was F Company commander Mike Ahearn, who took a machine-gun burst in the leg. The battalion commander, Lieutenant Colonel Horatio Woodhouse, called the company executive officer, Lieutenant Ed Pesely, on the radio to go forward and relieve Ahearn, but Ahearn refused to leave while the fighting continued. "Every time the stretcher bearers came to take Mike to the aid station, he would put another wounded man on the stretcher instead," recalled Pesely, a 28-year-old Californian who had won the Silver Star during the Guam campaign.

Finally Woodhouse came up to the Fox Company observation post in person and ordered Ahearn to get on the very next stretcher. Just to be sure the stubborn company commander did as he was told, Woodhouse stayed there until Ahearn turned the radio over to Pesely. By 1800 the tanks had to retire and the attack was called off. Ahearn was evacuated, things quieted down, and F Company began to dig in for the night.

On the left, 3/29, with H Company spearheading, moved forward about 300 yards before darkness and seized the forward slopes of a hill just northwest of the town of Makabe. Japanese on the hill had been firing on the left rear of 2/22 throughout the day. Despite that success, by the end of the day, the two assault battalions had pushed no more than 200–300 yards.

Meanwhile, the 3d Battalion, 22d had been directed to reconnoiter the northern outskirts of Naha. Patrols from the 22d Marines also entered the village of Amike, north of Naha Town. Accompanying one of those patrols was 18–year-old Private First Class Frank Shumann, a husky blond Yalie from Easton, Pennsylvania. Shumann had originally been assigned as a runner at division headquarters but that assignment hadn't been adventurous enough for him. He badgered his officers for frontline duty, finally talking his way into an advanced observation post where he spotted a number of enemy strong points. Then, typically, the boy the others called "Eager Beaver" offered to lead a patrol to the positions.

The morning patrol ran into an enemy machine gun and lost two men severely wounded. A stronger push, this one consisting of an L Company platoon supported by tanks, was mounted at 1400. Shumann was near the lead. "I think I know where that mortar pocket is," he said, referring to a particularly bothersome Japanese position. "I saw them when we were down there this morning."

Dead Japanese lay here and there along the road as the platoon pushed toward Amike, but the Marines saw no live enemy. They were 200 yards north of the Asato River when the Japanese finally opened up with mortars and machine guns. Shumann was among the first men hit, going down with a machine-gun bullet through his right knee. Pulling himself forward with his elbows, he worked toward the source of the fire, stopping every few seconds to fire his submachine gun. Fifty feet ahead he spotted the Japanese mortar position. "There!" he shouted, pointing. "There!"

Another burst of nambu slugs went through Shumann's leg, but he continued to inch forward, still shooting. He probably never saw the group of Japanese to his right as they pitched two grenades at him. The first grenade went over his head but the second exploded only inches from him, killing him instantly.

The enemy was well concealed within the village. Narrow streets hampered the Marine tanks. One of the Shermans was disabled by a satchel charge as it entered the village. The others pulled out. Another tank/infantry assault from the north also pulled back after running into heavy machine-gun fire. Regiment ordered the village destroyed. The tanks and troops leveled the buildings, killing an estimated 75 defenders, then withdrew at 1830.

During the day, the remnants of G Company, 22d, remained on the knoll facing Sugar Loaf. Jack Houston came back behind the knoll to get some chow. Later on he saw two Marines up on some high ground to the company left firing at random. "I was just a Pfc (private first class) without authority, but it seemed stupid to me," he recalled. The company had been shot up in the same area the day before and it was no place to take chances. Houston yelled at the pair to get down. Laughingly, they did, but ten minutes later they were at it again.

"What's wrong with—" Houston's warning was cut off by the *splat!* of a bullet slamming into flesh and bone. The rear man did a complete somersault and landed on his back. Where his left eye and nose had been was a huge hole with blood pumping out of it. "It sounded like the contents pouring out of an upside down milk bottle," recalled Houston. Seconds later, the other man, still up on the knoll, abruptly grabbed his neck and slid to the ground as a bullet hit him.

Houston called a corpsman. The two Marines were still alive when they were carried out.

The 22d Marines had taken a beating in the push from the Asa Kawa since May 10. Casualties numbered about 800 and the regiment's combat efficiency was clearly impaired.

Recognizing the erosion of capabilities, General Shepherd redisposed his troops on 13 May to maintain the impetus of the attack. The remainder of the 29th Marines went into position behind 3/29 where they could strengthen the division effort the following day. The 4th Marines, held in corps reserve, were sent south to take over the old positions of the 29th Marines, guard the division's rear areas and back up the armored amphibs posted to watch the open flank on the sea.

Working along the coastal area, Private First Class Ray Schlinder's K Company machine-gun outfit had been in action during the day. The fighting had not been as bad as 10 May, though they continued to take casualties. One of Schlinder's buddies suffered a crushed shin when a cave exploded after being squirted with a flamethrower. The Marine couldn't have been happier. He lay back on the litter, contentedly puffing on a cigarette and exhorting, "Go get 'em, boys! I'm going home!"

Late that afternoon Schlinder's machine-gun section set up along a seawall near a sheer cliff some 80 to 90 feet high. Schlinder's outfit had lost a number of men in the fighting along the rugged coastal heights. Now, told to face his machine gun out toward the sea in case the Japanese attempted a forced landing, he was jittery about the cliff to his rear and the possibility of bypassed enemy troops creeping up on him. The Michigan teenager built up a pile of rocks behind his position, thinking if "there was one sitting up there behind me he was going to use me like a rifle range."

It was just getting dark when Schlinder saw some men walking toward him behind the Marine front line. "Who's out there?" he demanded. The file identified themselves as members of the 2d Platoon with chow. Schlinder could see the boxes of rations as they trudged past. Twenty minutes later he spotted some more people walking by. "Hey, who's out there?" he called. Nobody replied and suddenly Schlinder realized the men were wearing round shiny helmets. There must have been eight or ten of them, not more than ten yards away—and behind him.

Schlinder searched frantically for his grenades, finally found one, and threw it. People started running in all directions as the other Marines also opened up. The next morning the Marines found 38 dead Japanese sprawled about the area. Schlinder suspected they had been bypassed earlier in the day and were trying to slip back to their own units.

Up on Queen Hill the bodies of Sergeant Munier and Private First Class Costa had not been recovered. The rest of the outfit had tied in for the night just to the north where they could bring the slope of the hill under fire. As darkness fell, Private First Class Ross Wilkerson spotted six or eight Japanese creeping toward the two dead Marines. Wilkerson was just about to open up on them when another man down the line shouted, "Halt!" It was a stupid thing to do—long experience had taught the Marines that anything moving around at night was Japanese—but it was done. The Japanese knew they had been spotted and reacted immediately.

"They just hit the deck right away and started throwing grenades at us," recalled Wilkerson. "There was a grenade that hit—I could hear it hit—but didn't know where it was at. I hollered, '*Grenade!*' and we all went to the bottom of the foxholes and the grenade went off between our foxholes. If we hadn't done that—gone down—it would have killed us."

The Marines returned fire, and in the morning found four dead Japanese, each with a demolitions pack tied to his body. "They were either going to blow up somebody or they were going to booby-trap these [dead] Marines," observed Wilkerson.

The evil little hill in Target Area 7672G had already been baptized in blood. But it was 14 May before it received the name it would carry into Marine Corps legend: Sugar Loaf.

Early on the morning of 14 May—a miserable day of clouds and incessant rain—Lieutenant Colonel Woodhouse assembled the company commanders of Easy, Fox, and George Companies to brief them on plans to continue the attack to the south toward Naha. The Okinawan capital was still hidden from view by three small hills that had held up the battalion on 12 and 13 May.

In his attack orders, Woodhouse designated the hills as Hills 1, 2 and 3 from right to left. Hills 1 and 3, each about 30 feet high, were closest, while Hill 2, the largest of the three at about 50 feet in height, was between 100 and 150 yards farther south. Colonel Woodhouse stipulated that Fox Company would make the attack with one platoon to capture Hill 1 on the right and one platoon to capture Hill 3 on the left. Easy Company would relieve the Fox Company platoon on Hill 1 and George Company would relieve the other Fox Company platoon on Hill 3. Then Fox Company, with all three platoons, would continue the attack to capture Hill 2.

By now the division had better intelligence on the enemy units manning defenses just to the south. Division intelligence reported the Marines appeared to be in contact with the 2d and 3d Battalions of the 15th IMR, the 2d Independent Battalion and the 223d Special Guard Force. Elements of the 7th Independent Antitank Battalion would also soon be identified. Total Japanese strength in the immediate area was put at about 1,650, which was probably an underestimate—and in any case did not take into account reserves which could be brought up from Naha and vicinity.

Woodhouse asked if there were any questions. One of the company commanders—apparently being of an orderly, logical cast of mind—asked why the hills were not numbered in the sequence they were to be attacked, with the two nearer hills being labeled 1 and 2 and the larger hill in the distance being Hill 3.

"Okay," said Woodhouse, "then this is how we will designate three hills: Hill 1 is the hill to the right, Hill 3 is the hill to the left, and the farther hill will be called Sugar Loaf instead of Hill 2."

Officers later recalled that during training exercises on Guadalcanal, Woodhouse had referred to at least one peculiarly shaped objective hill as "Sugar Loaf" apparently because it looked like a certain southern dessert dish. Hill 2 did in fact look like a loaf and Woodhouse's spur-of-the-moment nickname stuck.

The 2d Battalion's assault was to be one small piece of an attack by both corps of the Tenth Army to clear the western and eastern approaches to Shuri and envelope Ushijima's flanks. Woodhouse had specified that the attack wait until the 1st Marine Division on the exposed left flank came up on line with the 2d Battalion. But at 1130 the Assistant Division Commander, Brigadier General William T. Clement, arrived at the battalion command post and issued a written field order to Woodhouse directing that the battalion not wait for the 1st Marine Division to come up on the flank. The rest of the order was calculated to worry even the hardest Marine. The battalion was to move into the attack as soon as possible and continue it at all costs. Clement repeated the words "at all cost" lest there be any misunderstanding.

The appearance of an assistant division commander at a battalion command post to relay orders was extremely unusual. Beyond that, Woodhouse expressed muted doubts about the tone of the directive. He remarked to Lieutenant Ed Pesely, the Fox Company CO (commanding officer), that the "all costs" order was reminiscent of World War I. "He said it was not the school solution, but we had to comply," recalled Pesely of Woodhouse's reaction to the order.

Lieutenant Rodney Gaumnitz's 1st Platoon stormed up Hill 1 at about 1440. Hardly even meriting the title of "bump in the ground," the 30–foot hill was nevertheless hotly contested by Japanese using small arms and grenade launchers. Watching the assault from their positions to the west, B Company Marines were startled to see a Japanese soldier creep up over a mound in the field beyond and signal to someone below him. A grenade launcher coughed, sending a projectile toward Gaumnitz's platoon on Hill 1. The B Company Marines fired a hasty volley and the Japanese turned, eyed them with obvious surprise and scuttled out of sight.

By 1420, the 2d Battalion received information that Gaumnitz was on Hill 1, but was receiving considerable fire from Hill 3. "Need tanks to clean out draw between 2 and 3," reported the assault platoons ten minutes later. "F can't move out until they do." Meanwhile, Hill 3 was seized by Lieutenant Robert Hutchings. Hutchings lost most of his platoon to fire from the left flank and from the left rear—completely exposed because of the failure of the 1st Marine Division to come abreast. It was a problem that would plague the 6th Marine Division assault for days to come as the 1st Marine Division battled for the Shuri massif to the east.

By now the situation had become somewhat confused. At 1452 the 2d Battalion noted that tanks and infantry were moving in the draw between Hills 1 and Sugar Loaf. Eight minutes later the Battalion Journal noted that the Marines on Hill 1 needed help. "Plenty of Japs coming around right side," noted the journal.

What was happening was that E Company had relieved Gaumnitz's platoon on Hill 1 and Gaumnitz, accompanied by tanks, had continued the attack toward Sugar Loaf. Later, a fellow officer would remember Gaumnitz as a good-looking, stocky blond youngster. He had joined the battalion two or three months before, and he tended to keep to himself. "Nobody really got to know him," recalled another lieutenant. But he obviously had an aggressive nature in battle. Platoon leader Joe Bystry thought Gaumnitz's behavior was almost suicidal. "He was the only one that had a walkie-talkie," recalled Bystry. "They were bulky things. They didn't operate very well. And he was standing up there in the middle of nowhere and talking on it. He didn't crouch down, lie down, nothing."

Woodhouse contacted Pesely and told him he was scheduling another attack on Sugar Loaf with all the personnel Pesely could muster from Fox Company. The attack would be supported by a platoon of five tanks, said Woodhouse, and would be covered by smoke from artillery fire. Woodhouse subsequently called back and said the artillery had run out of smoke shells, but he would have the tanks start their attack five minutes before the infantry jumped off. The distance to Sugar Loaf was short, he observed, and the smoke from the tanks and the dust from supporting fires would somewhat shield the advancing riflemen. The G Company survivors were ordered over to Hill 3 to provide additional support for the assault. Down to about 75 men after two days of fighting, the survivors were consolidated into one rifle platoon to support Company F in the attack.

As he arrived, Private First Class Jack Houston saw a cluster of men at the bottom of the hill. He knew there was no way they could provide fire support from down there, so he climbed up to the crest and looked over to see a Japanese soldier just starting down the hill opposite him. Houston fired two rounds at the man, who jumped into a hole and disappeared from sight. As Houston fired the second round, a bullet snapped past his ear, so close he felt the breeze. He decided to withdraw and check up with the men below. "They told me they'd already lost three men up there before we came and all were shot right between the eyes," observed Houston, feeling that they might have imparted that information a little earlier.

Out on the plain, the tank and infantry attack was also in trouble. As the tanks neared Sugar Loaf, the base of the hill opened up in reply, exposing many more gun ports that the Marines had not noticed before. As the tanks moved forward, Pesely could hear a Japanese antitank gun located somewhere to the south of Sugar Loaf, placing direct fire on the Marine Shermans. Some shells ricocheted off the tanks with mournful moans.

Waiting in support along the railway cut, Lieutenant John Fitzgerald, executive officer of Easy Company, saw Major Henry A. Courtney come ambling up with the regimental chaplain, Father Gene Kelly. Courtney, the battalion exec, was a 29-year-old reserve officer from Duluth, Minnesota, a lawyer in civilian life. A veteran of Iceland and Guadalcanal, he was new to the battalion, having joined in the fall after the Guam operation. A big man with a slightly dour look—an impression enhanced by his quiet, reserved nature—he was an exceedingly devout Catholic. In chats with Father Kelly, he had indicated an interest in the priesthood. Friends and family called him "Bob." Those who were less enamored referred to him as "Smiley," in a less-than-enthusiastic tribute to his serious demeanor.

Unlike most executive officers, who generally stayed back to take care of "beans and bullets," Courtney had a reputation as "sort of a rover," recalled a fellow officer. He had suffered a slight shrapnel wound in the right thigh on 9 May, but stayed with the battalion. He had also spent the night with the frontline troops after G Company's bloodletting on 12 May, apparently feeling his presence might help steady the men.

Now, having moved into the railway cut as enemy fire buzzed about, Father Kelly began distributing the host to the waiting E Company Marines. Courtney had a chaw of tobacco in his mouth; he got down on his knees and spat the chaw into his hand and Father Kelly gave him the host. "Then Father blessed everybody and went about his duties," recalled Fitzgerald. Courtney just remarked, "See you guys later," and headed forward.

Then the tanks started coming back. One of them stopped by the rail cut and a crew member scrambled out the hatch. He had been wounded, though not badly, and was clearly agitated. "I got a kid badly hurt in there," he told the infantrymen. "We need help." The Marines summoned a couple of corpsmen and helped a red-headed freckled youngster out of the tank. The Marine looked to be about 17 years old and his arm was off to the elbow. Still in shock, he didn't seem fully aware of what had happened to him.

The tanks were falling victim to Japanese 47 mm guns set up to cover the killing ground in front of Sugar Loaf. Looking out to his front, Fitzgerald saw "the whole battlefield was just alive with flaming, burning and destroyed tanks." It was clear to him that whatever was happening on the hills, the Marines were losing the tank battle. One tank after another was methodically knocked out. Within about 25 minutes three of the Shermans were burning in the open ground fronting Sugar Loaf. But the tanks had destroyed a lot of gunports as they were being knocked out themselves. Meanwhile, Pesely's 3d Platoon under Lieutenant Joe Bystry seemed to disappear in the terrain in front of Sugar Loaf.

In fact, Bystry's platoon hadn't disappeared, but it was in trouble. The Sherman tank they were following stopped to fire high explosive rounds into a cave entrance, leaving the platoon stalled in the open under heavy fire. Caught without cover, the Marines pressed themselves into the ground and stayed as motionless as possible in hopes they would escape attention.

Bystry ran up to the rear of the tank and picked up the phone there. "What's the hold-up?" he demanded. "Jesus, our guys are exposed. There's no bushes or stones or anything to hide behind."

"There's Japs in that cave," replied the tank commander.

"Well, put in some phosphorus," said Bystry.

The tankers fired a phosphorus round into the cave. Two Japanese ran out, all ablaze, fell down, curled up and died. Still the tank didn't move. Down on one knee, trying to shield himself from enemy fire, Bystry demanded, "What's the hold-up now? Let's get going! We're getting the hell knocked out of us here!"

"We haven't got orders to move yet," replied the tanker.

Bystry slammed the phone down in frustration and stood up just as a knee mortar round exploded next to him, knocking him back down. Shrapnel sliced into his left knee, and a larger piece drove into his bowels. One of his Marines helped him back to battalion. Bystry noticed his vision seemed to be failing, but he could still see bullets hitting the ground around them. Somehow they made it back. One of Bystry's friends leaned over him and looked at the wounds. "Oh, Joe, that's nothing," he reassured him. "You'll make out okay." Soon afterwards, Bystry was loaded into a jeep ambulance. Dopey from morphine, later that night he found himself in a lighted tent. Two doctors were talking. "I'll do this one," said one of the doctors, indicating Bystry. "Doctor," protested the other, "you've been on your feet for 20 hours straight." The first doctor replied, "I'll just do this one." Bystry later learned he had been receiving blood transfusions for four hours before the operation. He didn't remember a thing about it.

By afternoon, Woodhouse was less concerned with seizing more ground than with holding what he had managed to wrest from the Japanese. He also wanted more men. At 1500, the colonel, "considering his losses and the obvious strength of the enemy to the front requested more troops to aid his battalion to hold what had been taken." Shortly afterward the 22d Marines reported that the 2d Battalion was only 60 percent effective, short 472 men from its normal strength.

Division was not particularly sympathetic. At 1515 Woodhouse logged a message from the regimental operations officer noting, "General Shepherd has ordered that the division objective must be taken before dark, without fail, regardless of consequences." As a concession to his losses, at 1545 Woodhouse was given K Company of 3/22 to bolster the attack. Hoping to make the assault while some daylight still remained, at 1630 he ordered E Company to support the attack by fire while F assaulted the hill. Supporting artillery battered Sugar Loaf and the two companion hills for

30 minutes before the jump-off F Company followed tanks and an artillery-laid smoke screen. The newly arrived K Company was kept in reserve.

Providing covering fire from Hill 3, Private First Class Wendell Majors and the remnants of G Company could see the Fox Company assault. Majors, an Arkansas farmboy, had been in college when his draft notice arrived. His older brother, a Marine, had advised Majors to get into another branch of the service, but when he went to join the Navy, a Marine gunnery sergeant put his papers to one side. "Majors, you're a Marine, too," he announced. That had been less than a year ago.

Now Majors watched as the assault emerged into the open. "The naval bombardment—you'd think that nobody could live up there in that kind of concussion—and within five minutes after the shelling stopped [the Japanese] were back there and they just cut us down like a mowing machine going through a hayfield," noted Majors. "I saw a machine gun cut across a platoon out there and it looked like . . . it reminded me of a mowing machine. The tanks had to go in and lay smoke grenades down and get all the wounded back out."

Also providing covering fire was machine gunner Dan Dereschuk. His 2d Platoon was set up along a ridge about 75 feet above the draw leading toward Sugar Loaf. It was open with very little cover or concealment and they were under constant mortar and machine-gun fire from the left flank. The fire wiped out the other machine-gun crew in the second section. Dereschuk was firing across the draw at a range of about 800 yards when a sniper put a bullet into the feedway of his machine gun, blasting a spray of metal fragments into Dereschuk's face. The corpsman dug out the powder and pieces of brass from the shell casings. "He painted up my face like an Indian warrior and put on some bandaids," recalled the machine gunner.

Undaunted, Dereschuk went over to where the other machine gunners had been knocked out, found their gun, mounted it on his squad's tripod and went back into action. Sergeant Milo Loveless, Dereschuk's section leader, came over and they noticed some troops moving across an open draw on their exposed right flank toward an adjoining hill. At first they thought the troops were Marines from the 1st or 3d Battalion moving abreast. "Then they headed straight into a cave at the base of the hill," observed Dereschuk.

The machine gunners knew no Marine unit of squad size would run into a cave, so they began firing on them. "The Japs kept coming and continued to head for the cave," recalled Dereschuk. "For the next half hour I had the best firing on the machine gun I'd had during the whole campaign. They continued crossing toward the cave and I laid in grazing fire around the cave opening." His only regret later was that he couldn't walk over there to see "the mess" he was making.

They also continued to fire on Sugar Loaf in support of the F Company attack, but that was becoming a lost cause. The gun ran out of ammo about the time F Company started to withdraw. There weren't many of them left.

Ed Pesely had lost contact with Gaumnitz and the 1st Platoon. Pesely didn't know whether Gaumnitz was a casualty or if the youngster's radio was out. "I saw a few members of his platoon that were passed through by Easy Company and I had them join me at my observation post," he recalled.

Pesely was contemplating the stalemate on his hands when Courtney appeared. Courtney told Pesely that Fox Company had troops on top of Sugar Loaf. He claimed he could recognize Lieutenant Gaumnitz. As they stood talking, someone on top of the hill, weaponless and without a helmet, appeared out of a hole and ran across the crest of the hill, looked at Pesely and Courtney for a few seconds, then disappeared into another hole before anyone could take a shot at him. Another man suddenly did the same thing. "That must be one of your Marines," said Courtney.

Pesely, described by a fellow officer as "a very quick, high intensity guy," was also an experienced man. He had served a hitch in the Marines before the war, later received a field commission, participated in the Marshall Islands campaign and had earned a Silver Star and Purple Heart on Guam. Now he expressed skepticism that the men on the hill were Marines. He told Courtney he had seen the same thing several times already. Why would Marines "be running on top of the hill looking at us and then disappearing down a hole instead of waving at us to come and join them?" he asked. Courtney left without resolving the issue.

Sunset was at 1908. It was getting toward dusk when Pesely joined Lieutenant Hutchings's group behind Hill 3. All that remained of Fox Company was gathered there except for the 15–man mortar section. There weren't many of them. Major Courtney joined them again. He continued to insist there were Marines on top of Sugar Loaf and said as soon as it was dark, that Pesely's men would join up with them. "Okay," said Pesely, still feeling Courtney was wrong.

Also present was Lieutenant Bob Nealon, one of only two officers left in G Company. Nealon was "a feisty little guy." Now he gave Courtney a bit of argument about the mission. Colonel Woodhouse had told him to relieve Fox Company on Hill 3 and that was what he was going to do, he said. "Courtney talked to several people who objected also in one form or another," recalled Pesely.

Courtney reiterated that Fox Company already had men on top of the hill and "we should join them also," noted Pesely. It would be easier to do it at night than to fight to take the hill tomorrow, added Courtney. "He slapped a few on the back and cajoled others until all agreed that we would go with him," recalled Pesely.

Pesely contacted Colonel Woodhouse on the radio. Woodhouse asked what Courtney planned to do. Pesely told him about Courtney's plan to get up on Sugar Loaf in the dark. Woodhouse agreed it might work. He also commented that Courtney was "walking wounded and he [Woodhouse] had lost contact with him for several hours." Pesely went on to say that Courtney did not appear to be carrying a weapon and that Courtney insisted there were Marines on top of the hill.

Over on Hill 3, Corporal Walt Rutkowski, one of the few survivors of G Company, saw his platoon leader, Lieutenant Nealon, approaching in the gathering gloom. Two days before, George Company had crossed the Asa Kawa with 215 men, about 35 men under its normal complement. Now Nealon told Rutkowski, "There's only 50 of us left from the company. You can take the first 25 and [Corporal] Steve Stankovich can take the other 25."

Rutkowski figured his troubles were over. "I thought he was telling us we were going back of the lines and take a rest," he recalled.

Nealon abruptly shattered that happy illusion. "At 1900 we're going to have smoke. We're going right up to that hill over there," he said, pointing toward Sugar Loaf.

Corporal Dan Dereschuk's group got word to drop back down to the draw below the high ground they were on. There they found Courtney with a supply of .30 caliber ammo and grenades. Wendell Majors was also among the group of Marines. Courtney told them, "After dark we're going up there, we're going to get on top of that hill and we're going to secure it. Every man will get his rations here and we'll be taking off after dark."

"Major Courtney told us we had to take Sugar Loaf Hill that night and hold onto it, or we would be overrun if we didn't," recalled Dereschuk. "He said he would personally lead us up there in the attack."

Private First Class Jack Houston also heard Courtney make his pitch. The major said the attackers were too exposed during the day; a night assault would provide concealment from the enemy gunners. Houston didn't like the idea. "We had a basic Marine Corps rule for a Pacific combat zone at night," he recalled: "*If it moves shoot it!*—because anything moving at night was Jap." From the expressions around him, it was obvious he wasn't the only veteran who doubted the wisdom of Courtney's plan.

While the Marines waited, Father Kelly held a brief service, then talked quietly with some of the men. Dereschuk told the priest he believed in God "and if I got back we would talk." Other men, he noticed, "seemed to feel they would never get back."

Rutkowski also went down the slope with his men and was waiting when Major Courtney spotted him. "What are you waiting for?" he asked Rutkowski.

"I'm waiting for my BARs (Browning Automatic Rifle) to give me covering fire on my flanks," replied Rutkowski.

"We don't have time for that," said Courtney. "It's getting darker and the smoke is gonna be shot. So we'd better get moving."

At 1900 F Company reported to Woodhouse, "Only Gaumnitz and two men still on Sugar Loaf. Their position is untenable. About 22 men (total) left in the 1st, 2d and 3d Platoons." Twenty minutes later the Battalion Journal noted there were many casualties in the draw between Hills 1 and 2. This was followed by a message from Courtney, reporting, "Heard nothing of Gaumnitz of late."

Star shells were starting to light up the area—the usual night illumination as the Marines got ready to set forth. By looking around the left side of Hill 3, they could see the rise of Sugar Loaf Hill looming across their direct front. Flares drifting down behind the hill outlined the skeletal trees on the skyline. Courtney said the signal to move would be the burning out of the last flare. He asked Pesely to call battalion and stop all flares so they could move out and link up with Lieutenant Gaumnitz on Sugar Loaf. It took only a few minutes for the last few flares to cross over them, ignite and drift slowly down before flickering out to leave all in darkness.

NOTES

1. Half Moon was also referred to as Crescent Hill. The Horseshoe was sometimes referred to as King's Ridge.

2. Zemlicka recalls several dead Marines already on the slope. H. Ross Wilkerson recalls seeing only two, obviously killed the day before and lying by some foxholes on the slope.

3. Zemlicka not only survived, he was able to rejoin his unit in Guam after the division returned from Okinawa.

Chapter 5

Night Attack

When the last flare flickered out, the Marines started toward Sugar Loaf, Major Courtney leading the column on a barely discernible footpath. Later estimates put their number at 45: 15 men and two officers from Fox Company, 1 officer and 26 men from George Company, and Major Courtney.

"It was dusk, but you could still make out objects and shapes," recalled Corporal Dan Dereschuk, moving up with his machine-gun section. Jack Houston noted, "it seemed almost immediately a machine gun opened up with fire going over our heads." Apparently the enemy gunner couldn't depress the weapon to bear on them since the column remained below the line of fire. Courtney yelled, "Keep going! Keep going!"

They were 50 or 60 yards out when a small light gleamed back on Hill 3. It appeared to be a candle in a cave. "I'm going to take a shot at it," said a Marine. He did and the light went out. "Hey, let's knock that off," snapped Courtney. "Let's keep moving so we can get to the top of the hill."

Private First Class Fred McGowan was an assistant BAR (Browning Automatic Rifle) man, having just joined F Company. "I was in the last fire team of the 3d squad," he observed. "So I was the last damn man in line. Which isn't too comfortable, you know. Your backside's bare. You feel just about like you're walking down Main Street naked on a crowded day." The BAR man, Private First Class John Brown, suddenly blurted, "I ain't staying back here." He started jogging up the line. Brown had passed six or seven men in the file when a Japanese emerged from nowhere and threw a grenade at the column. Brown caught the whole blast. He died on the spot. Lieutenant Ed Pesely told someone to pick up Brown's BAR and the column moved on.

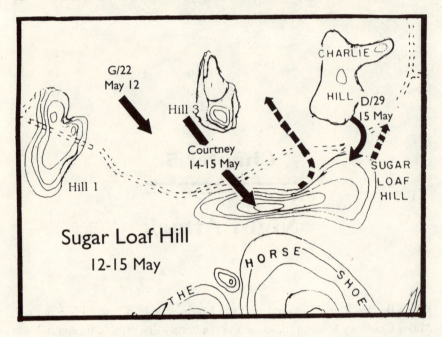

Sugar Loaf Hill
12-15 May

Dan Dereschuk's squad came abreast of a hump in the ground about two thirds of the way to Sugar Loaf just as two Japanese emerged from a cave jabbering to each other. They were only about 20 feet away. Dereschuk went to cut them down with his tommy gun. He had never had a problem with the gun before; now it jammed. He ripped out a phosphorus grenade and threw it after the two as they ducked back into the cave, then ran to catch up with the rest of the column.

As the column closed on the base of Sugar Loaf, Courtney began shouting, "Gaumnitz! Gaumnitz!" There was no response. As Pesely had believed all along, the only Marines left on Sugar Loaf from Gaumnitz's assault had been dead for hours. Courtney told the men to get up on the hillside and dig in. He moved around positioning the men. "Start digging in," he said. "We're going to stay here for right now." It was just 1930. The move to Sugar Loaf had taken about 20 minutes.

Among those digging in was Private First Class Wendell Majors. "The hill had been bombarded so much that it was just loose shale," he observed. "And it's hard to be quiet whenever your shovel is digging into loose shale." But it appeared they had completely surprised the Japanese. One enemy soldier blithely wandered up, apparently thinking the Marines were friendly troops. It was the last mistake he ever made. The Marines shot him down.

Pesely got on the radio and reported to Woodhouse that they had reached the hill and he could start the flares again. "He said to keep him informed and that he had lots of artillery support and naval gunfire," noted Pesely.

The Japanese were already reacting. "No sooner had we started digging when hand grenades started coming across the top of the hill at us," recalled Pesely. "After a shovelful dug here and there, a grenade would come over, we would move and pretty soon it was useless to move any further. We had to keep an eye open for incoming grenades while we dug. The flares lit the whole hilltop. We could see the grenades smoking as they came in our direction, so they were rather easy to dodge."

Dereschuk's men moved up to the middle of the hill. Courtney sent Corporal Stephen Stankovich's 2d Platoon and six or eight men to the left flank of the hill in case any Japanese tried to move around behind them from that side. Then he told Dereschuk to move his squad with two machine guns to the right flank of Sugar Loaf and set up his guns to cover the draw that side of the hill.

Jack Houston and his foxhole buddy, Rocco Pilari, were assigned to a hole toward the back of the hill to protect the rear. The hill was a mass of shell holes from three days of mortar and artillery fire, air bombardment and naval gunfire. Flares bursting overhead kept their surroundings almost as light as day, but with a garish, surrealistic edge. Houston was watching the crest when he saw a branch-festooned Japanese helmet appear over the top. "Look at that," he said to Pilari; then someone fired and the helmet disappeared.

Grenades started rolling down around their hole, thrown by unseen Japanese on the other side of the crest. A grenade exploded in a stack of BAR clips lying nearby and knocked one of the clips into their hole. Assuming it was a live grenade, Pilari pushed it into the ground with both feet, exclaiming, "Is that one?" Luckily for him, it wasn't, but Houston was impressed with his buddy's instinctive courage.

At 1945 Courtney informed battalion that he was on Sugar Loaf Hill. Fifteen minutes later he added, "Short on men, grenades and ammo. Have not found Gaumnitz."

Ed Pesely was still trying to dig in when Courtney came by and told him to commandeer an amphibious tractor they could hear working in behind Hills 1 and 3 to their rear. He told Pesely to take the tractor, go back to the battalion area and get all the grenades he could find. As Pesely started to leave, Lieutenant Hutchings came up and said, "Ed, you will never make it alive alone. I'm going with you." Pesely didn't argue with him. They started down the hill and were immediately caught in the bursting light of a flare.

They froze, waited for it to burn out and started again, only to freeze as another flare popped overhead. Pesely felt as if they were "as tall as Eiffel Towers" as they stood there; he expected to be shot at any moment. It also sounded as if the tractor was moving away from them. "The hell with this," he told Hutchings. "Let's keep running!"

As they ran, a wire suddenly snagged Pesely across the chest. He realized it was a communications wire he had seen Lieutenant Nealon's men stringing as they moved toward Sugar Loaf; he and Hutchings had somehow gotten turned around and were heading in the wrong direction, toward the 1st Marine Division area. Picking up the wire, he let it slip through his fingers as they ran toward Hill 3. "Several Marines came down from Hill 3 and said it was good that they recognized our voices because they were ready to shoot us," noted Pesely. "We told them we wanted that tractor. They told us that the tractor was picking up Fox Company casualties."

Waylaying the amtrac, Pesely demanded that the crew stop picking up casualties and take him back to the battalion command post. The driver retorted that he had orders from Colonel Woodhouse to pick up casualties, "and that was what he was going to do." Pesely was debating what to do, when someone in the back of the tractor piped up, "Hey Pese, give us a break. . . . We have been out all day fighting. Give us a chance to get back to the aid station after all we have done for you."

There wasn't much Pesely could say to that. He and Hutchings started to help pick up casualties. All of the bodies were pretty well shot up and cold," observed Pesely. "One body did not even have a head. It must have been hit repeatedly by machine gun fire." He saw a corporal from his outfit sitting at the edge of a water-filled hole. At first Pesely thought the man was sleeping. He pulled on him, but there was no response and the corpse fell sideways into the water. Looking up at Sugar Loaf Hill, he thought he recognized Courtney, "outlined by a flare, looking down at us. If he was hollering at us to go after grenades, I couldn't hear him."

Up on Sugar Loaf, the Marines were under fire both from the front and from somewhere to the rear. Within the first hour one of Dan Dereschuk's two machine guns was knocked out. One of the squad was killed and two were wounded. One of the wounded, Private Robert Steinhebel, had taken a machine-gun burst in the stomach. He kept screaming and moaning for morphine and water, but Dereschuk couldn't give him either one because of the type of wound. Steinhebel's cries were attracting even more enemy fire. Dereschuk pondered what he could do to keep the youngster quiet. "Then I did what only a young kid in a desperate situation might do," he recalled. "I crawled over and clipped him on the point of the jaw with a quick swing of my fist. He went out like a light."

Fred McGowan's sergeant decided to take a couple of men and clear the flank behind them. McGowan saw the old veteran reach behind, pull out his bayonet, and snap it on the end of his M1. "That kind of scared me a little bit," he admitted. He remembered an instructor he had had in basic training. The man had been wounded in the Marshall Islands campaign. One day the talk had turned to bayonets, and the veteran remarked, "Let me tell you something. When one of them sons of bitches comes running at you with a bayonet and gets real close, you want to have one more round in the chamber or be able to outrun the son of a bitch." McGowan had always considered that very sound advice. "I never had any intention of taking on one of those bastards with a bayonet," he observed. The old sergeant, bayonet fixed, disappeared into the night. McGowan never saw him again.

Over by Walt Rutkowski, a Marine by the name of Ed Tew had been wounded in the eye. In bandaging the injury, the corpsman had covered both eyes, so Tew couldn't do much except sit in his foxhole. Pretty soon a Japanese hand grenade sailed in and exploded, driving fragments into his legs. Tew came scrambling over to Rutkowski, having tilted the bandage over so he could see with his good eye. "I'm getting out of here," he announced.

"Just hang in for awhile," said Rutkowski. "We've got an amtrac coming to take you guys back."

"I'm going back to the first aid station," repeated Tew.

Rutkowski tried to talk him out of it. "Just wait here," he said. "You don't know what's in between us and the lines back there. The amtrac is coming, they'll be more than glad to take you back. Just hang in."

"I'm not waiting," retorted Tew. "I'm going right now." And he did. Though Tew survived, Rutkowski never saw him again.

By now, some of the men were out of hand grenades—a shortage the Japanese didn't seem to share. Over to Rutkowski's left, a couple of Marines were talking excitedly. They could hear the Japanese jabbering away just over the crest, but all they had left to throw at them were a couple of smoke grenades. "I'm going to throw a smoke," said one of the Marines. "Jesus Christ!" blurted Rutkowski. "Don't throw any smoke now. It'll help them more than it'll help us. It's not going to do them any harm." The Marine must have realized Rutkowski was right because he didn't throw the smoke grenade.

Wendell Majors couldn't even guess at how many hand grenades sailed back and forth over the top of the hill as the enemy woke up to the fact that the Marines were in possession of the forward slope. The Japanese would throw a grenade, the Marines would see the movement and shoot. "But then our rifles at night would always leave a flame for about two feet off the end of the barrel—when we'd fire, [the Japanese] would look and see that flash and here would come more hand grenades," recalled Majors.

Out by the base of the hill half a dozen tanks stood derelict from earlier attacks. At least one was still burning and giving off some light. A Japanese worked his way down by one of the knocked-out Shermans and began taunting the Marines, "Heeeeey, Americans! Heeeeey, Americans!" A Marine sergeant down on the lower part of the hill scanned the spot looking for the source of the noise. Suddenly he shouted, "Hey you, you yellow-bellied son of a bitch!" And he shot the infiltrator. "And I don't know where he hit him," said Majors, "but it must have been in the stomach because that Jap started squealing and his pitch was like a pig squeal. Somebody hollered, 'Hey Sarge, shoot him again!' And somebody else shouted back, 'No, don't shoot him again. Let that son-of-a-bitch squeal. It's good morale for us up here.' "

The sergeant didn't shoot, and the Marines listened to their victim shriek for nearly half an hour before the noise finally stopped.

Ed Pesely and Hutchings had finally arrived at the battalion command post, hitching a ride on the amtrac full of wounded as it rumbled on back to the aid station. Colonel Woodhouse was by their side almost immediately. In addition to grenades, he said he was sending an amphibious tractor full of supplies for the continuation of the attack the next day. "He said we were welcome to the whole tractorful," noted Pesely. "Besides grenades, the tractor had flamethrowers and food in that load."

Woodhouse asked if there was anything else he could do. Pesely said they could use some men. There weren't too many Marines up on Sugar Loaf and they were spread pretty thin, he explained. Woodhouse said Pesely could have all the replacements he had received from the regiment for command post (CP) security—a total of 27 men. If Fox and George Companies could not hold Sugar Loaf, there was no reason to have people back at the battalion CP, he observed. There were a couple of bakers and cooks and some communicators in the party. It did not take long to get them assembled, and they climbed on top of the supply-laden amtrac. "When loaded, it looked like a pyramid," noted Pesely.

Leading the reinforcements was Lieutenant Walter R. Jamieson. A veteran of Guam, Jamieson had argued and cajoled his way out of division headquarters to 2/22. Day after day, he had watched the jeep ambulances carrying Marine bodies back from the front, their feet sticking out of the racks and bouncing up and down as the jeep jolted along. He wanted to do more. On 14 May he had been given 25 replacements who had been in the Marine Corps for about eight weeks, and a second lieutenant with six months of service. At about 2130, Woodhouse had called for him. "I hate to do this, but I'm sending you right up now to the front," he told Jamieson.

Pesely was anxious to get back to Courtney, especially after the delay in picking up the casualties. He and Hutchings lay alongside the gunnels up front and directed the driver toward Sugar Loaf, looming up in the light of the flares. When they arrived at the base of the hill, Pesely tried to locate the path he had used going up the height earlier in the evening. The amtrac moved slowly along the base until Pesely told the driver to stop. He did and promptly dropped the rear ramp, letting some cases of ammunition fall off the ramp and under the rear of the tractor.

Courtney shouted for them to back up about 30 yards to the pathway leading up the hill, but the driver said he could not back up with all the cases of ammo that had dropped under the tractor. Pesely, Hutchings and a few other Marines started to clear the cases away. "Just then, about eye-level, the base of Sugar Loaf opened up with orange flashes, shooting point blank at us," recalled Pesely. "I felt the rounds hitting the dirt at my feet and passing between my legs."

The Marines ran behind the tractor and the shooting stopped. The driver repeated that he couldn't go anywhere until the ammunition was out of the way. The Marines ventured out again and cleared the cases without drawing any more fire. The driver backed up to the path and the unloading began. Boxes of grenades were passed up the slope along a human chain. It was about midnight, by Pesely's reckoning.

The newly arrived reinforcements were fed into the line. Private First Class Leon Paice noticed that most of the new arrivals were carrying carbines—an indication they had been scraped up from the rear areas of the division and were not experienced frontline troops. The men unloading the amtracs used bayonets and K-Bars to hack away the metal straps around each case of grenades. Each grenade was encased in a separate container wrapped with tape. They stacked the grenades in small piles and had the men come down one at a time and pick up all they could carry.

Dereschuk and some of the other Marines picked up the wounded and dead and loaded them on the amtrac. Among them were some Fox Company bodies from the assault earlier in the day, including one lucky "corpse" who started to groan when he was picked up and put on the amtrac. Steinhebel was also still alive as he left the hill; he would survive.

Still clinging to the side of the hill as the grenade duel continued, Wendell Majors was feeling a lot better after listening to the Japanese soldier squeal his life away down by the tank. It proved they were human after all. A Marine down slope called to the man next to Majors, asking who was with him. On the lines, Majors always went by the nickname "Deacon." A lot of the Japanese could understand English, the enemy liked to go after officers; Majors didn't want to draw unnecessary attention from some enemy soldier who mistook him for a major. But this time, the man with him forgot the precaution and shouted back, "Majors!" The shout brought a grenade sailing over. It hit right in front of Majors and bounced into his hole. Majors groped around for it momentarily, then leaped out of the hole and threw himself on the ground just as the grenade went off. Uninjured, he scrambled back into the hole.

Soon afterwards he looked up to see a Japanese soldier charging toward him with a grenade in his hand. Majors could hear bullets hitting the man—"we could hear them pop just like they were going through a wet paper sack"—but the Japanese kept coming. "I would say that roughly 20 rounds went through that guy before he finally dropped and as he was falling, he still popped that grenade on his helmet and tried to throw it, but he threw it wild." The enemy soldier collapsed not more than 15 feet from where Majors was dug in.

The incident had an amusing sidelight. One of the wounded Marines had been hollering for help, claiming he couldn't make his way down to the corpsman at the base of the hill. But after being on the receiving end of the one-man banzai charge, Majors recalled, "he found out he *could* move and he *did* move and went back down there where the corpsman was and got patched up."

By now it was clear to Courtney that they couldn't stay where they were indefinitely while the Japanese held the crest and pitched grenades down on them. Demolitions men had sealed up about three of the caves on the U.S.-held northern slope, but there seemed to be quite a bit of activity on the south side of the hill, as if the Japanese were getting ready to counterattack. Courtney decided to take the initiative. He told the men to each take two grenades; they would crawl up the slope and throw them both over the crest as quickly as they could when he gave the word. Then they would surge up to the crest and kill any Japanese who had survived the grenades. "We'll have our own attack—our own banzai," he told the men. Everybody was to fix bayonets.

Courtney also had the spotter bring the artillery in closer where it was hitting just on the other side of the hill. Shells suddenly began hitting the top of the hill and in among the Marines. Courtney yelled at the spotter to raise the fire and the explosions moved further out until the shells were striking just over the crest. Courtney had also requested more flares—three in the air at a time—so the terrain was starkly illuminated. "Let's take the goddamn hill!" he shouted. Lieutenant Jamieson saw him lead off and "all the rest of us, all together, as if a whistle had been blown to signal the start of a game, stepped out after him." There were about 50 Marines altogether, guessed Jamieson.

As Wendell Majors crawled forward, the sling on his rifle came loose on the lower end and he stopped to hook it back up. Lieutenant Nealon came up behind him. He apparently thought "I had chickened out," recalled Majors, for he slapped Majors on the back, gave him some words of encouragement and told him to go on. Majors explained what had happened and Nealon moved on.

Also creeping forward, Ed Pesely noticed a ladder sticking up a few feet out of the ground. He dropped a grenade down the hole, but it was so deep, he could hear only a muffled thump when the grenade exploded deep in the bowels of the hill. The ladder—and others like it—were too heavy to pull out of the holes, so the Marines had no choice but to leave them.

They were about halfway to the top when enemy grenades began sailing overhead, exploding back among the just abandoned foxholes. Peering over the crest of the hill, Pesely could see Japanese stretched out on the opposite slope. He heard them grunting with effort as they lobbed the grenades over to where they thought the Marines were on the other slope. "I was fascinated with the sight, to see live Japanese, almost within reaching distance," recalled Pesely. "One nearest me had his hand holding onto a bush and would grunt as he heaved his grenades."

Wendell Majors had already pulled the pin on his grenade and was holding it in his hand, just waiting for Courtney to give the word. He positioned the second grenade beside him where he could reach it quickly. Suddenly Courtney yelled, "Let them have it!" The Marines all pitched their two grenades as fast as they could. The dozens of grenades going off at once sounded like an artillery barrage to Majors. Shrapnel, dust and dirt showered the slope.

From his vantage point, Ed Pesely could see Japanese bodies tumbling down the hillside in the cloud of dust. "They were tumbling down, screaming and shouting," he noted. One of the Marines had thrown a white phosphorus grenade that raised a lot of smoke. Pesely threw his own grenade directly at the Japanese holding on to the bush. The grenade hit the man with such force, he let out an involuntary grunt of pain or surprise and let go of his handhold on the bush. The grenade took so long to explode, Pesely thought it might be a dud, but it finally went off with a bang further down the slope among the scrambling Japanese.

Scratching up to the crest with the others, Wendell Majors could hardly make out anything through the dust and smoke. Then he saw the Japanese running. They had obviously been caught completely by surprise and "they were running just like scared rabbits." The Marines opened up on them; "we were having a real turkey shoot," recalled Majors. Despite this momentary advantage, the Japanese position was nowhere near collapse. Two-thirds of the way up the Japanese-held slope, a narrow terrace curved across the hill. Shallow tombs had once dotted the terrace; these had been supplemented by man-made caves. The enemy soldiers could sit out the American barrage of grenades, then emerge from their caves to retaliate with their own grenades. Much larger caves opened at the bottom of the hill where reinforcements could wait before being fed into the fighting further up the slope.

As the shock of Courtney's attack wore off, Japanese grenades started to land among the Marines instead of behind them. Jack Houston saw a Japanese dart out of a cave, smack a grenade against his helmet to activate it, and pitch it towards Courtney. "Grenade!" yelled Houston, throwing himself backwards. The grenade landed near the major, but failed to explode. Houston popped back up to see Courtney firing his .45 downslope, shouting, "There they are, men! I see them! They're thicker than flies!" Earlier, Houston had doubted the major's sanity in taking them on a night attack, but seeing him now, he had no doubts about his courage and leadership.

Nearby, Ed Pesely's luck slipped a bit. He dodged one or two grenades thrown directly at him. Then, as he crouched down, he heard one thump onto the ground by his right foot. He immediately spun away to his left but caught a spray of metal fragments in his chest and neck. As the flurry of enemy hand grenades tapered off, Pesely heard Courtney ask if anyone was hit. Pesely spoke up. As it turned out, he was the only casualty. A corpsman took him back about 20 feet below the crest, cut off his blood-soaked undershirt, dusted him with sulfa powder from his chin to his belt and bandaged him up around his left side and under the right arm.

Up on top of the hill, Walt Rutkowski was standing next to Courtney and a BAR man. The BAR man turned to Rutkowski during the lull and asked, "What are we going to do?"

"Well," said Rutkowski, "we can dig in together, but I don't have a shovel."

"I'll get one," said the other Marine.

Rutkowski took the man's BAR and the Marine disappeared after a shovel. Soon Pesely also came up. He found he could still use his arm all right, so he went back over to Courtney.

There were still plenty of Japanese on Sugar Loaf. Peering downslope, Houston could see where a cave opened into a trench that ran in a straight line to a road below. He noticed Japanese soldiers jumping up out of the trench and running across the road. "Behind was a line of Japs wiggling and crawling one by one away from the cave," he observed. Houston set his rifle sights on the closest man and moved down the line, methodically squeezing off shot after shot, slowly choking the trench with dead Japanese.

Sheltered in a shallow hole three quarters of the way up the north slope, radioman Jim Hart had been talking with Woodhouse. The colonel asked for an update on their position so the artillery could be properly placed. Hart scrambled up to Courtney and relayed the message. The slope seemed to be crawling with Japanese and there were still more of them visible on the flats below. "Call in all the fire you can on those Japs down there and get the hell out of here and stay with that radio," directed Courtney.

Courtney also told Pesely to get on the radio and tell Colonel Woodhouse to call in artillery fire directly to their front. "Look at those Nips coming up!" he suddenly exclaimed. "They're in column formation!"

Pesely dashed back to his foxhole where the radioman was hunkered down. Courtney stood at the crest picking out targets for the men. Standing just to the right of him, Rutkowski heard him yell out, "There's 20 of 'em!" Rutkowski opened up with the borrowed BAR. He expended the clip and the BAR man suddenly reappeared and handed him another. Then there was a tremendous explosion almost at his feet—whether it was Japanese mortars or friendly artillery, Rutkowski never knew.

Rutkowski found himself lying on the ground between Courtney and the BAR man. He called a corpsman and the doc came over and checked on Courtney. "Jeez," he said, "he's gone." He moved over to the BAR man. "He's gone." A shell fragment had severed the major's jugular vein. Rutkowski suffered wounds to his arm. The corpsman bandaged him up and then vanished.

Only a quirk of fate saved Wendell Majors. Standing on the crest next to Courtney, he cranked off an eight-shot clip at the Japanese on the slope. As the empty clip pinged out of the rifle, he instinctively ran 15 or 20 feet back down the hill and was just shoving a new clip into the rifle when the explosion occurred. To him it appeared that the Japanese threw a barrage right across the top of the hill. He believed it was mortars, but it happened so suddenly and with such little warning that the effect was almost as if the Japanese had set off prepared charges along the crest. But whatever the source, the explosion wreaked havoc on the Marines along the top of the hill.

Majors jumped into a shell hole, expecting another barrage, but things seemed to quiet down. He had seen Courtney fall and groan when the explosions went off. Now he called, "Courtney! Courtney!" thinking the battalion executive might still be alive. There was no response and Majors knew he was dead.

Back with the radio, Lieutenant Ed Pesely was waiting for the message that the artillery was "on its way" when the enemy mortar barrage landed along the crest. Moments later Lieutenant Nealon scrambled down to the hole to tell him Courtney was dead. Pesely got on the radio and passed the news on to Woodhouse back at battalion.

Woodhouse radioed Easy Company over on Hill 1 to see if they could provide any assistance to Pesely. Easy said they were barely holding on themselves. They had nothing to spare. Executive Officer John Fitzgerald told Woodhouse that if Easy weakened its lines, the Japanese could conceivably break through and overrun the right flank of the Marines on Sugar Loaf. Woodhouse dropped the plan.

Among the wounded on Sugar Loaf was Lieutenant Jamieson. Earlier, up on the crest, he had escaped death when one of his green replacements fumbled a live grenade. Miraculously, no one was hurt in the explosion, but Jamieson gave the youngster a boot in the ass and some much-needed practical instruction in grenade throwing. Moments later a grenade or mortar exploded and hit the youngster lying to Jamieson's right. The boy started screaming. Jamieson crawled to him and found he had been hit in the left shoulder area. He yelled for a corpsman, and when none materialized, he picked up the wounded Marine in a fireman's carry. "Don't lieutenant, you'll get killed," pleaded the youngster. "Shut up," replied Jamieson. He carried the boy down the slope to a sort of ledge where the corpsman was working on the wounded. The corpsman started bandaging him, then left Jamieson to finish the job. There was an explosion and Jamieson found himself lying on the ground. The wounded boy was screaming and bleeding all over; he had apparently caught most of a mortar blast. "Some of the other wounded, lying nearby, but apparently not hit by this one, threw me a few bandages, but they were not adequate for the bleeding he was doing," recalled Jamieson. "I looked for his dog tags; he said they didn't issue him any. So I asked for his name and home address, which I wrote down and placed inside his helmet. He was yelling about his mother, and I told him I was going to see about a tractor coming up so he could be taken back to a field hospital where he'd be all right."

Jamieson found Pesely near the radio and asked him if there would be any amtracs coming up. Not until morning, replied Pesely. Earlier, carrying the wounded man down the hill, Jamieson had seen Courtney go down; "at the time it looked as though he had tripped or slipped." Now Pesely told him the major was dead. Jamieson also realized his right arm was bleeding; apparently he had been hit by the mortar round at the aid station. As he bandaged the arm, Pesely told him to spread his men out along the slope and send some more around to the right to protect the flank. It was about 0200.

Adding to Pesely's problems was the fact that Courtney had personally made the dispositions on the hill. Now, with Courtney dead and his force under heavy enemy pressure, Pesely found himself in command of a spread out, disorganized defense. Lieutenant Bobby Nealon had been killed shortly after leaving Pesely's foxhole. Few of the survivors, made up of a mix of units, had a clear idea of who was in command or even who else was on the hill with them. The Marines were fighting back, but more as stubborn individuals than as a cohesive unit.

In an effort to clarify the situation, Pesely asked if Easy Company could see what was happening on Sugar Loaf. He was told that his own position was not visible, but there were a lot of Japanese out front. Over on Hill 1, Lieutenant Fitzgerald was monitoring the radio exchange between Pesely and Woodhouse. Pesely was "Melvin Queen Fox 6" and Woodhouse was "Melvin Queen 6." Pesely obviously had real trouble. "Six," he told Woodhouse with audible agitation, "they're so close, they'll be in my vest before you know it."

One thing Woodhouse had at his disposal was artillery. He had told Pesely he had 20 batteries of Tenth Army artillery to draw from and naval gunfire too, if Pesely needed it. Now Pesely called in fire from several of those batteries. Word came back to Pesely that the slope was crawling with Japanese; they weren't being touched by the artillery. "We was looking ahead of us and shit they was behind us and all over," observed Private First Class Fred McGowan. "They didn't wear anything on their helmets and when it rained on them in the flares, they'd shine right out."

Pesely had the artillery drop 100 yards, then another 50. At this point, Woodhouse got on the radio and told Pesely the rounds were going to land too close to the Marines and he would not allow the request. Pesely also told Woodhouse he needed more troops. Could Woodhouse get them up to him? The colonel said he was working on it.

It had started to rain on and off. Pesely was eager for a cigarette, but his matches were all wet and he could not find any dry ones in his combat pack.

The Japanese were starting to use flares that landed on the hill. The flares floated only a few feet above the Marines before landing in their midst and burning out on the ground. One almost landed in Pesely's foxhole; the metal butt glowed red-hot on the ground. By touching a cigarette to it, Pesely was finally able to get a light.

As if the Japanese in front of them weren't enough of a problem, fire was also coming from behind. To the rear of his position Pesely could see a red flash and the crump of a Japanese mortar being fired, followed by the shell's explosion on Sugar Loaf. Pesely fired his carbine toward the enemy position and the Japanese responded with another mortar round that came in so close, it blew dirt in his face.

One of the U.S. machine-gun crews also spotted the mortar and fired at it. A retaliatory mortar round soon landed near the machine gun and silenced it. Pesely heard some movement from the position and some "good American cussing," then the machine gun went back into action again. Pesely radioed his own mortar section to see if they could knock out the enemy weapon. The lieutenant in charge said he would try. But a few minutes later he called back and told Pesely that battalion had refused permission because the target area was located behind the Marine front line.

Farther up the hillside, Wendell Majors was also taking stock. Creeping up to the crest he could see an American light machine gunner who had planted his machine gun in an exposed position just down the far slope. The field of fire was excellent, but the machine gunner's daring had cost him his life. Now he lay draped across the gun, almost as if in his final moments he had been trying to protect the weapon. Majors contemplated going out to retrieve the machine gun, but it looked as if it had been damaged.

Crawling off along to the left, he found shelter in a little depression where he had a good view of the Japanese-held slope. A huge boulder loomed at the base of the hill. All at once Majors saw a Japanese step out from behind the boulder and look off toward where Courtney had been killed. Then another helmeted head bobbed up from behind the rock. The second enemy soldier glanced quickly around, then ducked back down.

Majors was reminded of the 1941 Gary Cooper movie about Sergeant York, the World War I Medal of Honor winner. In the movie, backwoodsman York had gobbled like a turkey; the Germans would stick their heads up to look and York would shoot them. Majors knew he could easily shoot the Japanese standing in the open, but then he himself might fall victim to the soldier behind the rock—unless he put Sergeant York's backwoods stratagem to work and coaxed the Japanese to pop his head up again.

Earlier, he had ignored Courtney's order to fix bayonets, feeling the extra weight threw off the rifle's balance and maneuverability. Now he was going to put that maneuverability to the test. Sighting in on the boulder where the Japanese soldier's head had appeared, Majors gobbled loudly. The head popped up again and as it filled his sights, Majors squeezed the trigger, then came back down from the recoil, swung over, and killed the other Japanese standing in the open.

His victory did not go unnoticed. Not long after, a Japanese machine gunner crept up on the far right side of the hill and started working Majors over. Fortunately, the enemy soldier couldn't depress his gun quite enough to reach Majors in the bottom of the shallow depression. "He would hit in front of me and then on the other side of me . . . that guy wasted a whole belt of ammunition," recalled Majors. "He had completely fired that whole belt through there and the best that he did was that he clipped me across the leg on the calf."

Lying as flat as he could, Majors tried not to breathe for fear it would raise him up just enough so the Japanese could put a burst into him. The gash across the back of his leg burned painfully, and he carefully worked his hand around to check the seriousness of the wound. Finally succeeding, he discovered it was minor, "and then it quit hurting." At long last, the Japanese stopped shooting. "I slipped my helmet off and stuck it up, put my hand in there and I'd stick my helmet up and pull it down, then stick it up a little bit higher and pull it down and I kept teasing him to see if he'd reloaded and was going to wait for me to make my mistake [and] expose myself to where he could get me," recalled Majors. "But he never fired any more." Majors assumed his tormentor had "shot up all his ammo and quit."

Back down on the slope, Ed Pesely was trying to make sense out of the situation. One thing was sure: there were Japanese everywhere. During the night his radioman got up out of their hole to urinate and a burst of machine-gun fire from their left rear nearly sliced off his pistol holster. "He got down real fast," observed Pesely wryly.

Exhausted and weakened by his wounds, Pesely dozed off. In the early morning hours he awakened to hear his radioman. The man was informing Colonel Woodhouse that they were about to be overrun and he would save one grenade for the radio. Pesely got on the set and Woodhouse told him if they could hold out, he would send up King Company to reinforce the position. Guides were leading K Company to Hill 3. He told Pesely to look out for them and direct them up to Sugar Loaf as they came forward across the open ground between the hills.

The alert of K Company had come earlier. The company had been dug in back behind Hill 1 since evening. Following the evacuation of Lieutenant Paul Dunfey at the Asa Kawa two days earlier, the company had come under the command of Lieutenant Reginald Fincke. Scuttlebutt had it that Fincke came from a wealthy family and could have avoided combat. Instead, he chose the Marine Corps. "To tell you what a guy he was, I'd seen him walking, take the machine gun off some small guy, put it on his own shoulder to rest that boy up and he'd walk miles, holding one of those light machine guns . . . He was one of the finest men and thought so much of his men," recalled a K Company private first class.

At 2300 Colonel Woodhouse had ordered one platoon of King Company to advance to the rear slopes of Hill 3 and try to dislodge the Japanese located on the east slope. These enemy troops were directing fire into the rear of the Marines on Sugar Loaf. The platoon made the effort, but was forced off the exposed slope by enemy knee mortar fire. Only 10 of the 24 men who made the assault were left by that time.

At 0100 Woodhouse ordered King Company to prepare to move out to reinforce Sugar Loaf. Fincke reported to Colonel Woodhouse at his observation post (OP). Woodhouse told him, "The lines are extended and the Nips are counterattacking in strength. The situation on Sugar Loaf is very critical. Stand by to go to their reinforcement. Replenish your supplies."

An hour later Fincke was called back to the OP. Woodhouse told him, "There are only eight men left on Sugar Loaf. If we lose it, we will have lost all we've gained and paid dearly for. Take King Company to Sugar Loaf and hold it at all costs. I want to see you there in the morning."

"We were told to leave the bottom part of our packs . . . where we were dug in across the road from Sugar Loaf," recalled Private First Class Charles Pugh. "We were going up on this hill. I didn't know it was called Sugar Loaf and nobody else did. All we knew was that we were going up this hill. We were getting beat up pretty badly."

Also moving up in the darkness with King Company was Private First Class Ray Schlinder. A few hours earlier, he had been sitting around with his buddies and "talking about where the hell we're going to be the next week, the next day, where we're going to be in two hours, wondering if we're going to get through this mess. The word came along that we're taking a hill tonight no matter what the cost was. That was the word. Of course, that gives you something to think about. Real quick."

As they moved toward the hill, Schlinder saw that the area fronting Sugar Loaf was littered with dead Marines—there seemed to be hundreds of them sprawled grotesquely about. "There were men all over," he recalled.

He would have liked to stop and see if anybody was still alive, but there was no time for that. They had to keep moving.

Up on the slope, Pesely could hear King Company talking on the radio with Woodhouse. The Marines on Sugar Loaf could not get in direct touch with King since they were operating on a different radio band, so they guided the column in by shouting at them. It was 0230. The K Company reinforcements—4 officers and 99 men—had made it in without losing a man.

As he approached the hill, Pugh heard Lieutenant Fincke, say, "All right, men. Find a hole and get in it." The newcomers scrambled up the slope, lugging eight machine guns. It seemed to Pugh as if every foxhole already had somebody in it. "I couldn't tell if they were dead or some of our men had beaten us to those holes," he recalled. He and his buddy, Private First Class Gib Kanter, finally found shelter in a ditch overlooking the reverse slope.

Also scrambling up the hill was Ray Schlinder. The Japanese apparently realized something was going on. Knee mortars, heavy artillery and machine-gun fire began tearing up the ground. "That hill was literally splattered . . . it was alive with shells bursting," recalled Schlinder. Later he would wonder how he ever made it across, but he did and set up his .30 caliber machine gun in a trench on the forward edge of the hill.

As the K Company Marines approached Pesely's position, red streaks appeared from behind Sugar Loaf as the enemy mortar position opened up again. Pesely heard a K Company officer order a machine gun to be set up. Tracers floated toward the mortar as the machine gun opened fire. Someone behind the gun was giving corrections, "To the right, to the right," since they knew exactly where the mortar was located.

"Down! Down!" yelled Pesely as mortar shells started landing around the machine gun. It seemed to Pesely that three or four shells exploded near the gun, with one landing directly on the barrel, knocking out the gun and everybody around it. In an instant, all was quiet except for the soft grunting and moaning of badly wounded men.

One of the casualties was Lieutenant Fincke. The blast had caught him in the legs; now they remained attached by mere strings of flesh and muscle. Some Marines placed him on a stretcher in hopes of getting him off the hill, but one of the stretcher bearers slipped and lost his grip. To their horror, the lieutenant fell off and rolled all the way to the foot of the hill, his legs just dangling. If he wasn't dead already, he died soon after from the shock of his wounds. The men had no time to mourn, but one recalled later, "We sure hated to see him go."

Manning his foxhole, Pesely heard someone ask, "Where is Fox Company?" It was Lieutenant James Roe. Roe, executive officer of King

Company, told Pesely Fincke was dead. Pesely told Roe to get into position as quietly as he could and spread out his men over the top of Sugar Loaf. He also told Roe, quite sincerely, "that they were real heroes to come from behind the lines to join us in the darkness in the middle of a battle."

Settling in along the top of Sugar Loaf, nobody had to tell the King Company Marines they were in the middle of a first-class mess. Enemy fire had already knocked out the communications wire to Sugar Loaf, along with one of the two "300" radios. That left only one radio for communication between the hill and battalion headquarters. Grenades and shells were exploding, men were screaming . . . some were crying. Hunkered down in the ditch, Charles Pugh heard a voice calling out, "Why? Why? Why?" The cry became weaker and more distant and finally it stopped.

Grenades sailed back and forth over the crest as Japanese and Marines dueled for control of the hill. King Company had brought eight machine guns up on the hill, but any attempt to use the guns attracted heavy enemy mortar fire, so grenades remained the Marine weapon of choice. The Japanese were sheltered in caves and tunnels on the reverse slope, but they were close—from time to time Pugh could hear them jabbering to each other. The enemy troops would emerge from the caves and tunnels to toss grenades at the Marines on the crest, then duck back into their holes. "We'd toss a grenade down and they'd toss it back," recalled Floyd Enman. "We couldn't figure it out."

Peering out from behind his machine gun, Ray Schlinder caught sight of some Japanese soldiers working along a long dike-like fold in the ground about 60 yards to the front. They were a bit far out for grenades, but other Japanese were closer. "I was on the far side of the hill where it dropped right straight down," he noted. "So there were Nips right below me." Marines passed grenades forward and Schlinder, who in happier days used to pitch hardball, lobbed them out to his front. "There was one group that was about 50 yards off," he recalled. "I wondered if I could throw a grenade that far. I landed a little bit short, but I scared the shit out of them."

During one of these exchanges, something thumped into the side of Schlinder's right leg. Looking down in the light of the flares, he saw a Japanese grenade lying there. Without thinking, he grabbed it and tossed it back over the hill. "With all the noise going on I wasn't certain whether it went off or if it was a dud," he recalled. "But in either case the man upstairs liked me there because that would have been the end of R. J. Schlinder."

Among the K Company men holding the crest was an 18-year-old Kentuckian, Private First Class Jack Nuckols. But for his own impetuousness, Nuckols would have been in the Navy. Responding to his draft notice, he intended to join the Navy, but when he got to the induction center he encountered some Marines looking for volunteers. Nuckols stepped forward. "I thought, 'Hey, by the time I get in, everything will be over with,' " he recalled.

Now, lugging a Browning Automatic Rifle, he found himself part of the thin line on Sugar Loaf Hill. Eyeballing the Japanese-held slope he caught sight of four enemy soldiers moving along a trench not more than 50 feet away. Nuckols could see them bobbing up and down, but every time he moved to cut loose on them with the BAR, they disappeared. A flamethrower man climbed to his feet and started to ignite the flamethrower. He was shot to death before the flame could come out. Nuckols's best buddy, Private First Class George Dean was crouched in the shell hole with him. A bullet whacked into Dean's head. He died in Nuckols's lap.

Off to the left, a young Marine who had joined the division with Nuckols's replacement draft lobbed a phosphorus grenade over the slope. Some quick-handed Japanese threw it back. It exploded in white brilliance, showering the youngster with molten phosphorus. He burned, screaming, begging, "Somebody kill me!" No one could bring himself to do it, and the youngster soon died in agony. A piece of the phosphorus also hit Nuckols in the back but he wiggled and twisted and managed to scrape it off before it burned through his flesh.

Soon after, Nuckols's luck ran out as a Japanese grenade exploded by his left side, driving chunks of metal into his leg and tearing the side of his helmet off. Dazed and stunned, with no one else near him alive, Nuckols crawled back over the hill clutching his BAR. He finally encountered some other Marines who put him in a deep trench. Later that day he was evacuated to a hospital ship. Years later, he recalled ruefully, "Would you believe I didn't fire that damn BAR one time on Sugar Loaf? I only threw two grenades."

Sometime during the morning a replacement scrambled up to Walt Rutkowski. Since being wounded by the same shell that killed Courtney, Rutkowski had been waiting things out. He had his M1 and he'd taken Courtney's .45 off the major's body. The new man just materialized out of the dark and announced, "I'm a replacement. I've got a machine gun."

Rutkowski looked at the gun. "It's not going to do me much good," he replied. The back plate for the trigger assembly was gone, he pointed out. The gun was inoperable. "Where the hell is it?" he asked the other Marine. The man said he'd taken the part off and thrown it away because he didn't want the enemy to capture an operable gun. "It's not going to do me any damn good without it," said Rutkowski, dismissing him. The man disappeared, leaving Rutkowski alone. Sometime later another shell hit near to where Major Courtney's body lay stretched out. The blast tossed Rutkowski two or three feet into the air and hurled Courtney's corpse over him. When Rutkowski looked at the body he saw that the second blast had ruined the handsome officer's face.

Still pressed to the ground on the left of Sugar Loaf, Wendell Majors saw a Japanese soldier suddenly materialize down the slope and make a dash for some bushes. As the man came across an open spot, Majors swung on him, but the M1 wouldn't fire. Clogged with dirt, the rifle had failed to chamber a new round after his last shot. He was still pondering this latest problem when he heard one of his platoon members yelling at him. The man had been wounded, but could still fight, and he was warning Majors to get away from his dangerously exposed position at the edge of the hill. Nervous because his rifle had jammed and worried more Japanese would try to overrun him, Majors scrambled to his feet and "ran like a scared rabbit" toward the other Marine, sliding into an open shell hole "like going into third base in a baseball game." He never saw the bayonetted rifle propped up on the edge of the hole. As he slid in, the bayonet went into his thigh and came out his groin "like I was strung up for barbecuing."

Stunned for a moment, Majors was trying to move around and work himself off the blade, when he heard a Marine to his right yell, "There comes one! There comes one!" The other Marine threw up his rifle and it misfired. Then he picked up a BAR and it misfired too, so he threw it down, picked up his rifle again, ran out in front of Majors and bayonetted a Japanese through the neck. From what Majors could gather, the enemy soldier had been wounded earlier and was crawling away along the ground when the other Marine spotted him.

Still trying to get off the bayonetted rifle in the hole, Majors didn't waste any sympathy on his dead enemy. "I twisted around and I got braced in the hole and I gave that rifle a yank and it didn't even budge that thing out of my leg," recalled Majors. "I maneuvered around and got propped up a certain way so I had that rifle with plenty of space and I remember giving a big lurch and yanking that thing out of my leg. The moment it came out, blood spurted up about . . . it seemed to me about two feet that it went up. And I just knew that I had cut that main artery that was coming down there in my groin and I knew it was so high I couldn't get a tourniquet up above it there to stop the bleeding. And at that time I guess I thought that I had bought the farm up there."

But Majors wasn't done yet. Somehow he managed to get out his battle dressing. He worked the sulfa powder down in the hole, put some pressure on the wound and got the bleeding to stop. Soon afterward, Private First Class Jack Houston slid into the hole and patched up the wound with another dressing. Houston had also been hit. Earlier, as he moved back from the crest during a barrage, a knee mortar shell had exploded in a shallow hole next to him, "making the soft springy sound that knee mortars make." The explosion had driven bits of gravel and metal into his right side, but he was still mobile. Now, as he and Majors waited for something to happen, there seemed to be less than a dozen people on the hill—no officers, no noncommissioned officers—just buck privates and privates first class.

Subsequent events were confusing. After the knee mortars, an artillery barrage crashed into the hill, the explosions picking the men up off the ground and slamming them down again. Houston had never been more scared for so long a period. "When one particular barrage was over, I called out for Lieutenant Bob Nealon, who'd led our G Company group, hoping he'd agree with me that now would be a great time to move back," he recalled. "Someone hollered back that the lieutenant had been killed."

Hunkered in the hole with Majors, Houston heard Joe Futrell calling him. Futrell had been in Houston's fire team in the 3d Platoon and was an old buddy. Houston called back, asking him if he was all right, and Futrell said he was. But by the third time his friend called out, Houston knew Futrell was in trouble. He told Majors he hated to leave him, but he thought Futrell needed help. Houston scrambled over to Futrell and found he had been wounded. Shrapnel had punched into his back and arm. Houston poured sulfa powder over the injuries and applied two battle dressings to stop the bleeding. He had just about finished taking care of Futrell when a platoon sergeant materialized and said he needed someone up on the crest of the hill. Houston took Futrell's BAR and his own rifle and headed toward the top.

"When I got to the top, I realized it was now strangely and eerily quiet," he recalled. "As I was watching toward the enemy area, all of a sudden I heard voices and our flares showed that three Japs were walking along the road toward us, talking away without a care in the world. I lined up the BAR on them and started firing. But just then the star shell went out as I saw them scrambling. I don't think I got any of them."

He did manage to attract the attention of a Japanese machine gunner who probably spotted the muzzle flash from the BAR. Bullets started chewing up the ground around him. "I wasn't in a hole, only in a slight depression," observed Houston. "If his fire had been a little higher, I'd have been a gone goose."

Houston got a reprieve as U.S. artillery or naval gunfire began to slam into the area to his front. "I could see the light of their path showing they were coming in from the coast, almost as if they were tracer in machine gun fire," he recalled. "It finally dawned on me that it was probably friction. It was a fantastic display. But it couldn't stop the machine gun, which started on me again. It was a helpless feeling having chunks of earth knocked up over me."

Houston decided it was time to withdraw, so as soon as the next flare flickered out, he scrambled back down the slope. As he went, he took the precaution of yelling, "Look out, I'm coming down!" It was well that he did: sliding to a stop downslope, he found himself looking up into the muzzle of an M1. The handful of Marines there said they hadn't realized there were any Americans on the crest where Houston had been.

Houston moved downward along the slope. Japanese artillery fire began to fall nearby and he ducked behind a fallen tree for shelter. "I saw four Marine figures seated and leaning back against the incline, their heads tipped forward as if sleeping," he recalled. "Then a shell landed nearby and one figure fell against the man next to him and they all pitched over like dominos and I realized they all had been dead."

Still among the living were Corporal Donald "Rusty" Golar and Private Donald Kelly. They were a curious pair. Golar, son of an army officer, was a brawny, red-headed former San Francisco longshoreman. Ironically, the Marines had rejected him three times for poor eyesight, but Golar finally talked his way past the recruiters. He had won a Bronze Star on Guam. Kelly was a 16–year-old from Chicago's gang-ridden West Side; he had finagled his way into the Marine Corps after tricking his harried father into signing his enlistment papers, telling him it was a school permission slip.

Typically, Golar had been all over the hill that night. "Oh he was a wild man," recalled Fred McGowan. "He didn't know the meaning of the word fear." McGowan had laid out three grenades by his position. Golar scrambled up and said, "Give me them grenades" and "this crazy potlicker, he ran up the hill. He was all over that thing."

Now Golar and Kelly were manning a machine gun looking over the Japanese-held slope. Kelly was on the gun, firing short bursts at shadowy figures climbing toward him. There didn't seem to be any other Marines around, besides Golar, who was just behind him. As his ammunition ran low, Kelly called to Golar to get another box. "Hey, I'm down! I'm down!" yelled Kelly. He turned in time to see Golar sit down with his back against a slight embankment, his head down on his chest. Kelly kept yelling, but Golar didn't respond. Finally Kelly left the gun. He scuttled over to Golar. "Hey, Rusty," he said, pulling Golar's head back. There was blood on Golar's face. He was dead.

Kelly picked up a box of ammo and went back to the machine gun. The box was only about half full and he used it carefully. A bullet cut his heel open and a grenade or mortar drove fragments of metal into his leg. Kelly stuck to the gun. "The flares were up there," he recalled. "And it seemed to me when [each flare] started to go down and get dark, I'd see movement and then another [flare] would go up and they'd kind of duck down. But anything I could see I'd fire at. Here and there. They didn't come 50 or 20 together . . . I was running out of ammo. I started thinking, 'Gee, I wish they'd stop shooting flares, maybe I could sneak out of here.' " Finally, bleeding from his leg wound, he lost consciousness. When he awoke hours later, all he could see was bright blue sky. He heard voices and just had time to realize he was being carried on a stretcher before he passed out again.

In the early morning hours, a chill rain blew in off the East China Sea, soaking the dead and the living alike. Up in the ditch at the crest of Sugar Loaf, Ray Schlinder was still fighting. Sometime during the night an officer he didn't recognize crawled up the trench and told him, "Hold your position, we're going to get relieved in 20 minutes." The man returned every so often and repeated the promise. "I bet he come up 10 or 12 times," recalled Schlinder. "All night long." After a while Schlinder stopped paying any attention to him.

It was getting toward 0500 when his squad leader, Bill Enright, came crawling through the trench and said, "Hey, Ray, Farnsworth got hit." Farnsworth was Schlinder's number one machine gunner on the other gun. "Is he dead?" asked Schlinder. Enright said he didn't know. "Well, where is he?" asked Schlinder. Enright pointed out the direction and Schlinder said he was going to go see if Farnsworth needed help. "All right," replied Enright. "Good luck."

Schlinder had just started to get up when a knee mortar round exploded with a bang about three feet to his right. A chunk of shrapnel ripped down through his right lung and into his liver. Gasping for air, Schlinder's first thought was that he'd been affected by concussion. "I'd gotten hit by concussion before; it knocks the wind out of you," he observed. "And I'm gasping for air and all of a sudden I felt something hot running down the side of my stomach and I pulled my sweatshirt off and my shirt off and took a look down on my right and there's a hole in my chest about the size of a silver dollar."

Schlinder decided he would try to run to the back of the hill and dive over. And that's what he did. With a chunk of metal in his liver, he got up, zig-zagged across the hill to the back side, dived and rolled down the back slope. To his good fortune, he found a corpsman down at the bottom. "Hey, Doc," said Schlinder, "I need some help."

"I'm out of everything," replied the corpsman. But he took Schlinder's first aid kit and covered the hole in his chest, wrapped the bandage around his neck and tied it.

"Look, put me in that hole over there," said Schlinder when the corpsman was finished. There was a sort of ledge nearby with a hole underneath it. "Get me into that hole and I'll take my .45 and if they come over the top I'll take as many of those buggers as I can with me. Somebody's going to go before me."

The corpsman got him into the hole. Schlinder took out his .45 and lay there waiting. It was just starting to get light.

Guam, May 14—(Associated Press)—Japanese threw in fresh reserves today and laid down thunderous artillery barrages in an effort to halt a powerful American offensive which had reached the outskirts of Naha, shell blasted and heavily mined capital of Okinawa. . . .

Marines of Major General Lemuel C. Shepherd, Jr.'s Sixth Division, moving down the west coast of the Ryukyu Island only 325 miles south of Japan itself, fought fiercely to the northern bank of the Asato, which runs through the city. . . .

Fleet Admiral Chester Nimitz' communique today made no mention of Naha other than to say the Sixth Marine Division "was meeting stiff resistance" in a day of fierce fighting all along the tough line.

Pitted by artillery fire, denuded of vegetation, Sugar Loaf Hill viewed from the north following the battle (USMC/National Archives).

Dead Marines, casualties of the assault across the Asa Kawa, are loaded on an amtrac on 10 May (USMC/National Archives).

Machine gunners from L Company, 22d Marines, work forward in one of the assaults around Sugar Loaf (USMC/National Archives).

Following a tank up the railroad cut, men of 1/29 work toward Sugar Loaf and Half Moon Hill during the attack of 17 May (USMC/National Archives).

Captain Owen T. Stebbins (left) and Gunnery Sergeant Peter Maresh
(Courtesy of Owen T. Stebbins).

Colonel Horatio C. Woodhouse, Jr. (above)
(USMC). Private First Class James Chaisson
(top right) (Courtesy of James Chaisson).
Raymond P. Gillespie (right) (Courtesy of
Raymond Gillespie).

A wounded Marine receives aid behind a low hill shielding medical personnel from direct enemy fire (USMC/National Archives).

Lieutenant Edward Pesely (Courtesy of Edward Pesely).

Private Declan Klingenhagen (Courtesy of D. L. Klingenhagen).

Corporal Earl H. Curnutte (Courtesy of Earl H. Curnutte).

Major Henry C. Courtney, pictured here when he was still a captain earlier in the war (Courtesy Freedoms Foundation at Valley Forge).

Graves registration teams identify Marines killed in the fighting on southern Okinawa (USMC/National Archives).

Staff officers of the 6th Marine Division (left to right) Lt. Col. Thomas E. Williams, Colonel Victor A. Krulak, General Lemuel C. Shepherd, Jr., Brigadier General William T. Clement and Colonel John C. McQueen (USMC/National Archives).

Colonel Merlin Schneider (right) turns command of the 22d Marines over to Colonel Harold Roberts on 17 May (USMC/National Archives).

Tanks work around the eastern end of Sugar Loaf Hill. The hill in the background is Half Moon. The Shuri heights are visible in the background (USMC/National Archives).

Marines on top of Sugar Loaf look down on the "killing ground" they had to cross to reach the hill (USMC/National Archives).

Lieutenant Francis X. Smith (Courtesy of Francis X. Smith).

Private Donald Kelly (Courtesy of Donald Kelly).

K/22 machine gunners (from left) Ray Schlinder, Ray Kiman and James Whalen (Courtesy of Ray Schlinder).

L/4 machine gunners (from left) Paul Ulrich, Cal Frost and George Stovall (Courtesy of Paul Ulrich).

Supplies and debris clutter the northern slope of Sugar Loaf following its capture by Dog Company, 29th Marines (USMC/National Archives).

Marines set up home on Sugar Loaf's northeastern slope (USMC/National Archives).

Commander General Lemuel Shepherd, Jr., 6th Marine Division (left), and division operations chief Colonel Victor Krulak in front of Sugar Loaf Hill following its capture (USMC/National Archives).

Marines move up to the attack on 17 May, past the debris of battle (USMC/National Archives).

Sugar Loaf as it looks today, hemmed in by a concrete girdle and in the path of Naha's city sprawl (Courtesy of David Davenport).

Chapter 6

Counterattack

Sunrise on 15 May was at 0542. As it started to get light, Lieutenant Ed Pesely saw movement just below his position. Looking more closely, he realized it was a stick moving in the loose soil as a Japanese soldier in a cave or tunnel reopened a gun port on the slope. Suddenly the Japanese called out, "Hey, Marines, you are going to be dead by morning!" The voice continued its taunts, shouting, "To hell with the Marines," and then more bizarrely, "To hell with Mrs. Roosevelt!" Pesely observed wryly, "I suppose that was, for the Japanese, the ultimate insult."

Private Leon Paice, dug in on the forward edge of the hill with his buddy Vern Chandler, thought things "looked kind of bleak" as day dawned. They were about to look even bleaker. "As it got light, we could see out there and I could see a lot more Japs than I wanted to," he recalled. "They were everywhere out there." They all seemed to be heading for Sugar Loaf.

Crouched down in the low ditch along the crest of the hill, Private First Class Charles Pugh could hear a lot of Japanese talking somewhere below him as day dawned. He stood up and saw "quite a long line of Japs" moving at an angle as if they intended to work up the hill. Pugh singled out one of the enemy soldiers, sighted carefully, and shot him in the back. As the impact of the bullet knocked the man sprawling, Pugh ducked back down into the ditch. "Gib," he said to his buddy, Private First Class Gib Kanter, "they're just right over there. Get up and get yourself one of 'em."

Kanter stood up, shouldered his rifle and was taking aim when a Japanese bullet slammed into the M1 between the barrel and the gas chamber and ricocheted into his neck. Kanter dropped the rifle and clutched his throat with one hand. There was a lot of blood. Pugh couldn't see any other Marines around and he couldn't hear anybody. Unable to speak, one hand over his severed throat, Kanter crabbed off into the misty rain in search of a corpsman.

Alone now, Pugh noticed a little green bush just down the slope. The bush seemed to be moving toward him. As he looked again, the "bush" suddenly came into focus and he realized it wasn't a bush at all—it was a Japanese soldier. The man had stuck some vegetation in his helmet net for camouflage and managed to crawl within a few yards of the ditch without being spotted. As Pugh mentally reviewed his options—whether to stay down and throw a grenade at the intruder or stand up and shoot him—someone lobbed a phosphorus grenade over the crest. Bits of phosphorus showered down around Pugh without hitting him and when he looked down the slope again, the crawling Japanese was gone.

As the grenade indicated, Pugh was not quite alone on the hill. There were other Marines, though they were few in number. One of them was Floyd Enman. During the night both his squad leader and gunner had been wounded and Enman now had sole responsibility for the machine gun. It was getting toward morning when another Marine had called to him, "Come on, Enman, we're going back down."

"I didn't want to be called a coward," recalled Enman. "I was scared enough, but I didn't want to be called a coward." So he replied, "I'll stay." When daybreak arrived, he seemed to be all alone on the hill. Enman decided it was time to find some companionship, but he didn't want to leave his machine gun intact. As he started to disable the gun, a sniper put a bullet directly into the feed tray. That was persuasion enough. Enman turned to crawl away and was startled to find a dead Marine lying directly behind him. The man's side had been blown away by a grenade or mortar blast. Enman didn't recognize the man and had no idea where he had come from.

The sniper kept Enman under fire as he crawled over the dead Marine and down into the lee of the hill. "I went back down and the sergeant told me every man was for himself and that really got me," he recalled. A further indication that things were not well came when he saw his lieutenant talking on the radio. The officer "was broke up" and appeared to be telling the person on the other end that K Company was finished.

Even the indomitable Wendell Majors had finally had enough. Lying wounded and alone in the shell hole, Majors heard the firing taper off toward morning. Since he didn't have a watch, he had no idea what time it was. An occasional shell landed off to his right toward the center of the hill. Soon after daylight, he heard someone over in that direction yell, "Gotta get ready, here they come!" By now his injured leg was terribly sore. He couldn't maneuver and fight and there were no Marines anywhere near him that he could see. Majors decided the best thing he could do was get out of there, so he crawled out of the hole and just started rolling until he rolled all the way down to the bottom of the hill. Then, as sniper fire kicked up the dirt around him, he suddenly found he could use his bad leg after all, and he hobbled, crawled and hopped away from the hill until he found shelter behind the hulk of a knocked-out tank.

It was there that it became clear—if there had ever been any doubt—that the Marine attack had been hit terribly hard. Pausing to rest, Majors counted a dozen knocked-out American tanks and amtracs; some were still burning. The open field was strewn with dead. Majors had a horrifying realization: there were so many dead, he could walk on them all the way back to Sugar Loaf and never touch the ground. Instead he started back toward the rear where a couple of wiremen spotted him. They dropped the wire and ran to help him back to the battalion command post. "Man back from the hill!" yelled a sergeant.

Colonel Woodhouse came running toward him, carbine bouncing on his shoulder. What was the situation on Sugar Loaf? he asked Majors. There were still Marines on the hill, Majors reported, but he'd heard shouts that the Japanese were getting ready for a counterattack. He also told Woodhouse that Courtney was dead. "I'll send an attack up there and get those guys," said Woodhouse.

As Majors concluded, Woodhouse looked down at him with concern and affection and said, "Son, God bless you. Let me shake your hand." It had been raining and as Majors lifted his hand up, it came with about an inch of mud stuck to it. Woodhouse grabbed his hand and the mud squashed through their fingers. "It's a little muddy, Colonel," apologized Majors. Woodhouse just smiled, then he turned and left and that was the last Majors ever saw of him. Two days later, his leg covered in bandages, he was flown out of Yontan Airfield to a hospital on Guam.

By dawn there were less than two dozen Marines—many of them wounded—still able to fight, clinging to their positions on Sugar Loaf. Having already used K Company in an effort to hang on to the hill, Woodhouse needed more men. At 0630 D Company of 2/29 was attached to the 22d Marines to help "mop up" Japanese who were leaking into the 2d Battalion area. (The term "mop-up," as used in the official monograph on the action, would prove to be optimistic.) At 0800, Woodhouse ordered the seven survivors of Courtney's original group—including Ed Pesely— off the hill.

Woodhouse radioed Pesely and told him an amphibious tractor would come up soon to pick up the wounded. Pesely, Hutchings and the remaining Fox Company men were to come out, he said. Pesely turned over his radio and command to Lieutenant James D. Roe who had taken charge of K Company after Lieutenant Fincke's death only hours before. Roe and his few K Company survivors would hang on until D Company arrived.

Soon Pesely heard the tractor grinding toward him from the left side of Hill 3. As it drew closer, gun ports at the base of Sugar Loaf came suddenly alive, as enemy defenders directed fire on the amtrac. The tractor backed up and bogged down in a ditch. The crew bailed out and ran behind Hill 3. Back on the radio, Woodhouse vowed that the next tractor would make it to Sugar Loaf if he had to drive it himself.

Gib Kanter had made it back to the command post (CP) area near the base of the hill. He was lying on a stretcher awaiting evacuation, along with the many other wounded, when he suddenly noticed a Japanese soldier lurking under an abandoned Marine tank at the base of the hill. Unable to talk due to the wound in his throat, he waved his arms and tried to point. To his extreme frustration, the men near him thought he was cracking up, but someone finally got the message and took care of the enemy infiltrator.

The next amtrac appeared at 0800, raced to the bottom of the hill and spun around. Two Marines jumped out with Browning Automatic Rifles (BARs) and hosed down the gunports in the hill. The enemy activity abruptly stopped. "Okay," yelled one of the Marines, "you can bring your wounded down." Some of the wounded were carried down, others hobbled or rolled themselves down the slope. The ramp on the stern of the vehicle was about half way up when Pesely scrambled down the hill and jumped aboard, landing on top of the other wounded. As the tractor rumbled off, he could hear small-arms fire pinging against the side.

In less than five minutes they were back at the battalion CP. As Pesely felt himself being lifted out by four or five sets of hands and placed on a stretcher, a funny thought ran through his mind that he had forgotten his combat pack in the foxhole on Sugar Loaf. In addition to other items, the pack contained about $500 of military occupation scrip he had won in a poker game aboard the transport on the way to Okinawa. Pesely didn't waste any tears over the loss. . . . He figured he had been lucky to escape with his life.

Ray Schlinder was also still alive. Lying in the hole at the base of Sugar Loaf, the Michigan teenager had been getting worried. For some time he had heard amtracs trying to get forward. The amtrac would get closer and closer and suddenly there would be an explosion as the vehicle apparently got knocked out. The same thing happened several times. Schlinder kept telling himself, "One of them is gotta get through or I'm not going to make it." It was more along the lines of prayer.

Finally he heard one of the tractors getting closer and closer, and it pulled in behind the hill nearby, not more than 20 yards away. Schlinder thought he was just going to jump in the amtrac and go, but when he tried to get up, he found he couldn't move. He was so weak from loss of blood, he could not have squeezed the trigger on the .45 still lying on his chest if the whole Japanese Army was standing over him.

A corpsman grabbed him and put him on the amtrac. The vehicle was jammed full of wounded, maybe 35 Marines. "I thought I was in pretty bad shape until I got into that amtrac," recalled Schlinder. His buddy Don Siroky, a flamethrower man from Milwaukee, had caught a bullet in the neck and died on the way in. Another man also died as the vehicle lurched to the rear. "Everybody else was really busted up," observed Schlinder.

Schlinder was lucky. He ended up in an army hospital and was operated on that same night. They operated on his right lung and took care of another wound in his arm, but left the metal in his liver. He later learned that of the 65 men in his machine-gun platoon, all but three had been killed or wounded on Okinawa.

Assistant BAR man Fred McGowan was among the lucky few F Company men to make it off Sugar Loaf uninjured. Coming down off the hill, he had started to climb into the amtrac evacuating Pesely when another lieutenant asked him, "Is there any reason why you can't walk back to the CP?" McGowan figured he wasn't going to live much longer anyway, so he retorted, "No, I suppose there's not a damn reason." Making his way along a ditch full of dead Marines, McGowan was exhausted by the time he arrived at the CP. He crawled into an irrigation ditch and fell asleep in the rain. When he woke up in the afternoon, the ditch had four or five inches of water in it and the slop was running into his mouth. Things brightened a bit when the first sergeant came along and stuffed a pair of dry socks in his pocket. "He gave them to everybody," recalled McGowan. "Shit, there wasn't more than 20 men in the whole company."

Also among the survivors of the fight was K Company machine gunner Floyd Enman. Exhausted, he lay down on the ground and fell asleep. When he finally awoke, he found someone had stolen his .45 automatic. "I slept right through the whole thing," he said. "They took my pistol right off my hip."

Woodhouse still believed he could hold Sugar Loaf with the help of D Company, 29th Marines. Arriving at the 2/22 CP that morning, the Dog Company commander, Captain Howard L. Mabie, a tall, blond Idahoan, was told by the S-3, Major Glen E. Martin, to send one platoon forward to the battalion OP. The men were to carry grenades for further distribution. The 3d Platoon (reinforced), some 60 men led by Lieutenant "Irish" George Murphy, former captain and star end of the 1942 Notre Dame football team, filed forward.

From what Mabie could see of the situation from the battalion CP, located on a low rise just north of Sugar Loaf, it seemed obvious his company would soon be committed to the front lines. He stayed behind to phone his own battalion with that news. By the time he got to the forward observation post (OP) where Murphy had taken the 3d Platoon, the Marines were already on their way to Sugar Loaf to relieve what was left of K Company—now reported to have less than ten men still active.

Corporal Dan Dereschuk was also on the hill, still manning his machine-gun post. During the night one of his three surviving men was killed and they'd run through their last belt of machine-gun ammunition. When that was gone, they threw hand grenades, then used rifles and carbines they found lying around on the hill. Dereschuk threw so many grenades, his arm began to get sore. As the morning wore on, Dereschuk could see the D Company reinforcements coming up from the rear toward Sugar Loaf. The Japanese fire had momentarily slackened. As the Marines came up the slope, Dereschuk and his buddies went over to them. A lieutenant identified himself as being from D Company, 29th Marines and told them they could leave the hill.

Still in the ditch at the top of the reverse slope, Private First Class Charles Pugh looked up as a BAR man dropped down next to him. The man said he was from Dog Company of the 29th. "About that time we looked out in front of us, across this little valley to a high area and there was a Japanese looking straight at us down the barrel of his rifle," recalled Pugh. "And this kid maneuvered his BAR faster than I could move my M1. He shot that man and the fella jumped right straight up and fell over backwards and a Jap on each side of him grabbed him to let him down."

Pugh started back toward the other side of the hill where he ran into two buddies, Private First Class Homer Goff and a Marine named Williams. The three worked their way to the rear down a water-filled ditch with Pugh in the front, followed by Williams, with Goff just behind. Pugh suddenly realized he was alone. After a while Williams reappeared. He had been shot in the shoulder while running through the ditch. Goff was not so lucky. He had been killed.

Among the handful of G Company Marines surviving to welcome their Dog Company replacements was Private First Class Jack Houston. He had spent the early morning hours pressed to the dirt as Japanese knee mortars pounded the hill. The Japanese must have been very close because Houston could see the shells go almost straight up, reach an apex above him, and start down. He had one moment of extreme panic when it looked as if one of the projectiles was going to land directly on top of him. He started to run to another spot, but found he couldn't move; his legs had gone to sleep from lack of circulation. He crouched helplessly as the shell plummeted down and exploded—not on top of him, but close to the spot he had intended to run to.

Soon after this near escape, a knot of Marines appeared at the bottom of the hill and started toward him. Someone yelled that the 22d Marines was being relieved. As Houston made his way down the hill, he met "a young looking kid" armed only with a small caliber pistol. He asked the Marine where his rifle was and the youngster said he didn't know. Still lugging both Futrell's BAR and his own rifle, Houston handed him the M1 and admonished him to be sure to hang on to it.

Houston made his way back along the ditch toward the G Company CP. The first thing he saw there was the body of Glenn Mullooly, the company CP runner. The youngster had been killed two days earlier by the same machine gun that wounded Captain Stebbins, but the body had just recently been found where it had fallen into some vegetation. "Complete weariness was taking over and everything seemed to be happening in slow motion," observed Houston. He watched as a mobile rocket launcher pulled up and began firing a rack of missiles. One of the rockets misfired and fell near him. Houston didn't have enough energy to even duck. Luckily, the rocket was a dud.

He found two of his platoon mates—Rocco Pilari and Dennis Delcambre—who had also made it back off the hill. Someone told the company first sergeant, Pete Maresh, they were the last three riflemen in G Company. It wasn't far from the truth. Houston saw that Maresh had tears in his eyes as he sent the three Marines back to the battalion aid station. King Company hadn't fared much better. Of the 4 officers and 99 men who participated in the assault, only 3 officers and 30 men came off Sugar Loaf unhurt.

One of the G Company wounded was Dan Dereschuk, who found his way to the battalion aid station where he was checked by a doctor and tagged for evacuation to the Army's 82d Field Hospital. There were several officers present and while he and other wounded Marines waited, the officers questioned them about the location of Major Courtney's body. Dereschuk said he did not know, but he had last seen the major near the center of the crest of the hill. During the night a cluster of artillery rounds hit there in one sudden burst . . . anything at the center of the hill was probably hamburger at this point, he told them bluntly.

Plans called for the attack along the division front to resume at 0800 on 15 May. Naval and air preparation would last from 0630 to 0700. Artillery preparation would be fired right up to the moment of the attack.

On the right, Major Tom Myers, commanding 1/22, moved up to a forward observation post on the northern bank of the Asato overlooking Naha. Myers had a reputation as a "by the book" type of officer; he was a little too straitlaced for some of the combat mustangs, but Shepherd thought a lot of him. In previous days the major had lost a couple of his walkie-talkie people to snipers and the experience had apparently left him pensive. "I'm a bad man to be around," he remarked. "I draw fire."

Shortly after 0700 Myers gathered his company commanders in the lee of a red-tiled house to review the plan of action for the day. It should have been a safe spot, but the Marines were beginning to learn there were no safe spots on southern Okinawa. Some sharp-eyed enemy observer apparently marked the group. A mortar thumped from somewhere on the other side of the river. A single mortar shell landed directly on the red-tiled house. When the smoke cleared, Myers lay dead. Five feet away lay his orderly, Private First Class Guido Conti, also dead. Lieutenant Harrison P. Klusmeier, executive officer of C Company, 6th Tank Battalion was killed; the company commander was wounded. All three of the rifle company commanders were wounded. Major Earl J. Cook, the battalion executive officer, took command of the battalion. The attack was delayed as Cook worked to reorganize the battalion.

On the left, meanwhile, Woodhouse's battalion and D Company, 29th Marines, continued to battle for Sugar Loaf. Among the D Company Marines moving up to reinforce Sugar Loaf that morning was Private Declan Klingenhagen. The son of a career Marine, Klingenhagen had been in uniform less than a year. Up until 1 May, the 18–year-old Californian had been unloading supplies with the shore party. While other units had been taking casualties in the north, Klingenhagen's most serious injury occurred when he slashed his finger while opening a C ration can.

But on 1 May, he had been assigned to D Company, 29th Marines. Early on the morning of 15 May, his squad was told they were going up behind the front lines to help mop up Japanese who had infiltrated during the night. On the way forward, they trudged through the litter of the previous day's fighting, passing a Japanese who had been bayonetted. The victim sprawled face up on the ground, his right arm thrown across his forehead, an American bayonet lying near his head. Klingenhagen thought the enemy soldier looked terribly young, probably not more than 14 years old. Further along, an anonymous pair of legs leaned almost nonchalantly against a low stone wall. The torso from the waist up lay on the other side of the wall.

Meanwhile, what had started as a mop-up had now become a matter of helping the 22d Marines fight off growing Japanese pressure on Woodhouse's 2d Battalion. Stark evidence of that pressure lay at their feet as the men approached Sugar Loaf by way of a long ditch dotted with fighting holes. Some of the holes contained dead Marines. The newcomers were already under fire as Klingenhagen and another Marine were told to man a machine gun standing about 30 yards away toward the far side of Sugar Loaf. They headed for the gun, but never got there as a mortar and hand grenade barrage erupted around them. As Klingenhagen jumped into a foxhole, a hand grenade went off in front of his face and blew his helmet to the back of his head. "I did not get a scratch and I grabbed the helmet and reset it," he recalled. The explosion may have knocked him momentarily unconscious, for when he looked over at the machine gun he saw two newly dead Marines lying next to it.

Lugging a heavy machine gun, Private First Class Ben Bard would run a few yards, hit the dirt, then get up and run again. He was on the deck when a bullet slammed into his hip. Bard reached back and felt a flood of wetness. After one horrified moment, he realized that most of it was water from his shattered canteen. His leg had also been laid open, but there seemed to be more water than blood. Bard lay there for a few moments; then, realizing that his buddies needed the machine gun, he forced himself to his feet and staggered forward—toward Sugar Loaf.

Waiting with his squad at the foot of the hill, Private First Class Earl Curnutte, an 18-year-old from the West Virginia coal mining region, was told to climb up the slope and set up a machine gun. Up at the top, he found a heavy machine gun already lying on the ground. A dead Marine lay sprawled next to it. The hill seemed fairly quiet; there was no sign of any Japanese. He yelled down for the others to send up his machine gun. "There's one up there," someone shouted back. "Use it."

Curnutte set the abandoned gun up on a light tripod, put in a belt and aimed it out over the forward slope. "Is there any wounded up there?" someone yelled. "No, just one dead man," replied Curnutte, eyeing the dead Marine lying just beyond arm's length. The "corpse" twitched. "Hey!" he shouted. "This man's not dead! He's still alive." A couple of men crawled up to the crest and dragged the wounded Marine down, leaving Curnutte alone behind the machine gun.

A few minutes later he was startled to see about a dozen Japanese soldiers trudging up the reverse slope in his direction. They were carrying rifles and talking "like they owned the place." At about the same time, one of the Japanese spotted Curnutte and pointed toward him. Another enemy soldier immediately smacked a grenade against his side and threw it in a high looping arc toward Curnutte's gun. Curnutte had already opened fire and was cutting the Japanese to pieces as the grenade sailed toward him. Even as the enemy soldiers fell dead and dying, the grenade plummeted down between his feet and exploded. Curnutte looked down in shock and surprise to find his right leg had disappeared below the knee. The left leg hung useless, splinters of bone sticking out of the flesh.

Abandoning the machine gun, Curnutte dragged himself back to the northern slope, but the Marines seemed to be gone. Finally he came across a cavelike indentation dug four or five feet into the slope and crawled in. A Marine sat in the back of the cave, his rifle propped between his knees. Curnutte asked the Marine to help him put a tourniquet on the stump of his right leg, but the man just stared. Curnutte swore at him, then took a closer look. The man was dead, his eyes fixed. He'd been swearing at a corpse. Curnutte opened up his first aid pouch, found the tourniquet and tied off the stump. "I wasn't too worried about the other one because it was still hanging there, but the bones were sticking out," he recalled.

Though Curnutte didn't know it, Irish George Murphy's platoon was in big trouble. The Japanese he had shot down on the other slope were part of a larger counterattack all along the line. Back at the 2d Battalion OP, Captain Mabie's concerns mounted. Watching elements of the 22d Marines fall back from the hill earlier, it looked to him as if Murphy's platoon was being abandoned on the hill. He asked Woodhouse for permission to withdraw. Woodhouse refused.

Murphy's men had thrown all the grenades they carried—350 in all—but remained under heavy pressure. Murphy radioed Mabie and asked permission to withdraw. Mabie told him he would have to hold. Murphy reported that Japanese knee mortars were pounding the Sugar Loaf so heavily he could not hang on any longer. That was the last Mabie heard from him.

Up on Sugar Loaf, Earl Curnutte crawled out of the cave and managed to drag himself down to the foot of the hill. Two Marines suddenly materialized from somewhere and grabbed his arms. One was a new recruit, Private Roy L. Wilmot. The other was Irish George Murphy. They started to drag him along parallel to the hill when a bullet suddenly smacked into Wilmot's chest. He sank to the ground, convulsing as blood hemorrhaged from his chest, and died without a word.

An instant later, Murphy tumbled over backwards. When the former football hero raised himself back up, Curnutte saw he had been hit in the face by a bullet. It looked as if his eyes had been shot out. Blood was leaking from his mouth, his nose and ears. As Curnutte started crawling, Murphy tried to follow. Curnutte told him, "Murphy, wait and I'll get out of your way." But when he looked back again, Irish George Murphy was dead.

Curnutte left the lieutenant. He crawled parallel to the hill for awhile, then got into a ditch about 30 or 40 yards from the base of the hill. Too weak to go any further, he finally stopped. "I didn't see anybody. I didn't hear anybody. Just guns blasting and shells exploding everywhere," he remembered. By rights, he should have been dead of his injuries; oddly enough, he didn't even feel any pain from the stump of his severed leg.

Still up on Sugar Loaf's slope, Declan Klingenhagen was not sure what was happening. A few yards behind him a lieutenant was giving everyone encouragement. Suddenly Klingenhagen heard a *poof*. He turned and saw that the lieutenant had been killed instantly by a direct mortar hit. His body was a black husk. A little later a Marine further up the hill began calling for a corpsman. There was no response. All the corpsmen had been killed or wounded. The Marine finally quit calling and crawled to the rear of the hill. As he passed by, Klingenhagen saw that the man's leg had been blown off at midcalf.[1]

Klingenhagen had never been in heavy combat before. What he did next was a tribute to him and to his training. Expecting the Japanese to come swarming over the top of the hill in a banzai attack, he snapped his bayonet onto the end of his rifle and waited, holding the weapon ready. Instead of hordes of enemy soldiers, things seemed to quiet down. But soon afterward he heard a Marine up the slope yell, "We can't hold!" Klingenhagen went to the back of the hill to pass the word along, but nobody was there. Everyone had left. He went back to his foxhole and yelled, "Fall back!" Four Marines—one wounded helped by three others—came scrambling down the slope.

They made their way down to the bottom of the hill. One of the Marines broke off to help a wounded man lying on the ground. Klingenhagen went with him. The Marine crouched to help the wounded man, then fell dead as a sniper shot him in the center of his chest. "Since I was upright, all I could think of was that I was next," recalled Klingenhagen. "I took off for the cover of a disabled tank." As he ran, one of the other men yelled at him to leave his rifle, which Klingenhagen did, though all his training and instincts told him not to; "but he needed it and I could not refuse."

Sliding into a crater next to the disabled tank, Klingenhagen saw another M1 rifle lying there and immediately grabbed it. Three other Marines had also taken shelter in the crater. Looking up at Sugar Loaf, they could see Japanese soldiers moving back and forth along the crest. Klingenhagen examined the rifle he had picked up. It was very muddy and the bolt would not seat properly. He put the rifle on the ground and kicked the bolt home with his foot. Then, afraid the bore was clogged with mud and might explode, he test-fired the weapon, holding the bolt area away from his face. It seemed to work all right, but he had to kick the bolt home again. Satisfied, he began popping away at the Japanese on top of the hill, kicking the bolt home with his foot after every shot.

Lying in the ditch at the base of Sugar Loaf, Private First Class Irv Gehret could see the top of the hill silhouetted against the sky. "I tell you, you could see the stuff coming over there—it looked like people were throwing handfuls of stones over," he recalled. "There were just grenades and mortars and stuff like that coming over. And they were popping all over the place." The ditch was already full of bodies.

Corporal Jack Castignola was among the D Company men shifted into the 2/22 area to help mop up infiltrators only to find themselves involved in the full-scale counterattack. Most of his fighting was done along a nondescript rise which soon became known as Hand Grenade Ridge. "The Japs were in about the same position on the other side, and all we did was pull pins, give the grenade a little toss, and they'd roll down on the Japs," recalled Castignola. "We killed a lot of them with rifles, too. The first one I killed would have made a good end on any football team. He was over six feet tall and must have weighed over two hundred. He was the first one I saw dressed in a Marine outfit. He had on all our stuff except the helmet and that was one of the things that gave him away."

As the man strolled up to the Marine lines, Castignola glanced at him and thought to himself, "That guy has an awfully long rifle." He looked around just as the stranger ducked into a cave off to his left. That sharpened Castignola's suspicions. "I knew none of our men were casually walking into caves in that part of the country." When the man came out again, Castignola noticed his mushroom-shaped helmet and that was all the proof he needed that he was looking at a Japanese.

"There was a stone wall outside the cave and the Jap seemed to hide from something, pressing himself against the wall," recalled Castignola. "He stood just like he was in front of a firing squad. He sagged like a loose rope the first time I shot."

The Japanese counterattack against the few Marines left on Sugar Loaf had begun at 0730. The U.S. artillery preparation intended to support the Marine attack slowed up the enemy temporarily, but they soon regained momentum. By 0900 the counterattack had leaked out along a 900–yard front and into the zone of the 29th Marines. The virtual annihilation of George Murphy's platoon was recorded in the 2d Battalion Journal as Captain Mabie ("D 29th") talked with Woodhouse ("6") and the executive officer of Easy Company ("E 5"):

1136—D 29th to 6: Request permission to withdraw. Irish George Murphy has been hit. Has eleven men left in platoon of original 60.

1138—6 to D 29th: You must hold!

1143—D 29th to 6: Platoon has withdrawn. Position was untenable. Could not evacuate wounded. Believe Japs now hold ridge.

1144—6 to D 29th: Protect your unevacuated wounded.

1230—E 5 to 6: Japs are trying to put 47 mm gun on top of Sugar Loaf. Will have to fire regardless of troops.

1240—D 29th to 6: All wounded believed to have been removed from Sugar Loaf.

1500—D 29th to 6: Still evacuating wounded, send more smoke.

1522—D 29th to 6: Men sent in for casualties returned safely. Brought out one man. Could not find any more.

While 2/22 and D Company, 29th, struggled to contain the enemy counterattacks near Sugar Loaf, the rest of the 29th Marines had attacked abreast in an effort to seize Half Moon just to the southeast. The hill was named—as are many terrain features—by men who saw only one side of the position. The slope facing the Marines was a long arc, with the concave side opening to the north. Viewed from above, the hill appeared more T-shaped, with the stem of the T pointing south. Japanese troops on the stem could direct fire on the crest of the hill and enfilade any Marines trying to attack along the southern slope. The Shuri Heights, barely 800 yards to the east, also provided direct observation.

Both the 1st and 3d Battalions were engaged in bitter fighting on the approaches to Half Moon. By late afternoon, C Company had reached the valley north of Half Moon where its supporting tanks came under direct 150 mm howitzer fire. Private First Class H. H. Tayler was with C Company's 3d Platoon. Able Company had been in the assault the day before and returned badly shot up. "We heard what had happened to them and we knew we were going to catch it," Tayler recalled. As his platoon worked forward along the narrow-gauge railroad, dead Marines from the 14 May assault still lay on the ground, boding ill for what was to come. C Company soon began to suffer similarly. A youngster by the name of Pinner was among the first killed as the attack progressed toward Half Moon. Scuttlebutt was that he was heir to a toilet paper manufacturing fortune in Upstate New York. Tayler saw some people dragging Pinner's body off the hill in a blanket and he thought, "Oh boy, this is it."

Corporal Dean Wells, serving as a member of C Company's demolitions team led his men forward and they succeeded in destroying one of three strong points before enemy guns forced them to ground. Alone, Wells crawled forward across an exposed area to destroy another position. He then returned for more grenades and demolitions and assaulted the third strong point. His luck finally ran out and he was seriously wounded, but succeeded in neutralizing the third pocket of resistance, enabling his platoon to advance and secure the ridge.

Elements of A Company moved up on the right of C to link up with 3/29 while B Company linked the 1st Battalion's lines with the 5th Marines along the division boundary. Advancing over a wall with several other Marines, Private First Class Dom Spitale moved forward toward Half Moon. The man in front of him abruptly dropped, killed by a burst of machine-gun fire. The gunner turned his attention to Spitale. In the next instant, a bullet struck Spitale in the head, entering his right temple and exiting the left temple. Someone said, "Dom, you're hit."

Spitale felt an incredible flush of heat—so intense that he tore off his blouse, cartridge belt and other gear and then ran back toward the rear as bullets kicked up dirt around him. Wearing only his pants and shoes, he made it back to some other Marines who put him on a stretcher and lugged him back to an aid station. By this time Spitale had lost consciousness. A doctor gave him a quick once over and they put him in the "dead pile." But he wasn't dead. Miraculously, someone saw him move; they got some blood into him, and he was evacuated.

But Spitale's ordeal was far from over. In tearing off his gear, he had also torn off his dog tags. Now he had no idea who he was. It took him six months to remember his name: "Dom Spitale, United States Marine Corps," he blurted in a sudden revelation one day. A doctor replied, "Then what the hell are you doing in an Army hospital?" It turned out Spitale had been listed as missing in action for all those months. The war was over. His family thought he was dead. Spitale was discharged from Philadelphia Naval Hospital a year later.

Back by the wrecked tank in front of Sugar Loaf, Declan Klingenhagen and his three newfound friends decided it was time to get out. Huddling behind the tank, they held a consultation and decided to head back to the low ridge behind Sugar Loaf one at a time, at five-second intervals, just as they had learned in training.

The first man left. Five seconds later, the second Marine dashed out, followed by the third. Klingenhagen was the last man. Thinking about the regularity of their departure, he realized that if a Japanese were watching, by now he too would be counting off five seconds and waiting for the next man—who was Klingenhagen.

Klingenhagen hurriedly counted to three and took off. "As I ran across the field heading for the ridge, I saw stones and dirt kick up to the front and right of me," he recalled. "At the same time I heard the *dit, dit, dit* of a Jap nambu machine gun."

Klingenhagen ran faster. Coming upon a ditch, he dived into it and began crawling along toward the ridge. He was wearing two canteens, one on each hip and for a frantic moment he became wedged in the narrow ditch, but he soon freed himself. Finally leaving the ditch, he came around an embankment and found one of the other Marines. The other man ran out onto the open ground, making a beeline for the ridge. Three-fourths of the way across, he suddenly went down, wounded. Klingenhagen saw him crawling, still trying to make it to the safety of the ridge. "I saw four shell craters around the side of the field, so I went from crater to crater and got to the ridge at the same time as the wounded Marine," he recalled. "I helped him over the top of the ridge. He was wounded in the buttocks and seemed to be otherwise all right."

Also making it back was the rookie second lieutenant who had accompanied Lieutenant Jamieson and his 25 replacements to the front lines the night before. Severely wounded in the shoulder, he had heard the word to leave the hill that morning, but was unable to get up. "He heard the tractor pull out and he said a few minutes later the Japs were running all over the place," reported Jamieson. "He was lying face down in a ditch and lay still attempting to pretend he was dead, which worked." When the commotion let up, he started crawling, eventually making his way back to the Marine lines.[2]

By 1315, the Japanese counterattacks were finally halted, though the Marines had been forced to give up some ground immediately in front of Sugar Loaf to do it. By now the 2d Battalion of the 22d Marines was staggering from the constant fighting and heavy casualties. The battalion had lost over 400 men in three days. The wounded from this day alone lay on row after row of stretchers behind a small rise to the rear of the front lines. The suffering men reminded Sergeant Major Stanley Shaw of a scene in the movie *Gone With the Wind* where hundreds of wounded Confederates had lain crying and groaning in an Atlanta rail yard.

Concerned about a possible enemy breakthrough, Colonel Schneider had moved I Company over to back up Woodhouse's shattered battalion. Later in the day, regiment ordered the 2d Battalion withdrawn and replaced by the 3d Battalion. The relief was effected at 1700. Companies I and L were placed on the front line, and K Company was positioned slightly to their right rear.

Among the K Company men was Charles Pugh. Having survived his experience on Sugar Loaf, Pugh was sitting around with a handful of other lucky Marines, cleaning his .45. Word was that they would have to go back up Sugar Loaf. Pugh wasn't happy about the idea. "I wish I knew some way to get out of going back up there," he observed to no one in particular.

"Shoot your damn foot off," his platoon sergeant retorted. At that moment Pugh let the slide down on his .45 with his finger still on the trigger. The weapon went off, sending a heavy slug into the ground between his outstretched feet. The platoon sergeant looked at him oddly and remarked, "I didn't know you had little enough sense to do it."

At least three Marines remained on Sugar Loaf—and they were still full of fight.

On 14 May, Corporal James Day, a 19-year-old fire team leader with Weapons Company, 22d Marines, had led seven men—the remnants of two squads—up the western slope of Sugar Loaf where they found cover in a large shell hole. Of the seven men who started out, four were wounded on the way in, one badly. The Marines put their badly injured comrade in a cave at the base of Sugar Loaf where stretcher bearers picked him up a short time later. "The other three were wounded slightly, but later in the day they were very seriously wounded and they died before the afternoon was out," reported Day. Their bodies were placed in the cave at the base of the hill.

That left three survivors in the hole—Day, Private First Class Dale Bertoli and a Marine named McDonald. Day was an experienced man who had fought on Eniwetok and Guam. Bertoli was also a veteran of the Guam campaign. Day considered him very effective and courageous—"he knew what he was doing." McDonald was a youngster who had joined the outfit from a replacement organization a day or two before.

The three men defended the hole through the 14th. "During that night we received quite a bit of enemy fire and quite a bit of infiltration, but none of that infiltration was directly against us," recalled Day. The morning of the 15th, they heard the F and K Company survivors leaving the hill. Day,

Bertoli, and McDonald stayed put. "[It] was safer in that hole we were in than trying to cross that area to our rear that was about 300 yards across, that was completely covered by fire, most of it enfilade fire," Day observed.

The three Marines had four or five M1s and a carbine from the men who had been killed. They also had unlimited grenades and ammunition. A couple of amtracs had been knocked out behind them and the nearer one was loaded with ammunition. Whenever the little group of defenders ran low on ammo, they would delve into the amtrac for more.

During the day the hill was saturated with artillery and mortar fire. "To our right there were a couple of antitank weapons, 47 mm antitank rifles, and they had knocked out at least three tanks to our rear that had gone up with the initial assault of our companies and they had knocked out quite a few of the amtracs," noted Day. The gun couldn't reach the Marines in the shell hole because a sort of parapet had been thrown up on that side when the shell or bomb exploded. They were protected from fire from Shuri by the contour of Sugar Loaf itself. "They couldn't get into us because they were firing into the direct rear of Sugar Loaf," noted Day.

Through most of the day the three Marines kept the Japanese off with grenades. Day felt they were holding their own, but he wished he had a machine gun. Shortly before noon, he went back to get more ammo from the amtrac and ran into Lieutenant Dick Pfuhl of Easy Company. Pfuhl told Day that Easy was dug in directly to their rear and could give them any support they needed. "However, they could not move forward because they were the only blocking position between the Japanese force and the rest of the division, particularly the rear," noted Day. "So they couldn't leave that position."

Undaunted, Day returned to the shell hole. "We were in the enviable position that the Japanese in order to assault Sugar Loaf Hill had to come across our front, about 55 or 60 or 75 yards to our front," observed Day. "They were coming in from a place called Horseshoe and they were coming in from a small village that was to our right front. I say we were in an enviable position because we could bring flanking fire in on them and we did that for the entire day."

About 1630, Day got his wish for an automatic weapon when a machine-gun squad was shot down as it tried to get up on the hill. Day, Bertoli and McDonald retrieved the gun. "The only problem was we didn't have much ammunition for the gun," recalled Day. "I think we had two boxes. And we went through that in a hurry." They were able to obtain more machine-gun ammunition from the second knocked-out amtrac, but their success was short-lived. In their eagerness to put fire down on the Japanese they saw moving to their front, they exposed themselves to the 47 mm gun on their right. The gun put a round into them, knocking out their newly acquired machine gun and killing young McDonald. Now it was just Day and Bertoli.

At an aid station behind the 2d Battalion, Private First Class Landon Oakes saw firsthand what a beating the regiment was taking. All day long Oakes and his comrades in Weapons Company had been trying to suppress enemy fire from Sugar Loaf and surrounding hills with 105 mm guns mounted on M-4 tank chassis. They weren't having much success.

"The 22d was shot to ineffectiveness, utterly exhausted by the morning of the 15th and we were trying to pull survivors of a couple of rifle companies off the hill," recalled Oakes. Operating around the aid station, he saw dozens of Marines who had been brought in and died either at the station or on the trip in. "They had a pile of them," all wrapped up in ponchos or blankets, he recalled. "They'd been killed in the past few days. There was a lot of them and they weren't too well ordered there."

Oakes came close to joining them. Forced out of position by Japanese artillery fire, Oakes was helping to truck ammo to a safer area when a shell exploded beside the truck and drove fragments into his leg and side. He arrived at the aid station just as a graves registration detail finished loading the pile of corpses onto an amtrac. A couple of Marines picked up Oakes's stretcher and secured it on top as the amtrac started toward the rear.

"They put me up in there on it and I'm on a stretcher and there's two fellas driving it and it's full of dead men," recalled Oakes. "It's just plumb full . . . everyone you could pack in there. I was the only man on the stretcher. All the rest was dead." Though he was shot full of morphine and drifted in and out of consciousness, it seemed to him there must be 65 or 70 dead Marines packed into the vehicle. Oddly, the experience took on almost mystical proportions; he felt an overwhelming sense of brotherhood with the dead men. "To me, it seems like that should have been a nauseating experience, but it was far beyond that," he was to recall emotionally 50 years later. "I think I was quite proud to leave the lines with those men. They gave their all."

The amtrac left Oakes off at an old Japanese bus that had been converted into an operating room. He was vaguely aware of the surgeons trimming away flesh and tossing it aside. They were talking about stopping the blood and there seemed to be considerable conversation about irrigating the wounds. One of the doctors was swearing, saying somebody needed to bore some holes in the floor of that bus, it was so slippery and wet with water and blood.

A couple of days later, Oakes was flown out to a hospital on Guam. Though pretty well cut up by the shell fragments, he hadn't broken any bones. "I got just exactly what a man was looking for, you know," he said later. "It was one of those that was going to get me off the island, but wasn't going to kill me and I wasn't going to be permanently disabled." He was one of the lucky ones.

Also counting himself among the lucky ones was Earl Curnutte. Having crawled into the ditch fronting Sugar Loaf sometime before noon, he had been lying there, unable to move, ever since. Finally, some four hours after he had been wounded, he looked back toward one of the little knolls behind him and saw an entrenching tool rising and falling. "I didn't see anybody, but I saw the entrenching tool going up and down and I knew somebody was digging in," he said. Pulling out his canteen, he waved it back and forth in the air, trying to attract someone's attention.

Back where the survivors were digging in, one of the Marines saw the movement. "Hey, there's a man alive out there," he said. Somebody else retorted, "No, no. We've been all over that area. They couldn't live through the shelling." But the first Marine insisted he had seen movement and finally the other Marine saw it too. A sergeant took out a four-man rescue team. Under the cover of smoke grenades, they managed to rescue Curnutte from the ditch. All he wanted was water. He drank canteenful after canteenful and as soon as it hit his stomach, he retched it right back out. One of his best buddies sat alongside, watching him, tears running down his cheeks. "Man, we thought you were dead," said another Marine.[3]

"Nothing doing," said Curnutte. A few days later he was in Hawaii. His right leg was gone, but the doctors managed to save the left one, though it would never be quite right again.[4]

That night Charles Pugh had no one to dig in with. His buddy, Gib Kanter, had been hit in the neck up on Sugar Loaf and now Pugh was casting around for a foxhole buddy. The hole he had slept in the night before was pretty close to the crest of the hill. They were taking some long range artillery fire and nobody was enthusiastic about the spot. Pugh spotted one of the flamethrower men, Private First Class Arthur Kowalski, walking down along the foot of the hill and said, "Hey, Ski, do you want to dig in with me tonight?" Kowalski looked up the slope and replied, "No, that area is too exposed. I don't want to dig in up there."

As Kowalski walked off, Pugh heard a shell coming in. He hit the ground. The shell exploded at the foot of the hill and drove a piece of metal into Kowalski's back. "I didn't believe the dirty little bastards could do it," said Kowalski in surprise and pain. He was a big, strapping man, and he seemed to be in good shape as they took him out. But Pugh later heard that the bit of metal worked its way in and severed Ski's spinal cord. He died aboard a medical evacuation plane to Guam.

A Marine battalion at full strength numbered just over 900 men, though few units maintained a full complement. Since the assault across the Asa Kawa on 10 May, the 2d Battalion, 22d Marines had lost 400 men—leaving 286 effectives. The regiment itself was at 62 percent combat efficiency. The survivors showed the strain. Private Edward "Buzzy" Fox, a 20-year-old replacement from Elizabeth, New Jersey, arrived at G Company with most of his illusions intact. He was assigned to a machine-gun squad commanded by a care-worn Marine who looked to be at least 30 years old. Fox was stunned when he learned the man was only 19.

But though it seemed one-sided to the Marines beating themselves against the Sugar Loaf triad, the Japanese were also suffering. Some evidence of those losses lay on the field. Hundreds of Japanese corpses lay rotting in the division's zone, and hundreds more had presumably been killed by supporting fires or sealed in caves and tombs during mopping-up activities. As of 15 May, the division claimed 1,542 enemy killed and 1,912 presumed killed, since the Marines had entered the southern lines. The 'presumed' dead figure was pure guesswork. There was no way of knowing how many—or how few—Japanese had died unseen and uncounted in the caves and tunnels, or who had been dragged off by their comrades.

III Amphibious Corps (IIIAC) expressed skepticism over the figures. On 16 May, IIIAC cautioned, "It cannot be too highly emphasized that reported enemy dead must show as true a picture of the situation as possible, which case is often the exception rather than the rule. It is fully appreciated that counting and estimating enemy dead by frontline units presents a very difficult problem. Nevertheless, it is believed that reported figures usually tend toward an overestimate."

In any case, enemy casualties had been sufficiently high that the Japanese Thirty-second Army reinforced the 15th IMR on the night of 15–16 May with a "crack" battalion picked especially from service and support units of the 1st Specially Established Brigade. The help was badly needed. A POW from the 2d Independent Battalion told Marines his unit had been in contact since 9 May and had been "virtually annihilated."

Marines later captured another Japanese, a soldier from the 4th Company, 15th IMR, who had participated in the attack on Sugar Loaf the night of 14–15 May. He told his interrogators that the 2d Battalion, 15th IMR, had been "virtually destroyed" in the fighting south of the Asa Kawa. The 15th

IMR had had an original strength of about 2,500 men, he said. He also claimed there were some 10,000 enemy personnel available in Naha— 1,000–1,200 Army, 2,000 Navy and the rest Okinawan labor forces. The POW "stated that this position was a selected strong point and would be bitterly defended," noted the U.S. intelligence report. The prisoner did not mention, or did not know, that the 3d Battalion, 15th IMR had been directed forward to stiffen the Sugar Loaf defenses. When the Marines attacked again, they would be facing fresh troops.

Guam, May 16—(Associated Press)—United States Marines battled furiously on the edge of Naha, capital of Okinawa Island today. . . .

[A British broadcast of a Reuters dispatch heard by CBS in New York said Naha had fallen to the Americans. There was no confirmation from U.S. headquarters.]

At dawn one 22d Marine Regiment officer said, "We've been fighting like maniacs since midnight." [Associated Press Correspondent Al] Dopkins reported that before the battle was over, one American company had only two men left out of 240. Another company had only eight survivors.

NOTES

1. The man was probably Earl Curnutte.

2. The second lieutenant told Jamieson his story when the two met at a field hospital in Guam where both were convalescing from wounds. Fifty years later, Jamieson could not recall the man's name.

3. One published account maintains that Captain Mabie spotted Curnutte while studying Sugar Loaf through his field glasses; the account related here was told to Curnutte himself by his buddies.

4. Ben Bard was more fortunate. He was evacuated that night and his wound healed, though pieces of canteen continued to work out of his flesh years later.

Chapter 7

On the Line

The 6th Marine Division's difficulties were in large part beyond its control. General Buckner's unimaginative battle plan—and the restrictive terrain—precluded the use of large-scale maneuver. But the division also suffered at first from its failure to understand the magnitude of the Japanese defenses at Sugar Loaf. In hindsight, the expectation that Captain Stebbins's G Company would be able to seize the hill by itself would have been laughable had the results not been so tragic. Unfortunately, that unrealistic assessment of the enemy position seems to have persisted too long.

"Sugar Loaf was a tough nut to crack," recalled Colonel John C. McQueen, the division chief of staff. "I personally felt that initially we didn't put enough force in there. I felt, and I told General Shepherd, that I thought if we would put a battalion-size [unit] in there and take the losses . . . it would be cheaper in the long run. But several days went by when the smaller units went in there and it was tough going."

As the fighting continued, seven vital facts gradually became evident to General Shepherd and his staff:

—The 6th Marine Division's attack had uncovered the western anchor of General Ushijima's main defensive position.

—The anchor was made up of three terrain features—Half Moon, Horseshoe, and Sugar Loaf, each heavily fortified and mutually supporting.

—Each terrain feature was located at the end of a sort of geographical and tactical corridor and commanded all of the ground leading into it.

—The enemy was prepared to fiercely contest the three hills.

—If the hills could be seized, General Ushijima's line would be outflanked.

—Naha, the Okinawan capital, lay exposed, but could not be taken until the Sugar Loaf triad fell.

One more fact was also clear by this time, to generals and privates alike: it wasn't going to be easy.

For the Marine combat troops, far from the rarefied atmosphere of large-scale maps and colored pins, the fighting around Sugar Loaf dissolved into a seemingly endless blur punctuated by moments of extreme horror. Exhausted men performed like automatons. One survivor described himself as "like being on a drunk and in a daze and just functioning from necessity." It was an image that would recur again and again in later years as men struggled to convey the detached numbness that came over them as the battle dragged on. "I was just there," said Private First Class Ed Soja. "Like one of those tin soldiers . . . I just kept going and going and going."

Food came in a package—K rations, C rations, and the newer, more palatable ten-in-one rations. The individual K ration included a small can of hash and cheese or ham and eggs, soluble coffee or lemonade, some hard biscuits, a stick or two of chewing gum, a package of four cigarettes and some toilet paper. Few could eat much anyway. Living on cigarettes and bites of high-energy fruit and chocolate "D-bars," more popularly known as "dog turds," almost everyone lost weight—an average of 15 to 20 pounds for the line Marine. Bowels either worked not at all or functioned too well. "I was either bound up tight or loose as a goose," recalled Corporal James White. "There didn't seem to be any in-between."

Private First Class George Niland, an Irish kid from Boston, explained, "All you thought about was the little hole you were in, the little hill you were hitting. You didn't have any emotions, really. I loved my family dearly . . . but if I had received a telegram saying they all had been wiped out in a disaster, it wouldn't have affected me at all. Because all I was thinking about was killing Japs and surviving. That's it! End of subject! They reduce you to being an animal."

Fear increased in direct proportion to the immediacy of danger, but "there was always an underlying apprehension . . . a gnawing feeling of uneasiness," observed White. The time of the greatest fear, noted White, was during an attack.

"The word would be passed that we were moving out," he recalled. "We would saddle up. Cartridge belts were usually left on, but they would be buckled on if they had been taken off and the canteens would be aligned on the buttocks. The pack would be struggled onto the shoulders. Bandoliers would be looped over the neck. The rifle would be checked to ensure that a cartridge was in the chamber and that the action operated smoothly. The toothbrush would be taken from its usual place of residence, the pocket in the dungaree jacket—the one over the heart with the letters USMC and a Marine emblem printed on it. A fast brushing of real or imagined dirt particles from the rifle's action would follow."

The attack would begin.

"There were no immediate words to urge us onward, no waving of sabers or gallant cheers while we dug spurs into our horse's flanks and galloped forward. The platoon leader, usually in a normal voice, would say something monumental, such as, 'Okay, let's go.' The word would be passed, and we would begin to climb out of our foxholes and follow him. It is possible that there were men who wanted to get up out of a relatively safe foxhole and start moving in the direction of the enemy. I never met one of them. I would rather not be doing it, but following the platoon leader was just something that had to be done."

In front of them lay the hill so many of their comrades had already died trying to seize. "It looked just like hell is bound to look . . . smoking and blazing and eerie at night with the flares constantly above it," recalled a survivor. "It's impossible to describe. Horrendous noise, continuously, you know . . . from behind you and both sides of you."

Any time the assault troops reached the top of a hill, the Japanese would subject them to withering fire from supporting positions. "We couldn't get away from the goddamn mortars," explained Corporal Robert Fair, a veteran of Saipan and Tarawa. "If you stayed on the backside [of the hill] they'd beat you to death; if you got up on the top, they'd cut you to pieces. You either had to stay up there and fight . . . or run."

Private First Class Malcolm Lear, a machine gunner with L/3/22, spent most of the battle dug in on a little rise supporting the various infantry assaults on Sugar Loaf. They could see the Marine assaults through the smoke and dust; often men would drop, but it was hard to tell if they were hit or just ducking for cover. The open plain between Lear's position and Sugar Loaf had become a junk yard of wrecked vehicles and assorted debris: tanks with tracks shot off, blasted trees, "paper and cartons and shell casings and just plain old trash." There were bodies everywhere. A few, wrapped in ponchos lay behind the rise where Lear's outfit had set up. Victims of the attack on that little bit of ground, they lay there several days before graves registration toted them away.

Others were deprived of even that small dignity. They had been literally blown to pieces. The area around Lear's position was littered with body parts, arms and legs and unidentifiable pieces. Some of the parts were still clad in fragments of green cloth, so Lear knew they were Marines. The Marines tried to pick up the rotting bits and pieces. "They just picked up what they thought belonged to a guy," recalled Lear. "If he'd lost a leg or something, you'd gather up the nearest leg and put it in the bag or wrap it up in the poncho and hope to God you'd got the right parts."

Out in front of Lear's machine-gun position—in a spot dominated by enemy fire—lay a leg nobody could get to. It wore green. The Marines watched it putrefy over a period of days. "It went from green to greasy gray to greasy black," observed Lear. "You looked at that thing and you wondered, 'Is that going to be me tomorrow?' It was a sobering sight."

Moving up into the line one day, Sergeant William Manchester saw another line of Marines coming out. Among them was a normally "stolid imperturbable" corporal he knew well. Now, when Manchester spoke to him, the corporal seemed to be in an unfocused daze. As his column wound around a bend, Manchester got an inkling of what ailed his friend. About a hundred dead Marines lay by the side of the path. Each corpse had been wrapped in a poncho, secured with commo wire and neatly stacked like log wood. Manchester could see their boondockers sticking out of the wrapped poncho shrouds. "Every pair of boondockers looked like every other pair," he wrote later. "I looked down at my own. They were the same."

After a time in front of Sugar Loaf, death became almost more ordinary than life. It was not unusual, recalled Technical Sergeant Herman Kogan, to be greeted by a buddy with the half-surprised exclamation, "Hell, are you still alive?" But if death was common, the loss of friends still hurt. Kogan mused, "There was a sharp pain in your side when you heard about 'Pappy' or 'Ski' being cut to pieces by machine-gun bullets. It was even sharper and deeper when you saw them go down, their arms flopping crazily as they fell."

Death came in many, often undramatic, ways. Corporal James White remembered a sergeant who stood watching some men start to dig in. "All of a sudden he began to fumble with the clothes around his belt line," recalled White. "He sat down, then leaned to one side and fell over. He died soon after that." A bullet fired from long range had driven through his back and come out his abdomen. Later White found himself in a hole with a man who had been shot through the chest. A corpsman bandaged the casualty and gave him a shot of morphine before leaving to take care of other wounded. "The situation was hairy and the wounded man could not be evacuated," recalled White. "He was awake and alert. I asked him if he hurt much and he told me that he did not. A lot was going on outside our hole and I didn't watch the man constantly. When I looked back at him, after what seemed like only a minute or two, his face was gray and he wasn't breathing. He had gone into shock and died."

Others died with startling suddeness. Sergeant William Cromling was talking to a corpsman named James while their unit was under fire. "When James arrived he and I were kneeling behind a rice paddy wall and just his head was above the top of the wall. I was standing next to him, bent over with my hands on my knees telling him where I wanted him to go. At that time, the Japs were starting to register in on these tanks which were setting up about 25 yards behind us and a round came in and hit the top of the rice paddy wall, decapitating James and the same round wounded me and when I came to, the concussion had blown me about ten yards from where I was standing with James."

Frank Kukuchka's company lost four men killed on 16 May. One of them was Private John O'Leary. "Several of us were sitting on a low stone wall that supported a terrace, waiting for instructions for our next movement," recalled Kukuchka. "All had their helmets on and rifles ready to go except John O'Leary. He was wearing a soft cap, and I can still visualize the twisted wad in his green skivvy shirt at his belly where he kept his cigarettes. He was standing out from me on the terrace about an arm's length away when a shot came in and hit him in the temple. He made a short sound, 'Eh,' and nearly fell on me. It is even difficult to write about it. I never realized such a stream of blood could come from a wound like that. . . . He was rushed off in a jeep almost immediately, but he never made it." O'Leary, who came from Lawrence, Massachusetts, was two weeks short of his 19th birthday.

Private Ken Long, a member of I Company, 29th Marines, lost his foxhole buddy, a man named Sardo, on Half Moon Hill. Sardo, he recalled, was a nondescript Italian-looking man whose eyes always seemed to be darting around from here to there, never focusing on anything for more than a fraction of a second. Sardo never talked about home or family, his goals, what he had done in peacetime. "He was the type of person you would regard as a nonentity, but yet he was a solid person, someone I could depend on to fill in for my weaknesses, someone who would perform those hazardous jobs without even telling you he was going to do them. He was dependable, brave and my foxhole buddy," observed Long.

Sardo was killed by small-arms fire in one of I Company's final assaults on Half Moon. "A feeling of complete loneliness clouded my mind just as though I was the only person in the entire world," recalled Long. Though close as brothers, Long never even learned Sardo's first name until two years after his discharge from the Marine Corps. It was James.

"We tried to support those going up those lousy hills with our fire, but we came under severe mortar and machine-gun fire," recalled Private First Class Bill Pierce of Weapons Company, 22d Marines. "At times we abandoned our 37s and ran and dove into foxholes, burrowing down like moles. . . . Our area was showered with shells . . . I had on a small tan rope rosary that my mother had sent to me. I still have that rosary. I prayed. I said the Hail Mary 50 times or more, at least." Fifty years later his foxhole buddy, Howie George, still remembered the words to the Hail Mary—and he wasn't even Catholic.

Major Phillips D. Carleton, who wrote an analysis of the 6th Marine Division on Okinawa, credited the enemy shelling with having a major impact on the conduct of the campaign. "Artillery fire took a heavy toll of battalion commanders of troops marching to the front lines; it caused casualties among the troops resting in reserve; it made rest areas untenable; it made it impossible for Division to hold troops in ready reserve and at the same time to keep them safe," he wrote.

That analysis in no way conveyed the actual horror of being under artillery fire. Soon after arriving on the lines, one of the platoons in Private James White's company was strung out along a road by a hill, their backs against an embankment. A single shell exploded on the edge of the embankment. About a dozen Marines were hit, half of them killed. One man lost a leg. "I was walking up the hill, somewhere between 30 and 50 yards away from the place where the shell exploded and was hit in the right cheek by a piece of meat," remembered White. "I thought I'd been wounded at first until I saw what had hit me." Sometime later, White buried a severed hand which he found lying by his foxhole.

Private Donald Honis was digging in with his machine-gun section late one afternoon. He recalled, "PFC John Zuk was about 50 feet from me when a shell came in and landed right by his feet. I looked up and Zuk was gone. They could not find Zuk at all." A subsequent notation on Zuk's service record noted, "Remains interred unknown."

The strain was too much for some men. Private First Class Glen Moore recalled the almost constant enemy artillery fire on his 81 mm mortar outfit dug in some 1,000 yards from Sugar Loaf. "The Japs had naval guns on tracks deep in caves that our Hellcats and Corsairs could not reach during their daylight strafing and rocket attacks," he remembered. "During the night they would roll them out and rake our mortar positions and artillery with accurate fire. One night our number 1 gun with its three gunners and squad leader were in the pit awaiting firing orders and one of our ammo carriers, a 17-year-old from New York, began to cry and said he was coming over into the gun pit. I told him to stay there, and since we weren't getting any fire orders, I would come over and stay with him in his foxhole. He had his rosary beads wrapped around his Bible and was reciting his Hail Marys and kissing both with foxhole sincerity. Each time a round would go over or land close, he was sure it had his name on it. I began to recite as many Protestant hymns as I could remember and this seemed to help until the next round landed. Finally, one landed right between our foxhole and the gun pit. It wounded our squad leader and number 1 gunner who was hospitalized and joined us later in the campaign. The concussion threw the 17–year-old and me out of the foxhole. I still had my arm around him when we landed and I assured him that he was all right, as I felt to see if I still had all my own body parts. The next day the boy was taken away and we never saw him again."

Closer to the front, there were mortars, grenades and machine-gun and rifle fire to contend with. The Model 99 Nambu light machine gun had a cyclic rate of fire of 800 rounds per minute, not quite twice the cyclic rate of the United States .30 caliber M1919 light machine gun. "It sounded like a lady screaming," recalled a Marine of the high-pitched shriek of a nambu. Then there were the snipers. If the artillery was terrifying for dealing out indiscriminate death, the Japanese snipers were terrifying for their cool selectivity. The snipers were very patient and they seemed to have an uncanny knack for picking out officers. Often they would lie concealed while lesser targets passed, waiting for a shot at a leader or a radioman. Officers quickly discarded or concealed any sign of rank or authority. "If you were an officer with a .45 strap that went across you diagonally, they would kill you," observed Bill Pierce. "They were shot through the head and shot through the center of the chest. Dead shots. They didn't miss. You would be shocked at how many were hit dead center." Casualties were especially heavy among lieutenants. "These lieutenants come and go like a roll of toilet paper," recalled Private First Class Ronald Manson. "I can't even tell you the names of the company commanders. The officers lasted about 15 minutes and they were dead or gone."

A young platoon leader, weary and torn by the loss of too many friends, made no effort to hide his respect for the Japanese as he lectured a group of replacements just arrived in the lines and about ready to go into combat. Pointing his pistol at these bewildered lambs, he concluded, "And if I hear any bullshit about the Japs being lousy fighters, I'll shoot you. If one of you motherfuckers says they can't shoot straight, I'll put a bullet between your fuckin' eyes before they do."

His respect for the enemy was echoed in one of the regimental special action reports, which noted, "The terrain was broken by countless small hills, ravines, terraces and tombs. Every hill was a Japanese strong point and was undermined by elaborate tunnels with gun ports sighted for defense from all directions. They were all mutually supporting and the positions were well-camouflaged and impregnable to any kind of artillery but a direct hit. There was little concealment and troop movements were under constant observation from the dominating Shuri Hill mass on the left. The enemy was using mortars and artillery liberally and well." In the less-elegant phraseology of a line Marine, "There was quite a few nights there that you crawled inside your helmet and tucked your ass into your eyeballs and let it go at that."

Many Marines died without ever seeing a Japanese. The enemy soldiers just stayed in their holes and caves and gunned the Americans down as they came into the open. "We never saw a Japanese," recalled Captain Phil Morell, whose tank company supported the first assault on Sugar Loaf. "Never saw one. We saw people down and saw people bleeding, saw people shot, but we didn't see any Japanese. . . . We weren't attacking Japanese, we were attacking a hill. You didn't see anybody. It was a weird damn feeling. You used to say, 'Well, where are the enemy?' Just these damn slits in the hill where they were shooting at you and people dropping dead. It was just like looking at a hill. You didn't see anything. It was a weird type of thing, like you were on a Sunday morning walk and suddenly people are dropping dead. You're saying, 'What's happening?' "

Private First Class Tom McKinney was assigned to a four-man intelligence team which searched enemy dead for letters and documents and ventured into the caves to look for intelligence material. The first hole he went into led into a three-level complex housing a 47 mm antitank gun still surrounded by the rotting corpses of four or five of its crew. The entrances to the tunnels were three-and-a-half to four feet high and two or three feet wide. Inside, the passages opened up so that in places a man could stand. The passages were shored up with lumber at vital points; chambers were also well-shored up. Bits of gear, parts of packs and bags of rotted rice lay here and there. As the campaign continued, more and more of the tunnels were found packed with heaps of enemy, dragged there after they had been killed outside.

Entering one hole, McKinney could hear Japanese talking from somewhere deep in the hill. "It was disheartening," he observed. "Say you find a fresh-killed one [Japanese]. He was dry. We were wet and muddy. That told us he'd just come from inside someplace. He'd been in there, comfortable." McKinney noticed something else as well. Few of the Japanese dead wore packs. He had developed a taste for the hardball candy many of the Japanese carried in their packs as part of their rations, but he found few of the enemy dead with packs—never mind any candy. Finally he realized the enemy soldiers were leaving their packs in the caves and tunnels, emerging with only their weapons to man trenches and spider holes when the Marines attacked.

Those Marines who survived became experts in the science of violent death. "Funny thing, when you shot a Jap, he didn't bleed much," observed Private First Class George Niland. "But when they shot an American, he bled like hell. But Japs didn't seem to bleed much. They just seemed to die."

Then there were the flamethrowers, used to clean out enemy-held caves. "You pulled the triggers—there were two—just as soon as you thought your flame could reach them," noted Evan Regal, a flamethrower operator with the 22d Marines. "In it went and all hell'd break loose. You heard the shuffling and the screaming and almost always some would come running out, their hair and clothes on fire for the riflemen to pick them off. . . . Gasoline would glance off sometimes, just searing them, but napalm stuck to their skin like jelly glue even when they ran out, and we used napalm most of the time on Okinawa."

Recalled another Marine matter-of-factly, "If a body's been hit with a flamethrower, you can smell the burning flesh, of course, but that goes away in a little bit—you get used to that, unless the body's disturbed and that odor seems like it's all sealed in and that odor begins to penetrate your senses again. But if nothing's disturbed, it doesn't bother you. It's just when it's new and fresh that it's terrible."

The Japanese tried to counter flamethrowers by building caves with a sharp turn behind the entrance. Entrances were sometimes covered with blankets, shelter-halves or other heavy materials which could be wetted down. These measures, while of some limited success against brief attacks, were of little use against a prolonged assault. In those cases, unless the defenders could withdraw deep into the recesses of their cave or tunnel, they either emerged to be shot down, were asphyxiated or roasted alive. Fear of that prospect encouraged them to pay special attention to any Marine with flamethrowing gear on his back.

Once the operator squeezed the triggers, he was helpless for four to seven seconds while the flame came out. "You're also helpless when your tanks are empty—so you're as good as dead if lots of them come rushing out and the riflemen miss one," recalled Regal. "That's why the only thing you think about is killing them as quickly as possible. 'Oh God, let me get this job over fast. And let me get them *all* before I get shot.' " It was not an idle fear. Of the 16 flamethrower operators who tackled Charlie Hill on 10–11 May, Regal was one of just four survivors.

"When I was in the hospital, I remember them bringing a lot of flamethrower guys in," recalled Private John Oudstyn. "They'd all been shot in the shoulders." As the flamethrower men scuttled forward, hunched by the weight of the tanks, the terrified Japanese tried to shoot the tanks. When the bullet went slightly low, it would catch the flamethrower man in the shoulders.

General Buckner referred to the procedure of cleaning out the caves as "blowtorch and corkscrew." Corkscrew was the demolitions. Blowtorch was the flamethrower. It made good newspaper copy. Private First Class George Niland had a less-detached view than Buckner, one which would probably have been considered a bit too macabre for the folks back home: he thought the burned dead smelled horribly familiar, like fried chicken. But he had no sympathy for his enemy. "Shooting one of those people was like picking up a piece of popcorn," he said flatly. "It meant nothing emotionally."

That view was widely shared. Gunnery Sergeant Frank Habern was called up to carry ammunition to Marines on and around Sugar Loaf. During one trip across the no man's land fronting Sugar Loaf, Habern came across a Marine everyone knew as "Tex." Tex was standing on a dead Japanese soldier's uniform as he leaned over and knocked gold teeth out of the stripped corpse's mouth. He already had about half a tobacco sack full of gold teeth by Habern's estimation.

Habern was so jaded at this point he didn't think much at all about the fact that Tex was knocking out a dead man's teeth. He was curious about something else, however: Why, he asked Tex, are you standing on the dead man's uniform? It's simple, replied Tex, apparently oblivious to the fact that he was standing upright in the middle of a live battlefield. He said he planned to take the buttons and insignia for souvenirs and didn't want anyone to steal them while he was otherwise occupied. His curiosity satisfied, Habern left him to his macabre task.

At close range, the live Japanese "looked like badly wrapped brown paper parcels someone had soaked in a tub," recalled a Marine sergeant. "Jumping around on their bandy legs, they jabbered or grunted; their eyes were glazed over and fixed as though they were in a trance." He supposed he and his buddies looked much the same.

The enemy was extremely disciplined. A Marine special action report noted that Japanese troops encountered in the fighting at the Asa Kawa and around Sugar Loaf were "well-trained and disciplined army troops of exceptionally high morale and splendid physical condition." The individual Japanese fought with talent and tenacity, and he almost never quit. "It was implanted in their heads that they would not give up an inch of ground and they pretty well stuck to that," observed Corporal James Day, who would go on to become a major general. During the entire Pacific war, the only prisoner Day's platoon took was on the island of Eniwetok—and that man had been badly burned by a flamethrower. "We didn't see any on Sugar Loaf Hill," noted Day. "I don't think the battalion took any. Because they just wouldn't surrender."

Even massive U.S. artillery fire seemed to have little effect on the dug-in Japanese. "[Y]ou'd be laying there pinned down and you'd look up and there'd be a Jap poking his head up over the damned hill and firing on you," recalled Private Frederick Cross. "They never actually came over the hill. They'd get up real quick and shoot or throw a grenade or whatever and disappear."

At night the Marines would use hand grenades against infiltrating Japanese, "but if we couldn't use a hand grenade, we just let them go on through," remembered Private First Class Chris Clemenson. "To take a shot at anybody, there'd be a big ball of fire at the muzzle within three feet of where you were, so we didn't shoot at night. We'd use hand grenades or we said, 'Let battalion take care of them'—which they didn't appreciate, I guess. But it was a little safer that way."

Hunkered down in a foxhole near the bank of the Asato Gawa across from Naha, Private First Class Raymond Huestis was suddenly set upon by a Japanese soldier. The Japanese bayonetted Huestis in the right shoulder, right arm and neck. As his assailant drew back for another thrust, Huestis kicked him in the stomach, then leaped on him, clamped the Japanese's neck in the crook of his left arm and squeezed until the man soldier finally stopped kicking and died. Huestis survived his multiple bayonet wounds.

"Zahler and I were together and sitting so each of us was leaning against the opposite side of the hole with our backs—kind of feet to feet," recalled Private First Class Charles Miller. "A Jap came crawling over the edge and I got him with my knife and it was just like jabbing a pillow. I suppose the Jap hadn't gotten the word that the hill was in our hands."

Luck was a matter of fractions. A Marine in Private Donald Honis's machine-gun unit hit the ground as a Japanese shell screamed in. His buddies didn't. The shell exploded, peppering the standing men in the legs. The Marine lying on the ground was hit in the head and killed.

"I saw a miracle," remembered Private First Class Joseph Cormier. "You probably wouldn't believe this. Right below me was the 81 mm [mortars]. I'd say we were not quite to the bottom [of Sugar Loaf] with the 60s and we were lobbing them over on the other side. Trying to get where they were. And I just happened to look back, down below. And an artillery shell hit an 81 mm emplacement. And I saw—there was only one guy in there at the time . . . and that thing hit that hole and that man went up at least 50 feet. He came down, so help me God, this is the truth, he got up, looked around and laughed. This guy ain't lucky—to me, it's a miracle. He probably didn't believe it either. Probably never will."

Moments of extreme fright were relieved at times by dark humor. Newly appointed squad leader Charles Miller was assigned to take a small hill. He called his squad together and told them he planned to go right over the top to avoid the mortar fire. "You got that?" he asked. They indicated that they did. Miller turned to Private First Class Bill Cunningham and said, "Go ahead, Bill!" Cunningham looked at him and replied, "Miller, you fucking SOB, you're the squad leader you go first!"

Recalled Miller, "Seeing the look on Bill's face, I couldn't help but laugh. Soon the whole squad was laughing." They went over the top of the hill, lost a couple of men hit and had to come back. They could hear the Japanese talking on the other slope. All of a sudden a Japanese came over the top of the hill, yelling "banzai!" He had a helmet with a star on it and carried a sword in one hand and a grenade in the other. The Japanese struck the grenade on his helmet, but it was apparently defective, for instead of just lighting the fuse, it exploded and blew his head off. The Marines thought that was hilarious. "We started laughing," recalled Miller, "and said, 'Made in Japan! Made in Japan!' "

The fighting sent a flood of casualties to the rear. Such was the ferocity of the combat, that so-called "happy" wounds were frequently ignored as Marines stayed on the line to remain with their buddies. Corpsman Ralph Miller remembered a Marine named Jerry Shell who had been wounded three different times. "I got him off the line the third time and within an hour he snuck back up to the lines," recalled Miller.

"You always pick up some fragments along the line," noted Lieutenant John Fitzgerald. "Corpsmen throw some sulfa on it, this and that. Most of us never went back to battalion. Guys were getting so badly shot up, you felt terrible if you went back for a few superficial shrapnel cuts on your legs and that . . . when a guy just lost his arms or something. [Most men stayed] unless the company commander was adamant you had to go back."

Battalion surgeon Charles Veatch had joined the division on Guadalcanal where his predecessor packed his bags and was ready to leave in about ten minutes flat. "I want to tell you one thing, Doc," he said before leaving. "Don't crawl *over* a coconut log, crawl around the end."

Veatch didn't see any coconut logs on Okinawa. He carried his medical gear in a gas mask case—the issue medical case with the red cross made too tempting a target for Japanese snipers. He also packed a tommy gun, a .45 automatic and a K-bar combat knife. The battalion had about 40 corpsmen. Half were with the units—one to each platoon and two to each company headquarters—the rest were with battalion headquarters. Knowing the Japanese would show them no mercy, the corpsmen carried carbines—and they used them when they had to, the Geneva Convention notwithstanding.

Veatch set up his aid station in a foxhole behind the lines and checked casualties as they filtered back from the fighting. "My main job was to check the vital signs of patients that came through the aid station," he recalled. "The corpsmen in the trenches did such a good job that I rarely had to replace a bandage. Check his blood pressure was all right, he was breathing all right, and out he would go. Occasionally you'd have to cut a leg off or something like that."

Severely wounded by shrapnel in the side, Sergeant William Cromling vaguely recalled being carried in a poncho and then being loaded on the top rack of a jeep for the trip to the aid station. "I drifted between consciousness and unconsciousness on the way back to the aid station," he recalled, "but I do remember waking up at one point and hearing the wounded guy below me saying, 'Is that bastard above me still living?'

" 'Yeah, why?' replied the jeep driver.

" 'Because he's bleeding all over me,' said the other Marine."

Cromling was taken to an aid station in a cave, where it was determined his wounds were beyond their capabilities. Sometime later, he woke up in an army hospital tent, a naked light bulb hanging above him. Stripped naked, he was taken in to surgery. As he lay there, he heard a nurse say to the doctor, "Do you want me to catharize him?" Cromling thought she said *castrate*. "What did you say?" he interjected. The nurse replied, "Don't worry, Marine. We aren't going to take anything away from you." And at that point, they put Cromling under. He survived, but spent months in a series of hospitals from Guam to California before he recovered.

Technical Sergeant Herman Kogan, a Marine combat correspondent, chronicled the scene at the aid station of the 1st Battalion, 22d Marines, set up in the lee of some huge boulders about 1,000 yards behind the front lines.

"Down the road trundled a hospital jeep, dusty, dilapidated, and loaded with cargo," he wrote. Three men got out without help, but they shook with a palsy. Others came out feet first, on stretchers. One was a corpsman. 'Mortar shell exploded right near me and four other guys,' he told [the battalion surgeon, Lieutenant D. M. Thysell]. 'Damn it, I'm the only guy that got hurt.'

"The lieutenant, a corncob pipe gripped in his teeth, took one swift look. 'Take him to B Medical and get him there fast.' When the corpsman was gone, he said, 'They'll have to take off that leg.'

"The left side of one man's face, a lieutenant in a tank crew, was an ugly mass of blood and bits of flesh. Even before the first bottle of plasma had been administered, he died. A man in his crew, only slightly wounded in the leg, said in a dull voice, 'We were going along there, and some little Japs run out from behind a building with satchel charges—it blew us up bad.' His eyes kept staring fixedly ahead of him as he talked.

"Other jeeps brought in the wounded and the dead. Jack Riordan, of Columbus, Ohio, red-haired corpsman, his hand streaked with dried blood, bustled from one stretcher to another. . . . Then he went to another man. The Marine looked waxen. Flies swarmed around his blood-caked dungaree trouser leg. A bandage hastily applied at the front had slipped from his chest. A jagged hole showed above the heart. 'Hey, fellow,' said Red, 'we'll fix you up in no time.' Other corpsmen gave the Marine plasma and Red washed the chest wound.

"The Marine whispered something. Red bent down to listen. He jumped up. 'Nah, nah, kid, they didn't get your spine. What the hell gave you that idea?' "

Many, many others were less fortunate. III Corps Evacuation Hospital No. 2 listed each man who arrived at the facility alive, but who subsequently died of wounds: Gunshot wounds (GSW) and shell fragment wounds (SFW) tore young men's bodies beyond repair. The hospital listed the primary cause of death first—bullet or shell fragment—followed by the "contributory" cause:

—GSW lung—pulmonary edema, shock, transection of spinal cord.

—GSW head (penetrate)—shock, pulmonary edema.

—SFW head (penetrate)—shock, pulmonary edema.

—GSW abdomen—general peritonitis, cardiac failure.

—GSW abdomen—hemoperitoneum, lower wound, acute toxic nephritis.

—GSW neck—contusion of cervical cord (brain stem).

—SFW brain—brain abscess, meningitis.

—SFW brain—subarachnoid hemorrhage.

—GSW chest—generalized emphysema (mediastina), subcutaneous, scrotal frac-
ture, compound ribs, lacerated lung, and so forth.

Due to quick evacuation, the mortality rate among the wounded on
Okinawa was under 3 percent. III Corps Evacuation Hospital No. 3 treated
5,494 Marines. Of those, only 28 died. Many men were saved by whole
blood, donated in the United States, refrigerated and flown out to Guam and
Okinawa. Before the campaign was over, Tenth Army would use 15,000
gallons of whole blood.

About half the seriously wounded were evacuated to Guam aboard
hospital ships complete with nurses, comfortable beds and plenty of chow.
Thousands of others were flown out aboard four-engine C-54 transport
planes which could carry as many as 45 patients at a time. Less seriously
hurt men were treated on Okinawa and eventually returned to their units.
This became more and more common as the fighting continued—and the
definition of a "minor wound" became broader and broader. At least one
Marine recalled being sent back with a half-healed bullet wound in his
shoulder.

Private First Class Irv Gehret was wounded on 17 May, hit in the back
by fragments from a mortar shell. The corpsman dug the pieces out with a
steel probe. As far as Gehret was concerned, the cure hurt worse than the
injury. "I'd say, 'That's enough, that's enough.' He'd say, 'You've got to get
this out, it's getting infected. You've got to get this straightened out now. If
not, I've got to ship you back.' Well, I didn't want to go back. Because my
friends were there. I always thought—I don't know, maybe I was crazy, a
young kid, I was only 18—I felt that if you're gonna die, you're gonna die
with your friends."

Only five of Gehret's platoon made it through the whole campaign. "And
of those five, only two weren't wounded somehow," he observed. "Out of
52 men in the machine-gun platoon."

Back behind the lines with the handful of survivors from G Company,
22d Marines, First Sergeant Peter C. Maresh was approached by his new
company commander, First Lieutenant Hugh Crane. Maresh had always
thought of Crane, another of the division's Notre Dame alumni, as a "happy
go lucky type . . . one of these guys who tends to be in hot water all the
time." But Crane had undergone a transformation upon taking over the
company after its beating at Sugar Loaf, showing a responsibility and
maturity, Maresh had never noticed before. Now Crane approached Maresh

and tied a casualty tag on him. "What's this?" asked Maresh, a veteran of the Marshall Islands campaign.

"You're going back," said Crane, one of the few surviving G Company officers. "You've had enough."

"What about you?" asked Maresh.

"Well," replied Crane, "someone should stay with the company that knows what's going on."

Maresh tore off the tag. "Well, if you stay, I stay, too." And he did.

They weren't all heroes. Lieutenant Gene Folks, acting as forward observer for the 29th Marines, recalled a lieutenant who was a former football player, but had a reputation for not being particularly useful. As the outfit moved south, they were shelled fairly persistently by enemy artillery. "These shells weren't threatening, but they were close and we spent the night on the ground," recalled Folks. The next day, as they were approaching Sugar Loaf, the not-very-useful lieutenant came up to Folks and said, "Yo, Lieutenant, I've got an awful stomach ache. I feel just awful. I got diarrhea and a stomach ache and I've got to go back to sick bay." The man left, and Folks never set eyes on him again.

As more and more experienced men were lost to death or wounds, the quality of the replacements declined. "They brought up everybody, even cooks and bakers and military police (MPs) up on the line to fill in the vacant places," recalled Charles Pugh. Pugh was assigned a 48-year-old MP, a man much too old for combat, who promptly fell asleep on watch. Livid, Pugh snatched up his .45 and threatened to shoot him dead for his negligence. "Forty-eight years old, he sat there and cried like a baby," remembered Pugh.

Also vulnerable were the youngsters who arrived in the replacement drafts, some still sporting signs of their boot camp haircuts. "Sometimes they had been out of boot camp ten days," noted Private First Class Chris Clemenson. "They were either 17-year-olds who really couldn't hack it mentally, or they were 30-year-olds who couldn't do it physically."

Bringing up replacements for Captain Stebbins's shot-up company, Sergeant Irving Ortel got caught by darkness and had the rookies dig in, two to a hole, in a circle. He told them one man in each hole was to remain awake at all times. Ortel dug in alone in the center of the circle and went to sleep. When he woke up in the morning, every man was fast asleep. "Did I ever give them hell!" he recalled.

"Another time as I was bringing a bunch forward to the company, shelling from the Japs started," he said. "We all hit the deck. When it was over I found one kid had been hit in the thigh and bled to death. The guys near him had been too scared to realize and hadn't helped him at all. They got another lecture about that. But they were all just green kids and probably just as scared as I was when the shells started to explode around us."

Paul Brennan, a forward observer for the 15th Marines—the division's artillery regiment—recalled five or six replacements who came up the second or third day he was up at Sugar Loaf. They were strutting around and talking tough. "Where's them goddamned Japs?" All of a sudden the Japanese threw in an artillery barrage and the old hands went to ground. When they looked up again, the kids were all dead. "They looked like baby dolls laying there where one of those big shells hit 'em," said Brennan. "You know like a baby doll looks? The legs were thrown back around their necks, arms askew and everything. Just awful."

Many new officers were also received to replace those killed or wounded in the early assaults. Some of the second lieutenants fit right in, recalled Lieutenant John Fitzgerald. "But it got so bad for us in Easy Company, if we had a sergeant running the platoon and doing the job, we wouldn't put the lieutenant in charge until the sergeant or corporal said he was ready," noted Fitzgerald. "That's how nervous we became. We had a couple of them walk right up on the skyline and get shot right away."

Fitzgerald had one new lieutenant who had attended the University of Maryland. The newcomer discovered Fitzgerald had gone to George Washington University and started talking his ear off about old school days. "I finally had to tell him, it's a long way from Washington, kid. You're on Okinawa. You should be asking *me* questions," observed Fitzgerald. The lieutenant was killed the next day when he ignorantly showed himself on the skyline.

Private First Class Joseph Cormier remembered another replacement, a 90–day wonder, who arrived after their original lieutenant was hit. "He looked like he just got out of diapers," recalled Manson scornfully. The newcomer started to tell the veterans their business. Suddenly, a big California Marine spoke up. "You ain't been here long enough," he growled. "You keep your eyes open, your ears open and your mouth shut." Cormier recalled, "That poor lieutenant, he didn't know what to say."

For others, Okinawa was over. But new battles were just beginning. Hit on the morning of 15 May, Ray Schlinder was operated on that night in an army hospital, then he lay there three or four days with no one paying much attention to him. Other patients were being tended to by doctors, but "I'm not talking to anybody," he recalled. Schlinder put up a fuss and was transferred to a navy hospital and from there by plane to Guam.

"The night I got to Guam I thought I'd died and gone to heaven," he said. "They had electric lights and they gave me fresh cow milk and sunny-side eggs and fresh orange juice and after about 30 minutes, I gave it all back to them. I wasn't used to that sort of thing."

Schlinder started suffering severe stomach pains. The nurse thought he might have appendicitis. The doctor agreed. So they wheeled the 19–year-old Marine into the operating room, gave him a spinal and opened him up. "Hey, Ray, I screwed up," the doctor told a wide-awake Schlinder. "It's not your appendix at all, it's just blood clots in your stomach from the wound. But as long as I'm there, should I take it out?"

"You might as well," said Schlinder. So he did.

"From Guam they shipped me to Pearl Harbor," recalled Schlinder. "I got down to about 132 pounds—and I weighed about 180 normally. Of course I couldn't eat for three months, my stomach was all screwed up. Then the right lung collapsed . . . I was in San Francisco, then to a navy hospital in Barrett, Idaho. The worst part of that whole ordeal, about every second or third day they'd have to find that pocket in my right lung and tap it . . . all that fluid in there. They'd take an x-ray every day and I'd have to lean over a chair and they'd find that pocket and they'd stick that big needle all the way into my lung. I'm ready to shoot this guy."

Nine and a half months after coming down off Sugar Loaf Hill, Schlinder was discharged, still carrying a chunk of metal in his liver.

Chapter 8

The Bitterest Day

Seizure of Half Moon Hill to the east of Sugar Loaf was the key to the 6th Division attack plan for 16 May, a Wednesday. By now the division was beginning to grasp the true nature of the enemy defense, built around the three hills. It was felt that no grip on Sugar Loaf could be assured unless flanking fires from the area of Half Moon were neutralized.

The mission of seizing the crescent-shaped hill was given to the 29th Marines. Once they had cleared the high ground on the left flank, the 3d Battalion, 22d Marines would advance and capture Sugar Loaf. The entire action would occur on a front of only about 1,000 yards.

The 29th Regiment was under the command of Colonel William J. Whaling, a decorated World War I veteran who had taken over the regiment on northern Okinawa when its previous commander failed to live up to General Shepherd's expectations. Fifty years old, the ruggedly handsome Minnesotan had won a battlefield commission in the last war, commanded a battalion of the 5th Marines at Guadalcanal and won the Legion of Merit as commander of the 1st Marines at Cape Gloucester. He was known throughout the Corps as a crack marksman. He was also a keen woodsman.

On 15 May, Whaling's Marines had fought all day for the approaches to Half Moon, with only limited success. Now they would try again. Still up on Sugar Loaf, Jim Day and Dale Bertoli had a bird's-eye view of developments. The Japanese made several attempts to overrun their shell hole during the night, but the two Marines were able to pick them off by the light of the flares. Morning dawned clear and rainless.

"The next day we could look to our rear and we could see the whole battle shaping up," observed Day. "There was no one that could move to our rear that we didn't see. And we could see people from our battalion command post (CP) moving over to the different company areas; we could see the replacements coming up for the company. We could even see companies coming over to other areas to give the 2d Battalion, 22d Marines, a hustle on taking that hill . . . We were up high enough and we could see almost a panorama of the whole battle in that area."

As usual, one of the keys to the American assault would be the tank and infantry team. After the war, Colonel Yahara cited the American superiority in tanks "as the single factor most important in deciding the battle of Okinawa." Certainly few would dispute that the tanks provided a crucial element at Sugar Loaf. The infantry liked the support of the Sherman's 75 mm gun in taking out caves and dug-in Japanese automatic weapons, but considered the tanks a mixed blessing overall. "We would go up there," recalled Captain Phil Morell, commanding officer (CO) of A Company, 6th Tank Battalion, "and the infantry would say, 'Ah, you tanks draw fire.' And I'd say, 'No shit. You bet your sweet ass we do.' "

The heavy enemy fire was intended to break up the coordination between infantry and tanks. Japanese combat instructions noted, "if we do not attack the infantry soldiers accompanying the tanks, they will calmly guide the tanks into position, burn out our positions with flame-throwers, and then kill the remaining men. So will our fighting become passive—the root of our defeat. It is therefore necessary when tanks approach, to attack the infantry soldiers accompanying them with our full fire-power. Next, the tanks must be attacked by various methods. Our units have repulsed tank attacks on several occasions by annihilation of the infantry soldiers."

Inside the tanks "it was hotter than hell" for the five-man crew, remarked Morell. The crew would pass around an empty 75 mm shell to urinate in. "You try to get a shell that was fired 20 minutes ago so you don't burn your winkler off," explained Morell. "And if you've got to take a crap, you take a crap in that. What else is there? Sometimes we'd be in the tanks from 5:30 in the morning until 6 or 7 at night. If you ran out of ammunition, guys would say, *God, I can go back and take a leak!*"

Realizing they were outgunned by the tanks, the Japanese would wait with their antitank weapons in caves on hills the Marines had overrun or bypassed and then shoot the Shermans in the more lightly armored rear. "It would penetrate with a big hole on the outside and a small hole on the inside," recalled Morell. "It would flake off our armor and pieces of your own tank would become shrapnel and bounce around inside the turret and injure people." To counter the enemy guns, the tankers took to assigning one tank to follow behind, its turret turned backwards to watch for bushwackers.

"They had these satchel charges," observed Morell, "they would have like a suitcase tied to your body or on your chest and they'd run up to your tank and blow themselves up. These were not effective because they were not like a shaped charge. They'd blow outward." Mines were different. Most of the tanks lost around Sugar Loaf were knocked out by mines, though the very accurate Japanese artillery fire also took a toll of the Shermans.

The attack did not begin well. Support planes were a half an hour late, delaying the assault. "Heavy enemy fire swept the entire front as the assault companies attempted to jump off at 0830," noted a subsequent Marine Corps study of the action. Several tanks lost their way during the approach.

Day watched the attack develop. "Now the killing zone on Sugar Loaf wasn't really to our front and it wasn't actually on top of Sugar Loaf Hill," he explained later. "It was to our rear. It was about a 300 x 300 area back there —300 yards by 300 yards—that the Marines had to cross in order to reach Sugar Loaf Hill. And that's where the majority of them were killed or wounded."

A platoon from B Company, 1/29, backed by tanks, moved forward to clear the reverse slope of Charlie Ridge. The B Company Marines had no sooner moved out of defilade than they were hit by a storm of small arms, artillery, antitank, and mortar fire, much of it from the Shuri Heights only 800 yards to the east. It was the same for C Company, trying to move over the crest of the ridge. Heavy enemy fire from the reverse slope forced their attack to a standstill.

The only gain in the battalion sector was made by part of B Company, which advanced 300 yards along the division boundary with the 1st Marine Division until it came abreast of Company C. There it too was stopped by what Marine historians described as "Vicious frontal and flanking fire." The Marines tried to follow tanks forward, but the enemy fire was coming from so many different directions, the tanks provided no shield.

At 1400 the battalion CO, Lieutenant Colonel Jean Moreau was manning a forward observation post when a shell burst in front of him. First Lieutenant George Thompson, 50 yards away from the blast, assumed it was a mortar round since no one heard it coming. The blast shattered Moreau's leg—almost tore it off. "He was unconscious when evacuated, or I know that, leg on or off, he'd have raised hell about being taken away," observed Thompson. Moreau subsequently lost the leg. Major Robert P. Neuffer took command of the battalion.

Also injured during the day was General Shepherd. Examining the front, as was his habit, he was caught in an enemy mortar barrage and jumped in a shell hole for cover. An aide jumped directly on top of him and fractured the general's arm. Shepherd had the injury taken care of and continued his duties with his arm in a sling.

The 3d Battalion of the 29th Marines, commanded by Lieutenant Colonel Erma A. Wright, spent most of the morning moving into favorable positions for an attack on Half Moon, hampered by fire from Japanese heavy mortars and artillery.

At about 1400, tanks from Companies A and B of the 6th Tank Battalion churned through the railroad cut northeast of Sugar Loaf and nosed into the open valley leading up to Half Moon. Gerald Bunting's tank passed a Sherman that had bogged down in a shell hole and been abandoned during the 12 May attack. Two dead crew members still sprawled on the embankment next to the derelict. The B Company tanks fired into the reverse slope of the ridge in front of 1/29. A Company tanks gave supporting fire to the riflemen of Companies G and I rushing across the open ground to the northern slope of Half Moon. Japanese reaction was fierce. One Sherman took four 47 mm hits; the tank was disabled, but miraculously none of the crew was killed. Two other tanks were knocked out by mines. Mortar and artillery fire punished the tanks and infantry.

I Company rifleman Private Ken Long dodged from crater to crater, seeing, but not stopping for the many dead and wounded. The air seemed almost too heavy to breath, thick with the stink of rotting flesh, gun powder and damp, musty soil. "To our right, about 30 yards, were the bodies of about seven Marines that must have been caught in the fire of a nambu, as they were laying in a column spaced about five or six yards apart as though they had all decided to take a short nap alongside the narrow gauge railroad that crossed that area," he recalled. Fear, lack of sleep and the inability to eat for the past few days left him feeling weak and debilitated and he seemed to be having oddly inappropriate thoughts, two of which he later remembered: (1) He had never seen any birds on Okinawa and (2) Who was going to clean up this mess when the battle finally ended?

Private First Class Ed Soja, a 20-year-old assistant Browning Automatic Rifle man, was running across the open ground when he saw machine gun fire ripping toward him in the dirt to his left. Soja threw himself into a shallow hole, which had apparently been made by a phosphorus bomb since bits of the white stuff still lay around. The bullets stitched past him and hit the BAR man in the face. Soja snatched up the man's BAR and kept running.

Coming down off Charlie Hill and moving over the railroad track, Private Ross Wilkerson's G Company fire team made it onto the north slope of Half Moon. Wilkerson shucked off his pack, pulled out his entrenching tool and hit the ground a couple of licks with the blade when the Japanese opened up "with a nambus and rifles and everything else." The Japanese had waited patiently until the Marines were caught without cover on the exposed hillside.

Wilkerson pressed himself against the slope of the hill. Just ahead of him was a Marine named John Ryan. Wilkerson's head was laying by Ryan's feet. Their BAR man was just below them, with his head laying by Wilkerson's feet. In an instant Ryan was wounded by a machine-gun burst across both legs above the knees.

Wilkerson saw a shell hole just down the slope. There were two Marines in it: one was the 3d Platoon lieutenant, the only officer Wilkerson's outfit had left as far as he knew. Also crammed into the hole was Platoon Sergeant Mendel "Big John" Bons, who stood six foot five inches tall—when he was standing, which he was not doing now. Wilkerson rolled Ryan down into the shell hole and Big John picked up the wounded man, hoisted him onto his shoulders and lumbered down off the hill. "I guess he ran 100 yards or further," guessed Wilkerson.

Wilkerson crawled back above the BAR man. Bullets were striking all around. "And I'm looking back at him—course we were muddy as hogs, you know—but today it was pretty clear. The sun was shining. So we had dried off . . . but we were still muddy and dusty. And while I'm looking back I could see the dust fly from his shoulder." The Marine flinched.

"Oh, they got you, didn't they?" said Wilkerson.

"Yep," said the other man.

"You want me to patch you up?"

"Yeah."

So Wilkerson crawled back and got his first aid packet out and started to bandage the wound. Bullets were still kicking up dirt around them. Nonchalant up to now, the BAR man suddenly blurted, "The hell with this." He grabbed his arm and told Wilkerson, "I'm getting out of here and if I get hit again, you come after me."

"Okay," replied Wilkerson. "Get going." The Marine scrambled away and managed to get down off the hill without being killed.

Meanwhile, on the right of the division's attack zone, the 1st Battalion, 22d Marines ran into a hail of automatic weapons fire from the outskirts of

Takamotoji village when it tried to go into position to support the attack of the 3d Battalion. The Takamotoji area, just west of the Horseshoe, had been quiet until now; the new resistance by determined enemy defenders indicated the Japanese had moved reinforcements in to block any effort to flank Sugar Loaf from the direction of Naha. Due to the stiff resistance from Takamotoji and fire from Sugar Loaf and the Horseshoe, the 1st Battalion was unable to occupy the high ground it had been assigned.

Commanding the 3d Battalion, Lieutenant Colonel Malcolm O. Donohoo had planned to have I Company make the battalion's main push on Sugar Loaf from the east as soon as 3/29's attack progressed far enough to protect his flank. Donohoo, a rather stout, mustachioed man, was a friendly, outgoing type with an easy-going personality. "He never got flustered with anything," recalled Lieutenant Art Cofer, executive of I Company. Cofer, who had been wounded on Guam and briefly commanded I Company on northern Okinawa, considered Donohoo one of the best battalion commanders he ever served with. "He tried in every instance to give us every bit of support that he could get to us," recalled Cofer.

On 15 May, 3/22 had seized some 1,500 yards of the Asato's northern bank fronting Naha. Donohoo's plan now was for I Company to circle and assault Sugar Loaf from the left while L Company advanced its lines to the next high ground on the outskirts of the Horseshoe. L Company would then cover the assault with fire on the western and southern slopes of the hill. 1/22 would take the high ground further west where it would support L Company by fire.

Like most of the other companies in the regiment, I Company was well below strength. Of the 240 or so Marines they had started with a week before, the company was now down to 80 or 100 men. These survivors had been consolidated into two rifle platoons, rather than the company's normal three platoons. The company was commanded by Captain John Marston, Jr., son of a Marine Corps general. A slender man with a black brush cut, he was working on a handlebar moustache and seemed to be forever twisting the ends. He was respected and well liked by the I Company officers and men, known as a man who was willing to take risks himself, not one to sit back and order others into harm's way.

"It's funny because you don't really know what's going on over the next hill, really," recalled Cofer. "So we had no idea. We were told we were going to pull out of the lines down by Naha and swing over to the left towards Sugar Loaf Hill, but we didn't even know where we were at that point. We were getting ready to make the assault. Captain Marston had gotten the word that we were to attack the hill. Well, at that point, we were getting a lot of artillery fire. In fact, our mortars, 60 mm mortar section, took a round right in the middle of them and I think maybe two or three people got through that. So it practically wiped that unit right out. And then we ran into some K Company people and they were down to 20 or 30 people because they had been up on Sugar Loaf the night before and got chased off. . . . We really didn't know what we were getting into. We were just told to attack that hill up there and that was it."

Though 3/29 was not fully in possession of the high ground on the left, the I Company Marines moved out with tanks in support at 1500. The company reached the base of Sugar Loaf without meeting serious resistance. That changed when the Marines began scrambling up the slope. Enemy machine guns opened up and mortar shells began to whisper in.

Marston tried to work with the tank company, hoping to get the Shermans around to put fire down on the enemy-held reverse slope. The tanks promptly ran into a mine field. One was knocked out and the flanking effort failed. Despite that, and the heavy fire from the Japanese defenders, the I Company assault platoons fought to the top of the hill by 1710 and began to dig in.

Up toward the crest, First Sergeant Robert Stevens, a former Indiana State cross-country champion and University of Alabama track star, had just brought some ammunition up to the Marines digging in. He was about to take shelter in a foxhole when a volley of knee mortar shells slammed in behind him. Someone shouted, "Corpsman hurt! Corpsman hurt!" He looked around just as another shell exploded, riddling his legs. He later realized he had been lucky to have been standing when the shell exploded. "If I'd been down, I'd probably have gotten it in my body instead of my legs," he remarked. Stevens wanted to walk out. "Nope, you get down here," said a stretcher bearer, pointing to a litter. It was the right call—as it turned out, a good-sized piece of bone had been blown out of the front section of his right leg, putting an end to any thoughts he might have had about picking up his track career after the war.

Stevens was carried off the hill and back to a field hospital. He was later transferred to a hospital ship bound for Saipan. "I didn't mind that," he recalled drily. "I had a fried egg sandwich and a milk shake."

L Company never managed to get into position to support the attack on Sugar Loaf. Moving out shortly after 1500, the company was pinned down almost immediately by fire from three sides. "L Company of our battalion was supposed to be on our right and a unit of the 29th Marines was supposed to be on Half Moon Hill and supporting us by fire," noted Cofer. "But they were taking so much incoming fire themselves it really was quite ineffective."

With 1/22 and L Company unable to get into a position to deliver supporting fire on the right and with 3/29 in trouble on Half Moon on the left, I Company's position on Sugar Loaf was untenable. Noted the Marine Corps monograph, "Excessive casualties inflicted by enemy gunners on both flanks and the determined defenders of Sugar Loaf itself forced the company back down the hill."

Corporal Benton Graves, section leader of the I Company machin-gun platoon, set up a light machine gun in an exposed position to help cover the displacement. According to his subsequent citation for the Silver Star, "Although he was under constant heavy fire, he knocked out two enemy machine guns and killed several Jap riflemen. His action played a big part in the successful withdrawal of his company with a minimum of casualties."

Division and corps artillery put down harassing and interdictory fire to dissuade the Japanese from attacking the I Company survivors as they withdrew. The survivors numbered perhaps 40 to 50 people, recalled Cofer. They took up positions on a small rise dubbed Mole Hill "because that's the way we were living there," recalled a Marine. I Company had made its first and last assault on Sugar Loaf Hill.

As 3/22 was organizing its night defenses, Japanese artillery pounded the lines for over half an hour, injuring still more men. Among the casualties was "Blizzard 6," Lieutenant Colonel Donohoo. Wounded in the legs when shells fell directly on his command post, he had to be evacuated. An intelligence scout logged the incident among the events of the day:

1910 Shells falling region of CP

1918 Shells now falling directly in CP

1934 Blizzard 6 wounded

1940 Shells stopped falling

1945 Blizzard 6 removed to CP

The battalion executive, Major George B. Kantner, took command. By day's end, the battalion had lost 8 killed, 67 wounded and 1 missing. The Marines claimed 76 enemy dead.

Corporal James Day had felt sure the latest push would finally secure Sugar Loaf. Artillery had pounded the hill all morning. "It looked like every artillery piece we had in the division was zeroed in on the hill," he noted.

His optimism faded as the attacks broke up. "We could see from our position the casualties being carried back, the casualties being inflicted, and it was a horrendous day," he recalled. "The tanks were coming up and trying

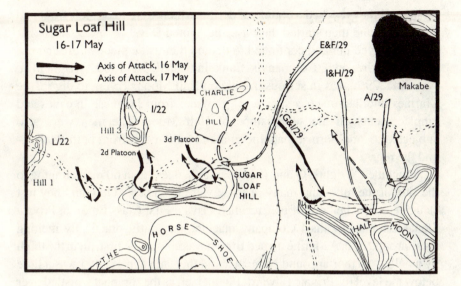

to extract the casualties, trying to give cover and trying to get them out. The tanks, more tanks, were being knocked out. Additional amtracs were knocked out that day."

The tactical dilemma was the same as before. Secure on their reverse slope, the Japanese could not be dislodged by mortar or artillery fire. Tanks could not slip around the hill without being shot up by well-placed antitank guns or knocked out by mines. Caught in interlocking fire from Half Moon, the Horseshoe and Shuri to the left rear, the Marine riflemen could not continue. "There was just no place to hide," said Day of the assault troops. "There was no foliage on Sugar Loaf Hill. The only place they could get were into holes."

Three men wandered over to Day's shell hole during the fighting. All three were wounded, two fairly seriously. The third was losing so much blood he was unable to help the other two to the rear. Dale Bertoli took the two worst cases back to the knocked-out amtrac where they had some protection and could be evacuated by stretcher bearers. The third Marine, who had waited behind with Day, was killed by small-arms fire as he tried to reach the safety of the amtrac. The small-arms fire, noted Day, came from the left rear.

By now the squally weather had lifted and Day and Bertoli could see well past the Horseshoe to the Asato River from their perch on the hill. What they saw was not calculated to raise their spirits: Japanese reinforcements were plainly visible as they moved toward the battle line. "We could bring fire on them from about 500 to 600 yards away and we could keep fire on them until they reached a couple of defiles which were to our left front and right front, and then started their assault," noted Day.

They stayed put and continued to defend their little piece of ground.

As the fire on I Company's flank indicated, by 1500, Wright's 3d Battalion, 29th, was in serious trouble on Half Moon. Trying to dig in, the Marines huddled under a shower of grenades from Japanese in caves and emplacements on the south slope of Half Moon. The men were also subjected to small-arms, machine-gun and mortar fire from both flanks—and the rear.

Altogether, Wright's G and I Companies had less than 60 men clinging to the side of the hill—and many of those were wounded. "Oh man, they just slaughtered the hell out of us," recalled Private First Class Ed Soja. Private Donald Honis saw his I Company machine-gun outfit practically melting away around him. A Marine named Brown was among the first, hit in the thigh by a bullet. "A mortar round came in about then and apparently I was a little below the level of [Private Edward] Finkbeiner, as the shrapnel whistled over me and peppered Finkbeiner in the rear end and back. The entire area was one big melee. [Corporal Norman] McCool got hit in the neck and it was a miracle he wasn't killed as I felt if the bullet had been 1 mm in either direction he would have been killed or at least it would have severed his spinal column. [Another man] was hit in the chest and killed. Pfc [George] Breaux was at one of the guns and a Nip bullet hit his machine-gun belt, exploding a round of ammo and his face was hit with the brass from the exploding casing—none went into his eyes. At this point we are literally getting blasted off of the hill with artillery and mortars and guys are dropping all over the place as we're receiving fire from three sides."

Directing the assault from Charlie Hill, Lieutenant Colonel Wright called for smoke in an effort to help the exposed Marines. It made little difference. Just before dark Wright bowed to the inevitable and authorized a withdrawal.

Scrambling down the hill with the other survivors, Private Ross Wilkerson found himself in a little field. The Marines stayed low as Japanese machine-gun fire clipped the tops of the tall grass. Another Marine came running, but tumbled as a bullet hit him in the leg between the ankle and the knee. "Oh, don't leave me!" the man yelled. "Don't leave me! Don't leave me!"

Wilkerson glanced at the knot of Marines with him. "You, you and you, let's go," he said, tagging three of them. They trotted over to the wounded Marine, put together a makeshift stretcher with two rifles and a poncho and started to lug him, feet first, out to the relative safety of the railroad track. Wilkerson took the left corner and Private First Class Francis West was carrying the right corner down by the wounded man's feet "and these bullets are going—I don't see how they're not hitting us," recalled Wilkerson. All of a sudden one of the slugs spanged into West's helmet. West dropped the stretcher, grabbed his head and just started running. Wilkerson scooped up the end of the stretcher as best he could and the three carriers stumbled down the railroad track to get out of the fire zone.

Further up the track, they found West sitting up against the embankment. He had his helmet off and was rubbing his hands. He had thought the liquid running down his face was blood from a bullet in the head, but now he couldn't find any blood. Wilkerson put the wounded man down and saw it wasn't blood on West's face . . . it was sweat. "West, you're not hit," he reassured him. "That's not blood."

West pulled his helmet liner out of the steel shell and a Japanese bullet fell out. "It had gone right around his helmet, made the nicest little grove around it you've ever seen," observed Wilkerson. Greatly relieved, West reached down and grabbed the slug. "That's my souvenir out of this war," he announced.

Lying on the ground, the wounded Marine piped up. "Fellas," he said, "thank you for saving me. Would you do me another favor?"

"Sure," said Wilkerson. "What?"

"Straighten my leg out."

Wilkerson looked down and saw that the leg was lying at an unnatural angle and the bone was protruding. The Marines straightened the leg, sprinkled the wound with sulfa powder and splinted it up with a bayonet scabbard.

Enemy fire was still falling on Charlie Hill as Wilkerson and the other survivors tried to work their way back along the railroad track. There was a knocked-out tank nearby and a lieutenant was using it for cover as he directed traffic. The lieutenant would shout at the Marines hauling the wounded out along the railroad track to come up a few at a time so they wouldn't bunch up around the tank. Pretty soon it was Wilkerson's turn. His little band lugged the wounded man up behind the tank and rested for a couple of minutes.

"You boys about ready to go?" asked the lieutenant. The Marines said they were. The lieutenant had his helmet in his hand and was down on one knee as he looked around the tank. As he looked around the corner, a bullet creased him along the top of his head—an inch lower he would have been killed outright. This lieutenant was tough as well as lucky. He lurched back, reached up to his head and found some blood. "Boys," he addressed the waiting Marines, "let that be a lesson to you. Don't *never* look around without your helmet on."

Wilkerson and the others got the wounded man out to the other side of Charlie Hill where an amtrac took him away. The company had been badly hurt. By one estimate there were less than two dozen men left of the 240 who had landed in April. Some of them had strayed and would return, but most were dead or wounded. "All the officers in the company, with the exception of one, had been wounded," recalled a G Company Marine. "The remaining officer had cracked up. He kept crying and repeating that the day was his 19th birthday."

The handful of survivors climbed back up the hill and dug in by the light of the flares. Wilkerson dug down about eighteen inches and hit water, a miserable finish to a miserable day.

The division was later to call 16 May the "bitterest" day of the Okinawan campaign. The 6th Marine Division special action report conceded that its "regiments had attacked with all the effort at their command and had been unsuccessful."

That lack of success was evident in the dozens of dead Marines strewn on the slopes of Half Moon, Sugar Loaf and their approaches. Peering through his lieutenant's binoculars from a nearby hill, an I/3/22 Marine, Anthony Cortese, was stunned to see the battle area literally covered with dead Marines—a few Japanese, too, but mostly Americans. As darkness gathered, he could also see live Japanese busily rebuilding their positions.

Among the day's casualties was Private Donald Honis, shot through the leg while helping to carry a wounded Marine off Half Moon. Bandaged and shot full of morphine, he was loaded onto an amtrac. Two or three of the most badly hurt were on stretchers; the remainder were lined up along the walls of the vehicle. One G Company man had lost both feet and his right hand. As shell fragments spanged off the outside of the vehicle, the driver stopped long enough for a corpsman to get plasma going into the G Company Marine, then the amtrac lurched off. "The guy I was sitting next to on my right was bleeding on me, the guy on my left was bleeding on me [and] I'm bleeding into my shoe," recalled Honis. "Because of the amount of blood and the number of men in the amtrac (about 15 men) when we went over bumps, of which there were many, the blood would slosh from one side to the other." The battalion aid station was under Japanese artillery fire, showering dirt and shrapnel on the wounded. Transferred to an ambulance, Honis suddenly realized how quiet it was. He could actually hear the sound of the ambulance's motor. After the din of the front lines "the silence was absolutely deafening."

It was midnight before all the Marine wounded were retrieved. "Artillery fire continued to drop throughout the regimental zone during day and night of 16 May making evacuation and supply difficult," noted the special action report of the 29th Marines. "The enemy had excellent observation over our entire zone of action making any movement hazardous."

The 22d Marines had also been shot to pieces. Assessing his losses after the day's assaults, Colonel Schneider reported that his regiment's combat efficiency was down to 40 percent. A Marine Corps study of the action later noted that "the offensive capabilities of the 22d Marines had been reduced to a point where further effort was inadvisable."

General Shepherd also had growing concerns about the effectiveness of Colonel Schneider. In Shepherd's opinion, Schneider wasn't pushing hard enough; he was showing too much caution. There were signs of trouble for those who knew where to look. For instance, on 14 May the assistant division commander had arrived on the front line to issue a direct order to one of Schneider's battalions—a very unusual occurrence in the field and an indication that all was not well.

Schneider, a 1923 graduate of the Naval Academy, had been overseas most of the war. He had been to Samoa, participated in the Marshall Islands landing and the fighting on Guam. "I think Colonel Schneider had the feeling that this operation might be his last," recalled Shepherd. "So he became overcautious and spent most of his time in his regimental command post established in an Okinawan tomb. I couldn't get him to go up front to see what the hell was going on."

Shepherd's view was that a troop commander must spend much time in the forward lines to maintain a feel for the pulse of his advance units. He had "given him [Schneider] the devil about it" two or three times already. "You've got to visit your battalions," Shepherd told the colonel. "You're a regimental commander. You don't even know where they are."

Though Schneider's regiment had been pretty well used up, Shepherd had no intention of backing off. The attack would be pressed, but now the 29th Marines would carry the burden of the fighting the next day. The regimental boundary was shifted to the west to include Sugar Loaf within the 29th Marines' zone. The realignment would also ease coordination of simultaneous attacks on both Sugar Loaf and Half Moon.

Back at the 82d Army Field Hospital, Dan Dereschuk heard the Marines were desperate for troops and needed every man who could walk. He asked for his Thompson submachine gun and headed back for the front. When he found his company a day and a half later, there was hardly a face he recognized.

Though the Marines in the line could not have appreciated it, General Ushijima was feeling the pressure—not just the 6th Marine Division's repeated efforts, but the U.S. push all along the Shuri Line. On 16 May Ushijima sent urgent signals to Imperial General Headquarters and to his immediate superiors at Tenth Army Headquarters on Formosa. His situation was desperate, he reported. He had committed his last reserves. The Shuri Line was weakening by the day.

He would be able to prolong the battle, he continued, if arms were sent for 25,000 men presently without weapons (he did not specify whether these were Okinawan recruits or simply Japanese short on equipment). Another possibility was to fly in several battalions of paratroopers to reinforce his position. Still another option would be to send all remaining airpower against the U.S. fleet off Okinawa, depriving Buckner's army of supplies and support.

Ushijima probably knew the answer from Imperial General Headquarters before he even asked the question. He was told, in essence, he would have to do the best he could with what he already had.

Chapter 9

A Hard Day for Easy

General Shepherd, accompanied by his operations officer, Lieutenant Colonel Victor H. Krulak, had come forward in the late afternoon of 16 May for his usual daily visit to the front. It was clear why the day's attack had not been successful: the Sugar Loaf defenses had been reinforced and strengthened during the past 24 hours. Worse, the intense enemy fire from the division's left and left rear was chopping up the Marine assaults. There was no way to deal with this fire, which came from the Shuri area in the zone of the 1st Marine Division, which had itself been held up for days.

Conferring with Colonel Whaling, the officers noted there was a long depression to the east of Sugar Loaf. This depression ran north and south and while far from being "a valley," it offered some protection. Some Japanese fire had fallen into it, but it did not seem to be specially targeted. Men had passed through the depression safely on several occasions.

Shepherd decided to try a power play through the depression on 17 May. The plan was to move the 29th Regiment—what was left of it—through the little valley in column. Emerging from the valley, the battalions would each engage one point in the defense system. Each attack would begin as soon as the one preceding it was well underway. The 1st Battalion would lead, placing the southeastern corner of Half Moon under attack; the 2d Battalion would assault Sugar Loaf from the east; and the 3d Battalion would push through to Half Moon on the right of the 1st Battalion. This would bring both elements of the enemy defensive structure under simultaneous attack, preventing any one part from supporting the other. With luck, occupation of the forward slope of Half Moon would allow elements of the 2d Battalion to loop around and gain Sugar Loaf from the east. The push on Sugar Loaf would be led by Easy Company.

The plan brought relief for Day and Bertoli up in their shell hole on the slope of Sugar Loaf. After dark, the Japanese had drifted over their way in some force and they had battled almost continually through the night with both grenades and rifle fire. Both Marines had already suffered minor shrapnel wounds in their face and hands. During the night both were also spattered with white phosphorus, fire which hurt the Japanese more than it hurt them. "It was friendly fire that came in, but it was welcome fire," observed Day. "We weren't burned to the point that we couldn't operate. It was just minor burns."

Elements of the 29th Marines reached their hole during the morning. A lieutenant told Day they were going to try to set up a base of fire and assault from the left flank—the fire would probably come over into their section "so that was the cue for us to come off," recalled Day.

Day and Bertoli each grabbed a wounded man from the 29th Marines and trudged back to the command post (CP). A doctor at the aid station dug out some of the shell fragments and gave them some ointment for their white phosphorus burns. The two then returned to Weapons Company, "and that was the end of the battle of Sugar Loaf for me," remarked Day. Fifty-eight dead Japanese were later counted in front of their shell hole position.

Artillery and naval gunfire laid down a heavy preparation before Whaling's 29th Marines jumped off at 0855. The intensive softening up included the fires of 16–inch naval rifles, 8–inch howitzers and 1,000–pound bombs on the regiment's objectives. The assault companies set off behind "a heavy and continual" artillery barrage. Each infantry battalion also had the support of a company of tanks.

Leading the 2d Battalion's push on Sugar Loaf was Easy Company, commanded by Captain Alan Meissner. Before the war Meissner had been a business manager in Minneapolis. He was quiet and not at all flashy. A fellow officer recalled him as "an awfully nice guy. Not very aggressive; he wasn't a gung ho sort of guy. A real nice, very capable guy. A good commander of troops."

Like so many others before them, Meissner's E Company Marines were unimpressed with the appearance of Sugar Loaf. "[It] was just kind of a little lump in the ground," recalled one Marine. The whole area was a moonscape from the constant artillery fire. "It looked like a plowed field."

Meissner wanted to send three tanks through the railroad cut east of the hill to get behind Sugar Loaf. This maneuver would allow him to put fire on the enemy reverse slope defenses. The tank officer demurred. Concerned about the lack of maneuverability, in the cut and the ground beyond, he kept his tanks in the valley between Charlie Hill and Sugar Loaf. Easy jumped off without the tanks in a wide turning movement, using the railroad cut for cover.

The company's first effort was halted by enemy artillery fire as soon as the Marines emerged into the open. Artillery located on Shuri and mortars dug in on the Horseshoe pounded the assault platoons. Private First Class Chris Clemenson, a rangy 6–foot youngster from South Dakota, lost most of his platoon right then and there. "They sent our platoon up the railroad track," he recalled. "We got halfway through the cut, they laid in on us with mortars and machine guns . . . and the platoon I was attached to—the 2d Platoon—lost everybody within 15 minutes except three of us." The attempt failed. A second E Company effort, a close flanking attack around the left of Sugar Loaf was checked by the steepness of the southeastern face of the hill.

Incredibly, one Marine had already made it to the top of Sugar Loaf—alone. A corporal by the name of O'Connor, who was serving as a machine-gun section leader in Item Company, 22d Marines, took advantage of a quiet interval at about 1000 to make a one-man assault on Sugar Loaf. Tanks continued to fire in the valley between Charlie Hill and Sugar Loaf, but O'Connor managed to get under the muzzles of their guns and started up Sugar Loaf with a bag of grenades under his arm and a pistol in his hand. The tankers, presumably astonished, stopped shooting as O'Connor dodged along the summit firing his pistol and throwing the grenades until both bullets and grenades were gone. Then he returned across the draw.

The I Company commanding officer (CO), Captain John Marston, Jr., had been told there was a Marine on top of Sugar Loaf. He watched O'Connor's attack through his field glasses, believing O'Connor was only one of many Marines who had finally secured the top of the hill. Only later did he overhear one of his men remark, "Here comes that crazy Marine of ours back from Sugar Loaf." Incredulous at first that O'Connor had mounted a one-man assault on the hill—and survived—Marston had him brought in for a talk. The corporal told Marston he had lost a lot of buddies killed or wounded in the I Company assault the day before and he wanted to get even. Marston sent the youngster to the rear for 24 hours to have him examined for psychoneurosis.

Meanwhile, Easy Company reoriented the assault platoons and at 1700 launched an attack by 1st and 3d Platoons up Sugar Loaf's northeast slope. Among the 3d Platoon Marines was Private First Class Jim Denny, an 18-year-old West Virginian who had joined up right out of high school and was now acting runner for his platoon. "When we made the first rush on Sugar Loaf, we came across that big field, that real big field," he recalled. "And we were being shelled . . . We were just hopping and skipping and hitting the ground." One of the first to be killed was Gunnery Sergeant James Kriener. "He was a pretty tough old bird," observed Denny. "He was the heavyweight champion of the service, I think, in '30 . . . We were just running 15 or 20 yards and hitting the dirt. Shells were coming in. He got a direct hit with a shell."

The platoon made it onto Sugar Loaf. Denny's platoon leader, Lieutenant Gilmon Wales, sent him back to inform Meissner and ask for instructions. Denny ran back and delivered the message. "Well, you go back and just tell him to hold on," replied Meissner.

But by the time Denny got back to Wales, the Marines had already been pushed off the hill. By now there were only ten men left in the 1st Platoon, only 25 in the 3d. Wales and the remnants of the 3d Platoon had taken shelter in a ditch about 50 yards from the hill. Japanese were visible along the crest, "sticking their heads up real fast" as they fired on the ditch. The Marines crouched low, firing back at the bobbing heads.

Denny was known to have a strong throwing arm, and after a time, Lieutenant Wales called him over. He told Denny to take a case of grenades and make his way up to the left of the hill at the base. "He wanted me to throw the grenades and get their attention over there and do it pretty fast so they'd think it was more than one person. Their idea was to go around the other side," recalled Denny.

Denny scrambled forward with the case of grenades and found cover by a big shell hole at the base of Sugar Loaf near the eastern corner. "It was five feet deep, I guess and probably seven feet at the top," he recalled. "It looked like a hell of a big shell had hit there." Pulling out the grenades, he began hurling them over the top of the hill as fast as he could.

The Japanese retaliated, showering Denny with grenades of their own. He caught quick glimpses of a head or an arm as they bobbed up to pitch grenades at him. The Japanese were so close Denny could hear the metallic click as they armed the grenade detonators by rapping them on their helmets. As Denny pitched his last grenade, he ducked back into the bottom of the shell hole. An enemy grenade landed in the hole with him, but he managed to grab it and hurl it back out before it exploded. A second grenade plopped into the hole, and he tossed that one out, too. Then a third grenade dropped in. "The third one rolled right down against me and I picked it up and just as I was getting ready to throw it, I got real nervous and the thing hit the top of the bank and rolled and then I dove back into the hole," he recalled.

"It was just a big round crater like. And that thing rolled against my leg. And I kicked and when I did, it moved a little bit and I guess that really saved my leg." Even so, the explosion drove chunks of metal through the top of his foot and out the bottom and peppered his legs, arms and body with fragments. As Denny struggled to climb out of the hole, a Japanese rifle slug ricocheted off the ground and hit him under the arm, driving through to the base of his neck.

Back at the ditch, the attack had not gotten off and one of Denny's buddies, a Marine by the name of Jim Doyle, saw that Denny was in trouble. The next thing Denny knew, Doyle was running toward him across the open field. Doyle dragged him to his feet and "we run back and I had that doggone blood coming out of me everywhere, you know, but I was able to [run] with him, hanging onto his shoulder. He saved my life."

The Marines reorganized and pushed up again. Again they were swept off the hill. A third attempt to take the top failed. "A lot of the fire was coming out of caves and you weren't sure which cave it was coming out of," remarked a Marine of the fighting among the hills. More men were hit. Lying in the ditch, Denny saw one of his platoonmates killed without warning. "A shell hit him right in the neck and he just lost his head," said Denny. "It just shot his head off."

Private First Class Calvin Christopher was shot while following his sergeant's orders to try to locate some fire support. The bullet hammered through the magazine of his rifle, exploding the full clip before glancing off and driving into his right shoulder along with fragments of metal and wood from the rifle. It also ripped open the last two fingers of his right hand. "I was all done after that," recalled Christopher. "Some machine gunner—I can't remember his name, helped dress my wound at that time. I congregated with a guy named Kincheloe (from Indiana) who was shot through the shoulder blade, and another fellow named Price, shot through the calf of his leg . . . and Ryder, from Revere, Massachusetts, shot through a cheek of his ass. We all made it off the hill about the same time under cover of a smoke screen made by our tank men to hide their tanks from Jap artillery fire." One of his buddies helped him stop the bleeding, gave him a sulpha tablet, then watched crying as Christopher was loaded onto an amtrac and evacuated. Jim Denny was also taken out by amtrac late in the afternoon. He faced 11 months in the hospital, but he would keep his leg.

Late in the afternoon, F Company's 2d Platoon was sent over to climb the western nose of the hill under covering fire from Easy. Private First Class Warren Wanamaker's machine-gun section was attached to the 2d Platoon. The platoon leader was Lieutenant Charlie Behan, a big strapping man who had captained the Dekalb University football team and in 1942 played end for the Detroit Lions. Somewhere along the line Behan had been hit in the lip or mouth by a piece of shrapnel. He had a big patch on his mouth and had trouble talking, but refused to be evacuated. "He said he could handle things with arm and hand signals if he had to," recalled Wanamaker. "He was determined not to be taken off the line."

Behan was one of several well-known pro or college football players in the 6th Marine Division. He had been particularly good friends with former Notre Dame star Irish George Murphy, killed on Sugar Loaf during D Company's assault on 15 May. News of Murphy's death the day before had hit Behan hard, and he seemed eager to avenge his friend. He got his chance late in the afternoon when his platoon was sent forward to assist the Easy Company Marines on Sugar Loaf. They got forward only to run into a hail of mortar and small-arms fire.

Wanamaker and his buddy, John Blanchard, had their .30 caliber machine gun mounted on a light tripod, a trick which improved mobility in the assaults. Another gun crew set up on the hill to their front and was cut down almost immediately. "We had the gun loaded and were trying to get into some position to fire, but it was just impossible the way those mortars were falling," observed Wanamaker. Behan and the platoon sergeant got to the top of the hill just as a Japanese mortar concentration slammed in. It "just wiped out a whole bunch of them right away," said Wanamaker. The dead included Behan and the sergeant.

The survivors in Wanamaker's small area were pinned down and useless. Men began to pull back. "It was just, 'Well, what do we do now?' And I said, 'Well, let's get out of here.' It was dumb to stay there," he recalled.

Wanamaker's gun crew was among the last to fall back. For some reason they happened to have a lot of smoke grenades. As Japanese came around the edge of the hill, the Marines would pitch smoke grenades toward them, fire into the smoke and then leapfrog back. The Japanese weren't attacking in great numbers, mostly separate groups of five or six. "They were as scared as we were," observed Wanamaker. "They were peeking around, looking at us, pointing, trying to fire."

There was no real organization left. "It was all helter skelter," recalled Wanamaker. "We didn't have any officers and we only had a couple of noncoms. Nobody really knew where the hell we were going. But we got back." Wanamaker's gun crew fell back on defenses manned by elements of the 22d Marines. As they got squared away, Wanamaker overheard a lieutenant say, "Why the hell didn't someone tell us you guys were going up there? We could have given you some covering fire."

The whole incident had lasted perhaps 30 minutes by Wanamaker's calculation.

Easy Company's troubles stemmed in part from the situation of the 1st and 3d Battalions. Both had managed limited advances, but neither had been able to seize its designated objective, leaving Easy open to fire from Half Moon.

According to the plan, the remnants of H and I Companies were to assault the western nose of Half Moon just to the east; Able Company, still further east, was to drive down a draw between Charlie Ridge and Half Moon, protecting the left of the 3d Battalion. Tanks moved through the ruins of a village at the foot of Charlie Ridge to support the A Company attack. Japanese lay hidden among the rubble, waiting until the tanks were nearly on them before throwing grenades at the accompanying Marines. The rest of the 1st Battalion was also in action, trying to clean out Japanese dug into the reverse side of Charlie Ridge.

While B and C Companies tangled with enemy troops on Charlie Ridge and the adjoining ground, A Company renewed the attack and advanced quickly across the valley floor to the forward slopes of Half Moon. Lieutenant Wilbur J. Gehrke, a 27–year-old North Dakotan in charge of Able's machine guns, rushed over the crest, but quickly reappeared to report the Japanese were massed in trenches on the far slope—more Japanese than he had ever hoped to see. His men had thrown all their grenades and sprayed the trenches with automatic fire before scrambling back to the protection of the Marine-held side of the hill.

Spared some of the enfilading fire from the left thanks to Able's advance, How and Item Companies also fought across the valley floor to Half Moon. By midafternoon the companies—now down to less than one third their normal strength—were digging in on the northwestern nose of the hill, but there was a gap between their positions and those of Able Company. I Company asked for more men. At 1635 Colonel Whaling ordered two platoons of F Company to close the gap.

A Company was also in trouble. Completely exposed to enemy fire from their left, they were barely holding on. "Men were clinging to the hill as men would cling to a reef in heavy surf," a Marine officer wrote later. "They could not go forward; while they were in partial protection, they could not attack, only endure."

The company commanding officer (CO), Captain Jason B. Baker, asked B Company to send up a platoon to stiffen his weakening line. The B Company CO, Captain Lyle E. Specht, a veteran of Tarawa, had been wounded shortly before; the acting CO, 1st Lieutenant Charles Gallagher was having trouble with his radios so he trotted forward to confer with the officers handling the defense of the slope. Huddled in a knocked-out Japanese machine-gun bunker, Gallagher, Captain William A. Gamble of H Company, 1st Lieutenant John P. Stone of I Company and 1st Lieutenant Warren B. Watson of A Company debated what to do. Watson said he had already lost half his men. He thought trying to put more men on the hill would only result in more dead Marines. Stone and Gamble thought they could continue to hold.

Gallagher went back and placed one of his platoons, commanded by Lieutenant Robert H. Neff, behind Able Company, so their machine guns could cover Watson's men. Enemy fire continued to rake Able from behind. Watson finally spotted the source of the trouble—an overlooked gun emplacement on a hill to his rear. He went down into the valley and sent a tank up with orders to blast the enemy gun, warning the crew not to fire to the left where Neff's platoon was located. The tank knocked out the gun, but on the way back the driver became confused and the gunner fired his 75 into Neff's machine-gun section, which didn't help matters any.

As dusk fell and the tanks withdrew, enemy fire picked up; yellow tracers streaked toward the Marine positions. On the left, A Company men began sliding back down the hill. Their withdrawal had a domino effect: the line simply peeled back. Both Gamble and Stone were now calling for permission to pull back. Major Neuffer authorized a withdrawal to a defiladed area approximately 150 yards north of Half Moon. In the gathering gloom, the Marines got down into the draw and across the road where they dug in.

Just before dark, the exhausted Easy Company survivors somehow managed one more try at Sugar Loaf. They made it to the top and though the Japanese tried to drive them off, they managed to hold their ground. But it couldn't last. They were down to a handful of men and "not enough ammo for a weekend hunting trip," observed a Marine correspondent.

Among those who made it to the top was Private First Class Homer "Pop" Noble. The nickname "Pop" came by virtue of his great age—he was 25. His presence in the Marine Corps was a bit of a mystery to him. He had gone to enlist in the Navy, heeding the advice of a family friend, a World War I Army veteran who had spent too many cold, scared nights in water-filled shell holes. But when he got to the recruiting station, he found a dozen or so Marines "hanging around talking up the Corps" and one of them asked if anyone in Noble's group wanted to join up. For some reason—he was never sure why—Noble stood up. He was the only one. "Well," said the recruiter, "I got the best of the lot."

Now "the best of the lot" and two other Marines had scrambled up the left side of the hill and taken shelter in a shallow depression gouged out by an artillery shell. There were dead men strewn all over. Japanese machine-gun and mortar fire from the left had cut Easy Company to pieces. Marines Noble had known for a long long time were now among the litter of corpses on Sugar Loaf's slope.

From their position at the edge of the hill, they could see the Japanese were in stand-up foxholes on the reverse slope not more than 200 feet away. Japanese soldiers habitually kept their bayonets fixed at all times; now Noble could see a veritable forest of bayonets sticking up over the edge of the holes on the slope. There seemed to be hundreds of them. Now and again a mushroom-shaped helmet would rise up over the lip of a hole and the Marines would knock it back down with rifle fire.

They had the Japanese pretty well pinned down—fortunately, the enemy did not seem to realize how few Marines were holding the crest. The Japanese stayed low and retaliated with knee mortars. The "beer-can size" grenades were raining down all around, but many of them failed to explode. Noble suspected that the detonator buttons on the grenades were not hitting properly, perhaps because of the angle of fire or the angle of the slope.

Firing whenever one of the Japanese exposed himself, the three Marines eventually ran out of rifle ammunition. Private First Class Joseph Bogdan started to stand up. "Don't stand up there!" warned Noble, seeing what he was doing. Bogdan said he wanted to see what was happening further down the slope. He stood up and blurted, "My God! They're going to banzai!" At almost the same instant, a bullet struck him under the armpit and came out his chest. Bogdan pitched over dead.

Noble and the other Marine pitched their remaining grenades down the slope and scuttled back to the northern side of the hill. It was starting to get dark. "Hey!" yelled somebody down below. "Get the hell down off that hill!" They didn't need to be told twice. Scrambling down, they spent the rest of the night helping load Easy's dozens of wounded into amtracs.

Private First Class W. R. Lightfoot was with a Dog Company squad sent up with an amtrac to deliver grenades and help evacuate the wounded. He had no idea what was going on, but things were obviously bad. "There was all confusion and running around and screaming and all of that," he remembered. "They got most of the wounded out. But you could still hear some of them crying."

With ammunition exhausted and casualties so heavy that no one could be spared to help the wounded back, the Marines couldn't hang on. At 1840

Colonel Whaling ordered the survivors to withdraw after dark. The attack cost E Company 160 killed and wounded.

Among Easy's casualties that afternoon were Lieutenant Edgar C. Greene and Corporal John A. Spazzaferro, both of the 2d Platoon, which had been trapped in the initial assault. Spazzaferro, a big, rugged Italian, stood about 6 feet 2 inches tall and was said to have been a coach for the Pittsburgh Steelers. He started the withdrawal with just two men remaining of his 14–man squad. Greene later described Spazzaferro as "the toughest guy I ever saw," but the corporal wasn't indestructible. A bullet went through his left arm, two more went through his right arm, breaking it above the elbow. Another bullet nearly took off his trigger finger, while the fifth entered his back and came out just above the left hip. A sixth grazed his right hip.

Greene, a former reporter for the *Detroit Free Press*, was also hit. He took four slugs in the chest and fell beside the rail of the narrow gauge railroad along the draw between Half Moon and Sugar Loaf. He raised his head and saw "Spazz" standing there, still firing his weapon. When the enemy fire stopped, Spazzaferro started to move, then collapsed about ten feet from Greene. Greene thought he was probably dead.

Four Japanese suddenly emerged from the landscape and came toward them. Greene feigned death, assuming a grotesque attitude. One of the enemy soldiers took his wrist watch, then reached a hand into Greene's pocket, only to draw it back out in disgust as it became covered with warm sticky blood.

After the Japanese had moved off past Spazzaferro, Greene lifted his head and called, "Spazz!" To his relief, the tough corporal managed a grin in return. Both were too badly hurt to crawl back to safety, but they were—incredibly—alive.

Also miraculously still alive was a K/3/22 Marine, Private Samuel O. Bradford. Bradford had scaled Sugar Loaf to reinforce Major Courtney's group the night of 14–15 May. Sometime during the night, a Japanese mortar shell had blown off his lower legs and his buddies had left him for dead. The young Georgian had the presence of mind to pack the stubs in mud to stop the bleeding. He had been lying on the hill, drifting in and out of consciousness, for two days, hearing Japanese wandering about during lulls in the fighting. Some Marines finally found Bradford on the morning of 17 May and he was carried to safety.[1]

Nineteen-year-old Private First Class H. H. Tayler dug in with the survivors of C/29. The company had gone into action two days earlier with 252 men. Now Tayler guessed there were maybe 50 or so left. He and a handful of other Marines had taken shelter in an abandoned Japanese trench. After dusk, they could hear the Japanese out front. It sounded like hundreds, screaming and yelling as if they planned a banzai attack. Tayler was terrified.

None of the Marines was saying anything. His BAR man, a 27-year-old private first class, was scared speechless. Tayler was on the far right of the position. Corporal George Scott was on the far left. Tayler was sure they were all going to die. As he recalled it, what happened next was just short of bizarre. Accepting his own imminent death, he turned to the man next to him and said lightheartedly, "Stand by for an important message. This message is addressed to Corporal George Scott. George, there is nobody in command on the right flank. This message is signed H. H. Out." Moments later a reply came back down the line: "H. H., I have complete confidence in you. Take command of the right flank."

It was pitch dark except for the occasional star shell. They had no communications with the rear to call up mortars or artillery or naval gun fire. "We're all going to die tonight," thought Tayler. A Marine jumped into the trench next to him. "Who are you?" asked Tayler. The Marine laughed and said, "I'm the new forward observer. Is this the front line?"

"You have a line to the rear to the 105s and 155s?" blurted Tayler.

"Yeah," said the Marine.

Tayler told him to get on the line and call up his captain. "Give him the coordinates immediately." The Marine did and the artillery officer came on the line. "My captain wants to talk to you," said the observer. "What are you, a major?"

"No, I'm a PFC," said Tayler. He got on the phone and said, "PFC Tayler." The officer swore at him and demanded, "Give me the lieutenant."

"There's nobody left," said Tayler.

"What's that noise?" said the officer.

"That's the enemy," Tayler told him.

"Who?"

"The Japs. They're going to banzai us."

That got the officer's attention. Tayler told him they needed artillery fire to their direct front. "All right," said the officer. "I'll fire a round for effect."

"No you won't," said Tayler. "No rounds for effect."

"Why not?"

"They run back into the cave with one round fired. They know it. No rounds."

"We're going to kill all our men," worried the officer.

"You stupid asshole," said Tayler. "We're dead anyway."

By now the once happy-go-lucky forward observer was suffering from an acute case of terror. "When the young forward observer found out it was Japs yelling like that, he started crying and then he got into it with the captain over his crying . . . This captain was giving him a hard time," recalled Tayler.

As the thin line of Marines waited for the barrage, a Japanese started sniping at them from the right rear. A flare drifted down and Tayler suddenly saw the man silhouetted from the waist up as he popped up from a hole to take another shot. Tayler dropped him with a shot from his M1. Then the barrage came in and whatever Japanese were gathering out front either died or hid.

The Japanese in front of C Company's position were probably part of the reinforcements Ushijima attempted to bring forward after nightfall. U.S. observers spotted large numbers of enemy troops moving across the open ground beyond Sugar Loaf. Artillery spotters called in fire from 12 artillery battalions on the hapless Japanese and completely smashed the attempt.

Only a small portion of Okinawa remained in enemy hands by 17 May, but American forces had paid a terrible price for their gains. To date, Tenth Army had lost 3,964 men killed in action, 18,258 wounded and 302 missing, plus 9,295 nonbattle casualties. Naval casualties among the offshore fleet totaled over 4,000.

The reason for the 6th Marine Division's failure on 17 May was all too clear. In a postwar study of the action, Marine Corps historians observed, "So well integrated were the enemy defenses on Half Moon and Sugar Loaf, capture of only one portion was meaningless; 6th Division Marines had to take them all simultaneously. If only one hill was seized without the others being neutralized or likewise captured, effective Japanese fire from the uncaptured position would force the Marines to withdraw from all. This, in effect, was why Sugar Loaf had not been breached before, and why it was not taken on the 17th."

Nevertheless, the division historian found hope in the day's events. The 29th's attack had failed to take Sugar Loaf, which was the key objective, "but a considerable measure of security had been gained by the advances on the left flank and the regiment was in a good position to resume the assault on the next morning," he wrote.

The 22d Marines would continue to play a major role in the battle, but their CO, Colonel Merlin Schneider, would not be with them. General Shepherd had tired of trying to spark Schneider to action. At 1430, Schneider and his executive officer, Colonel Karl K. Louther, were relieved.

"The scuttlebutt we got was that [Schneider] refused to go back up there the 12th or 13th time," remembered a junior officer of the 22d Marines. "Schneider was a good man and we respected him. You don't know a hell of a lot about what's going on at his level. We just heard that he stuck up for the battalion, the regiment. . . . The regiment was used up and he couldn't in good conscience keep sending us up there."

The scuttlebutt was apparently not true. Shepherd had decided that Schneider was just plain worn out; "fatigued physically and mentally, combat fatigue," he had, in Shepherd's words, "faltered." He was relieved without prejudice. "I thought it was time for him to go home for a rest," explained Shepherd. "No disgrace. He was a nice fellow, so I pinned a Bronze Star on him and sent him back to the States."[2]

The message to the rest of the division was unmistakable. Shepherd also wanted results—and Schneider was not providing them. Lieutenant Colonel August Larson, who served on the division staff, recalled that Shepherd never hesitated to relieve an officer who, in his opinion, didn't push hard enough. "He wanted you to achieve your objectives every day," noted Larson. "He always wanted to keep the pressure on." Shepherd also realized the 22d Marines was badly in need of strong leadership. "They had been badly mauled at Sugar Loaf Hill," he recalled. "I mean that was a hell of a fight. We lost a lot of people there and I think the regiment's morale was pretty well down."

To bring the regiment back to trim, Shepherd named Colonel Harold C. Roberts from his division staff to take over for Schneider. Forty-six years old, Roberts had served as a corpsman with the Marines in France during World War I, receiving the Navy Cross for heroism at Belleau Wood. After the war, he applied for a Marine Corps commission, receiving it in 1923. He had received a second Navy Cross while acting as second in command of the Coco River Expedition in Nicaragua in 1928. Before coming to the 6th Marine Division in January, 1945, he had served as Chief of Staff for the Corps Artillery Officer, V Amphibious Corps during the invasion of the Philippines. Lieutenant Colonel August Larson was named executive.

The first thing Roberts did was establish his command post immediately behind the front lines. When Shepherd saw this, he blurted, "Roberts, what the hell did you come up here for? You'll damn well get shot." Roberts replied, "I want to show the men in this regiment that this is where the regimental commander is so they will follow me in the next attack. They need somebody to get them out of their foxholes, get them to move forward." He thought it would help if the men could see him, he said. "Brace 'em up."

Shepherd knew then he had picked the right man.

NOTES

1. Bradford survived and sired three children. His eldest son also served in the Marines and was killed in Vietnam.

2. Merlin Schneider's combat record up to this point speaks for itself. He was only one of many good men who were worked to exhaustion during the war. He retired in 1948 as a brigadier general.

Chapter 10

Sugar Loaf Falls

On 18 May Secretary of the Navy James Forrestal told reporters in Washington that casualties in the naval support forces operating around Okinawa now totaled 4,720, including 900 killed in action, 2,746 wounded and 1,074 missing in action. Forrestal said he made the announcement as a "sobering fact to make the country aware that continuing support by the Navy of a major land operation is a costly and serious business."

There was an implied criticism there for those able to read between the lines: Buckner was moving too slowly.

Buckner was feeling the pressure from above. He chafed visibly at the slow progress along the Tenth Army front and urged his corps commanders to speed up the assault. The Tenth Army Marine Deputy Chief of Staff, General Oliver P. Smith, observed, "Buckner was under considerable pressure to make faster progress as the Navy was sustaining heavy casualties by being forced to remain in the vicinity of Okinawa." On 11 May alone, the day after the Tenth Army launched its general offensive, four ships were seriously damaged by kamikazes. One, the aircraft carrier *Bunker Hill*, lost 396 men killed and 264 wounded.

Japanese hopes that the fleet would be forced to abandon Buckner's army would not be fulfilled. Nevertheless, on land, Yahara's defensive tactics were costing the GIs and Marines dearly in blood. All along the Shuri Line it was much the same as the GIs from XXIV Corps and the Marines from IIIAC measured their gains in yards. The 1st Marine Division was being shot to pieces in assaults on the Shuri Heights. The 6th Marine Division was being decimated in front of Sugar Loaf. XXIV Corps was not doing any better.

The Japanese were also suffering, their capabilities steadily eroding under the American onslaught. The slide in Japanese morale was evident in the entries of a diarist from one of the naval units now serving in as an infantryman with Ushijima's composite battalions opposite the 6th Marine Division.

9 May   Due to good weather, enemy planes came and bombed us heavily. We are moving our troops again.

10 May   At 0500 we moved to new positions about 500 yards away and I am with about 6 fellows from the 3d and 4th squads. Strafing by enemy planes is becoming severe.

11 May   We moved again before dawn—the 3d and 4th squads, the boat personnel, in fact, the entire force. Naval gunfire has become intense and the positions we were in before received a direct hit. Thank God our lives were saved.

12 May   Clear weather today. The enemy is near. We changed positions this night. We used cloth sandals; use of shoes was forbidden. We heard that the army has been ordered to defend this island to the death. All the ship's crew has been put into the army as 2d Class Privates. We got two sacks of dry bread today. Miyakawa went into the Suicide Unit and was killed. This area is devastated.

14 May   Since we entered Naha Harbor two months ago, conditions have continuously deteriorated. The trouble is that victory depends upon control of the air but no friendly airplanes are in the skies. One of the ship's crew went out for vegetables but was killed by shellfire. Enemy planes came in large numbers. This morning, since the word was that we would move before dawn, I went up to establish communications but was prevented from doing so by fire.

15 May   We got some tobacco issued as a present from the Emperor and some cakes. I got one cigarette, about a quarter of one cake, and two packages of nutrition ration. It looks like we are to die at last. The enemy has halted at a distance of about 1,000 yards from us. We have some Type 38 rifle ammunition left and also 65 rounds of Type 3 ammunition for use in machine-guns.

16 May   We have placed our machine-guns in position on the high ground. Our food is only half-cooked and filled with sand. I can see the figures of enemy soldiers within 1,500 yards of us.

17 May   Eating canned food. I am on duty as an observer of enemy activity. Two or three hand grenades per man have been issued. One of the Ishi platoons was annihilated by enemy naval gunfire. At best, a concentration of 60 rounds dropped within an area 30 feet square is extremely deadly. There is talk that the Grand Fleet will come and destroy the enemy by Navy Memorial Day.

18 May Our forces are without planes, warships, or tanks. Because we are abandoned we have no hope other than to die resisting. This is said to be the resolution of everyone from the army commander down. Our medium artillery is destroyed and we have not even one piece left. Since we are serving our daily allotment of food in two meals, we are hungry. We have come to our end in this despicable land. How I would like to return safely!

That wish was not to be. A few days later a Marine from K Company, 22d Marines, took the diary from the writer's corpse.

Dug in facing Sugar Loaf, the outlook facing the 2d Battalion, 29th Marines seemed especially grim the night of 17 May after the survivors pulled back from the hill. The battalion had expended all its grenades in Easy Company's first two attempts to take the hill. That in itself had contributed greatly to the company's problems on the hill, along with the usual dilemma of being exposed to enemy fire from Shuri and other points. There seemed little reason to think the next day would be any different.

But battalion commander Lieutenant Colonel William G. Robb remained optimistic. He sensed that the Japanese were being worn down. Talking with Colonel Whaling on the field phone that evening, he said, "We can take it. We'll give it another go in the morning."

Closer to the front, the D Company commander, Captain Howard Mabie, found out Homer Noble was one of the few Marines who had made it to the top of Sugar Loaf during Easy Company's attack that day. He quizzed Noble on what he had seen. Where was the enemy's greatest strength? What had gone wrong? Why did the assault fail? Noble told him the Japanese fire on the left flank was murderous. The way to go, he advised, was around the right. Mabie listened and began formulating a plan.

In front of Half Moon, less than half a mile to the east, Private First Class H. H. Tayler, former "commander of the right flank" who had resigned himself to death the night before, was still miraculously alive when the sun came up. His Browning Automatic Rifle (BAR) man, who had been scared speechless through the night, stood up. A nambu chattered shrilly and the automatic rifleman clutched at a bullet wound in his wrist. Tayler snatched up the automatic rifle and charged directly at the nambu he had spotted in a cave mouth 40 feet away. He survived only because the machine gunners were trying to reload. There were three of them gathered around the nambu "and they were just all thumbs" as they rushed to get the gun back in action, he observed. Tayler gunned down all three with a long hosing burst from the BAR.

Also up on the front line that morning—and glad of it—was a 23-year-old lieutenant from Woodside, New York, Francis X. Smith. Nicknamed "Bobby Sox" due to his passion for swing music, the boyish-looking Smith had been assigned to 2d Battalion headquarters since the landing in April. Day after day he had endured the emotional pain of seeing the casualty lists of the dead and wounded—many of them officers he had known for months—pass through battalion headquarters. Finally, in desperate need of officers for the frontline platoons, Colonel Robb assigned Smith to D Company, 29th Marines. "I thought it was great," recalled Smith, whose brother had been wounded on Iwo Jima in February. "But that's the beauty of youth. You never thought it was you that was going to be hit."

Mabie gave Smith the 1st Platoon. They were "pretty well beaten up," recalled Smith, but the fight hadn't gone out of them. They were ready to go. The plan had been worked out between Mabie, Robb and Captain Phil Morell of A Company, 6th Tank Battalion. Mabie gathered his platoon leaders and told them what he proposed to do: the 1st Platoon under Smith would flank Sugar Loaf, moving down the valley and up the western nose of the hill, pulling enemy attention to that side. Fire teams would peel off along the slope to form a continuous line from the base to the top. When Smith had gotten halfway to the top, Sergeant Ernest Ellison would take the 2d Platoon directly to the top to hold the left part of the hill. The 3d Platoon, which had been shot to pieces under Irish George Murphy on 15 May, would remain in reserve across the valley, prepared to provide protective fire with machine guns and rifles.

Mabie's company had not been committed to an actual assault since 15 May, but his Marines had not been entirely out of harm's way. Declan Klingenhagen's squad lost one of its members just the day before when they headed back into the lines and were pinned down in a ditch by an enemy machine gun. "During the wait," he recalled, "we heard a rustling in the group and suddenly one of the group threw his rifle away and began crying and crawling back towards the rear. A few of us retrieved the rifle and, according to the book, stripped it down and threw the parts in all directions."

Now, Dog Company was going to tackle Sugar Loaf. The key part of the plan was the tanks. Mabie and Robb realized from hard experience that when Smith got onto Sugar Loaf, the Japanese would emerge from the caves on the southern slope to contest the hill. At that point, the tanks would sweep around the flanks and catch the emerging enemy troops in the open. If the

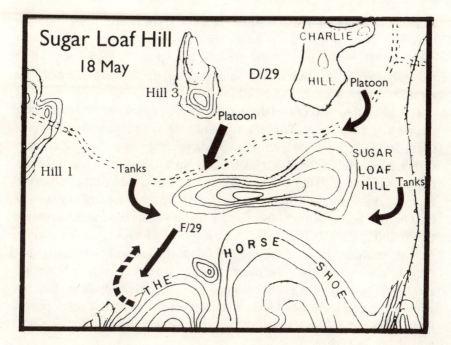

Sugar Loaf Hill
18 May

maneuver worked, the 29th Marines would gain possession of the hill; if it didn't, the regiment probably would not be able to mount another assault. All hands knew they were getting down to last efforts. The regiment had been badly hurt over the past few days; if this attack failed, the division's last reserves, the 4th Marines, would have to do the job.

As Dog Company got into position, the battalion forward observer punished the enemy defenders with artillery. The battalion's 81 mm mortars added to the din, dropping their shells just over the crest of the hill.

The assault began with tanks from the 6th Tank Battalion attempting a double envelopment of Sugar Loaf. The maneuver did not get off to a promising start. Antitank fire and well-placed minefields quickly disabled six tanks. Despite those losses, tanks from Captain Morell's A Company and Captain John Clifford's C Company, managed to get into position on either side of the hill, preparatory to enveloping the position. A dozen rocket trucks raced up and delivered their salvos, dodging enemy artillery fire as they scampered back into defilade. Then D Company's 60 mm mortars started pounding the crest.

At 0830, the assault platoons—about 80 men in all—started forward. As Smith loped toward the hill, he noticed they were being fired on. There wasn't anything he could do about it. "Everything was coming right at you and you just kept running," he recalled. "If you were lucky, you got through." A corpsman assigned to the company took note of Smith's coolness. "He was fearless," observed the corpsman. "If he was scared, he never showed it." Another Marine said simply of the boyish lieutenant, "He turned out to be a mean, tough little bastard."

Days of killing had turned the approaches to Sugar Loaf into something resembling a cess pool. Working forward with D Company, Private First Class Irv Gehret passed putrid heaps of decomposing flesh. Two days earlier, some of them had been his friends. Now they were unrecognizable, black and bloated. "They tried to take Sugar Loaf eleven times," observed Gehret. "And each time they went up there they threw an artillery barrage on it before they assaulted. Then, when the Japs came back after us, they'd throw stuff at us. All those bodies were just laying there . . . out in the open. Nobody could get to them. Although the Japs tried to pull their dead away, they'd be laying all over the place. Parts . . . parts of bodies. When we assaulted [18 May] it was almost impossible to actually walk up that hill without treading on bodies. Ours and Japs. There were just that many people there. They weren't in the best of condition. It was just like walking up a pile of smelly garbage."

Scrambling past the putrefying dead on the torn and blasted hill, Smith's platoon made it to the crest. "Make a line along the crest of the hill!" Smith shouted to the men. He had made sure his men had plenty of grenades—some were loaded down with as many as 15 or 20. "Let 'em have it," he yelled, and the Marines heaved grenades down the slope as the Japanese began to emerge from their holes. As the grenades exploded downslope, Smith directed other Marines to set up machine guns. "Keep up the fire!" he shouted as they sprayed the reverse slope with bullets. Smith was slightly wounded in the head and hand by shell or grenade fragments, but he ignored his injuries.

Suddenly the Marine tanks rumbled around the flanks of the hill. A Company of the 6th Tank Battalion sent three tanks down the railroad cut and around the eastern end of the Sugar Loaf. C Company sent theirs around the western end. The minefields were behind them. The Japanese antitank net had been worn thin by days of attrition. At long last the tankers were able to lay direct fire on the enemy reverse slope defenses, even as the Japanese emerged to fight off Smith's assault. Tank Lieutenant Donald R. Pinnow noted, "We pumped a few more shells in the caves when suddenly the Japs began running down from the crest. We fired . . . and blew them all over the landscape." A Japanese suicide squad carrying satchel charges emerged from a cave and ran toward the tank. Sergeant Charles M. Scott opened up on them with a machine gun and hit one of the charges. The team vanished in the explosion. Two other suicide teams were also shot down.

Pinnow's tank, driven by Sergeant Gerald Bunting, came on a long trench running south off Sugar Loaf. The trench had been dug to give shelter to enemy troops as they attacked or fell back from the hill. Pinnow told Bunting to drive the tank so it spanned the trench. Bunting did, then turned and looked up from the driver's seat to see that Pinnow had the hatch open and was throwing grenades into the trench. He killed a lot of Japanese, recalled Bunting.

Another tank commander, Corporal Whalen R. McGarrity, saw a Japanese officer standing by a cave entrance. The enemy officer was using his sword as a pointer as he directed his men to take cover. McGarrity put the tank's main gun on him and fired, atomizing the man. Recalled Lieutenant Richard Peterson, "His sword went flying 50 feet through the air. We could see it glittering in the sun."

Following in the command tank, Captain Phil Morell saw a Marine reel up from the torn earth at the foot of the hill and start banging on the back of the tank in front of him. Realizing no one could hear the man, Morell radioed the other tank, "Hey, you've got a Marine banging on your tank. Twist your turret and open your pistol port and yell at him." The other tanker did and told the Marine to drop down and they would pull him through the escape hatch in the bottom of the tank. A few minutes later the forward tank informed Morell, "Hey, he's been wounded. He's been on the hill all night." It was Lieutenant Edward Greene, wounded the day before in Easy's assault on the hill. Somehow he had summoned up the energy to stagger out and feebly hail the tanks. Both he and Spazzaferro were rescued and survived their ordeal.

Greene had one more contribution to make to the battle. "The Japs had come up and taken his wrist watch off him and felt around him, they thought he was dead," recalled Morell. But they didn't take his compass. "There was a big gun in the hills beyond Sugar Loaf that was raising hell with us. And he got an azimuth on that gun and he saw the flash and counted, one one-thousand, two one-thousand, until he heard the bang. So he got the direction and the distance. When we got back he reported where that gun was and they radioed out to the *Tuscaloosa*, I think it was, and they fired in and laid a big barrage and knocked it out."

After an hour of furious fighting, the Dog Company Marines were firmly dug in all around Sugar Loaf Hill. Japanese resistance was weakening. "I could see down into the corner where this railroad was and you could see them bailing out, running down the railroad there," said Irv Gehret. "Away from us."

Morell could also see that the enemy had broken. "We were up there and there were some Japs running around; they didn't have helmets on and they didn't have any weapons and they were trying to get out of there," he observed. "We knocked them out with machine gun fire from the coaxial gun." It was the first time in nearly a week of fighting that Morell had actually seen Japanese on the hill. Morell's tankers later claimed 100 Japanese dead. None of the tank crews were killed or wounded.

As the enemy fire subsided, Lieutenant Smith waved his men forward. "Let's move down and clean this thing up," he called. Accompanied by his runner, Smith walked around toward the front of the hill "to make sure we were really holding it" and to check on the Japanese caves. The next thing he knew, someone grabbed him. He assumed it was one of his Marines trying to get his attention, but when he glanced around, he found two Japanese soldiers trying to drag him into a cave. A couple of Marines instinctively grabbed Smith on the other side and pulled the other way. "It was a tug of war," said Smith. "A ridiculous thing that you would see in a Keystone comedy. Nobody could shoot for fear of hitting us and we were all pulling and shoving."

Fortunately for Smith, his men won the tug-of-war. The two Japanese ducked back into a hole, followed by a couple of Marine hand grenades. The incident left even the fearless Lieutenant Smith somewhat shaken. "If I was a little older I would have had a heart attack," he admitted. "But I wasn't smart enough to have a heart attack."

Private Declan Klingenhagen had been held back from the initial D Company assault. He was never sure why; it might have been because his sergeant felt his first frontline combat had been so ferocious two days earlier. Perhaps it was just good luck. "I was sitting in a trench dug out of the bottom of a small hill and I was apprehensive," he recalled. "I wasn't hiding because there were other Marines around, but I hoped no one would see me. I guess I was feeling fear. . . . At one point, a longer time member of my squad saw me and asked why I wasn't going with the assault. The sergeant was nearby and told the member to leave me alone; it was all right."

Now, ordered to join his fellow Marines on top of Sugar Loaf, he started off, passing the body of a dead Japanese along the way. The man had been eviscerated by a grenade. The chest was blown open and maggots teemed on the rotting flesh. As he climbed the hill to his position just over the top of the hill on the forward slope, he stumbled over a dead Marine whose body was mostly covered with earth from shell explosions. The man's feet stuck out of the dirt. Like some of the Marines, this man wore his dog tags in the laces of his boondockers. Klingenhagen paused to read the name: it was the same name as a seminarian upper classman he had known two years before. The upper classman had left the seminary before Klingenhagen and also joined the Marine Corps. Klingenhagen took some comfort in the fact that it was a common name.

At 0946 Lieutenant Smith triumphantly radioed Captain Mabie. Sugar Loaf was secure, he reported. "Send up PX supplies." Despite Smith's optimism, by 1300 Dog Company was still digging in under heavy mortar fire. The Marines were on Sugar Loaf. Now all they had to do was stay there.

The combat efficiency of the 29th Marines had been seriously diminished by the week-long fight for Sugar Loaf. Since the start of the Tenth Army attack on 9 May, the 6th Marine Division had suffered 2,662 battle and 1,289 nonbattle casualties—almost all of them in the 22d and 29th Marines. Clearly, a fresh unit was critically needed if the attack were to continue. General Geiger released the 4th Marines from IIIAC reserve at 1830. Having seized Sugar Loaf, the 29th Marines were to go into division reserve, subject to IIIAC control. Attack plans for 19 May called for the 2d and 3d Battalions of the 4th Marines to relieve the 29th and consolidate the gains made on 18 May.

Meanwhile, the Marines on Sugar Loaf were still under pressure. Though the hill was in U.S. hands, heavy fire continued to come from Horseshoe Hill just to the west. Particular trouble was caused by mortars set in the defiladed areas at the Horseshoe beyond the reach of Marine weapons. At 1630 Lieutenant Colonel Robb ordered F Company to seize the height.

Hindsight indicates that Robb underestimated the difficulty of this mission. Enemy troops remained in large numbers all through the area between Sugar Loaf and the Horseshoe, as well as on the Horseshoe itself. Fox ran into trouble almost immediately. The lead platoon had no sooner descended into the depression between Sugar Loaf and the Horseshoe than the Marines came under fire from a machine gun *behind* them. The gun was emplaced in a cave at the base of Sugar Loaf; its crew had apparently either dug their way out, or ducked into the recesses of the hill during mop-up operations. Informed of the problem, Captain Mabie sent a demolitions team and flamethrower down the hill. He also persuaded one of the tanks to come back and fire into the cave openings.

A Dog Company flamethrower operator, Private James Lore, edged up to the cave and spotted seven Japanese at the entrance. When they saw Lore with the apparatus on his back, three ran to one side of the cave entrance and four to the other. Lore roasted the group of four with one searing blast, then turned on the remaining three. A squirt of flame set their clothing on fire, but before Lore could complete their incineration, the flamethrower sputtered out. The enraged Japanese started after him. Weighted down by the hose and tanks on his back, Lore turned to run, but tripped over a communications wire. As the smoldering Japanese closed on him, he sprayed them with the only thing he had left—the incendiary fluid. The enemy soldiers went up like torches as the fluid ignited on their burning clothes.

The Fox Company Marines drove through to the lip of the Horseshoe depression where the advance developed into a close quarters brawl with grenades. D Company, now deployed along the crest of Sugar Loaf, provided fire support, which helped F Company seize the forward slope of Horseshoe. They dug in there under strong enemy counterfire. Private Kenneth Wells, a Fox Company replacement undergoing his first real combat, had been in high school in Vaughsville, Ohio, a year earlier. He couldn't see any Japanese, but he fired back anyway. The Marine alongside him was suddenly hit by a bullet which entered his left chest just under the collar bone. Wells tried to apply a compression bandage to stop the bleeding. The casualty passed out from shock; in his inexperience, Wells assumed the man had died, so he went back to shooting at the unseen Japanese. A corporal came by, pointed out the enemy positions, then dropped as a bullet hit him in the thigh. Wells slit the corporal's pants with his K-bar and put a tourniquet on the wound. The corporal passed out from shock. Thinking this man too was dead, Wells went back to his rifle.

The Marines did not have a good position. They found themselves in what was basically a deep salient into the Japanese front. The long ridge occupied by the company was honeycombed with caves at and slightly above the level of the floor. These caves presumably sheltered Japanese troops. The Fox Company CO, Lieutenant George S. Thompson, who had taken over the company after Captain Bob Fowler was wounded on 15 May, made note of one particular bad spot—a defile at the very western end of the ridge where a road led down to Naha. The road could be covered by L/3/22 located just to the northwest, but Thompson could not get in touch with them, nor was anyone visible in their supposed position. He compensated by hooking his right flank back along the road and placing machine guns to cover the weak spot. Unfortunately, the machine guns could only deliver plunging fire into the defile. As darkness fell, the 60 mm mortars of the three companies began pumping out flares—at least one every two minutes.

Private First Class Warren Wanamaker and two other Marines had taken cover in a shell crater. Wanamaker and Private First Class John Blanchard manned a machine gun, the other Marine carried a rifle. "We were trying to get the machine gun set up, trying to figure what the hell we were going to shoot at," recalled Wanamaker. "Because it was pretty dark. We had a lot of flares going. But it was almost suicide sticking your head up over that hill."

They could hear Japanese chattering on the other side of the crest, the rattle of canteens and equipment and loud whispers, "banzai! banzai!" As they tried to figure out their next move, a flare popped overhead "and there was a big Jap sticking his head right up over the hill looking down on us." They all took a shot at him and the head disappeared. But a few minutes later a couple of grenades came sizzling over the top of the hill. One of them went off with a bang in the crater and all three Marines were wounded. Wanamaker had taken some shrapnel up and down his right side. He wasn't sure he could walk—his leg felt as if he had a charlie horse—but he could still fight. His two buddies were also hurt, but still mobile.

The first sounds of the gathering attack had started at about 2300. There was much yelling and jabbering from the darkness below and enemy mortars began to work over the Marine positions. The rounds included white phosphorus, a weapon many Marines did not realize the Japanese possessed. After much probing, the full force of the attack hit at 0230. The Japanese chose their route well, concentrating on the very spot that had concerned Thompson most—the open right flank. Feeding reinforcements through the deep defile, the enemy continued to rake the F Company Marines with a heavy bombardment of white phosphorous.

The Marines had plenty of grenades and they used them lavishly to keep the slopes in front of them clear. But after a while groups of Japanese managed to get up the road through the defile. Climbing up on the bank of the defile itself, they set up a machine gun that could enfilade the Marine lines. Fox Company machine guns knocked out the gun twice, but other guns were set up in the same spot. The steady fire became too much to bear. The platoon nearest the gun began to pull back as a unit; then men began to run for the safety of Sugar Loaf. The platoon leader of the next platoon in line gave the withdrawal order, and the Marines began to abandon the Horseshoe.

Wanamaker's group was among those told to withdraw. The three wounded Marines fired a few slugs into the water jacket of their machine gun and then "limped and crawled and scratched" their way back to the secondary position. The Japanese were close behind. The Marines killed 33 Japanese as small groups attempted to reoccupy their old positions on Sugar Loaf. Others apparently succeeded in reaching the caves, joining those defenders who had escaped death earlier in the day by retreating into the honeycomb of tunnels.

Among the heroes of the night was Corporal Charles V. Horvath, a squad leader with the D Company Marines on Sugar Loaf. As enemy pressure built against his outpost position, he crawled forward to an unmanned machine gun, set it up and took the counterattacking Japanese under fire. The Japanese just kept coming "right in front of the gun, in bunches." Wounded twice, Horvath stuck to the gun until daylight. "I must have been out of my mind," was all he could say later.

Through the night and early morning hours, the Marines on Sugar Loaf could hear the Japanese digging in the hill beneath them. "We didn't know what the hell the noise was," recalled Lieutenant Frank Smith. "They were just digging through and popping out these holes again. We didn't dare shoot at night. Fortunately, they didn't jump into any of the holes we were in."

"They were like rats," remembered Horvath. "You could see this earth move and they were coming up from nothing." Horvath was crouched under incoming grenades and mortar shells when he saw something squirm out of the dirt in front of him. A Japanese officer, sword in hand, suddenly rose out of the ground and reared back to decapitate a Marine in the adjacent foxhole. "I just put the M1 in his back and emptied the whole clip," said Horvath.[1]

Irv Gehret was among the thin line of Dog Company survivors clinging to the hill. Gehret and his buddies dug a hole that was big enough for a couple of men and set up a machine gun on the edge. It was a "pretty scary place," admitted Gehret. Now and again their own artillery fire skimmed over them "damn close to the top" of the hill. A little while later the Japanese guns would reply and shells would skim over the other way. Occasionally a shell would plow right into the crest.

During the night, the Marines realized someone was out to their front. "We heard this sound, we couldn't see it," said Gehret. "It was walking." As the sound got closer and closer, one of the Marines drew a bead on a shadowy form and fired. The form went down. "It was a Jap," recalled Gehret. "His leg was bandaged up, he'd been shot in one leg. His head was bandaged up, he could only see out of one eye. And his arm was wrapped up in a sling. He had grenades in there. He couldn't even walk, he was dragging his leg." That was the sound they had heard . . . the cripple's leg dragging on the ground as he stumbled toward them. Later, whenever talking about the incident, the Marines referred to the unfortunate apparition as "the mummy."

As morning grayed the eastern sky, Corporal Tom Crunk, part of a forward observer team on Sugar Loaf, thought he heard faint cries for help from the foggy valley below the hill. During F Company's nighttime melee on the Horseshoe, many Marines had become separated from the company. Now, listening closely, Crunk distinctly heard someone calling, "Help! Help!"

Crunk, a former railroad switchman from Missouri, rounded up a couple of men. Venturing down into the shell-torn valley bottom they found a big, well-built Marine lying in a hole. During the night the Japanese had lobbed a grenade in his hole. He had thrown it out, but it was followed by another that exploded and riddled him with fragments. Unable to walk, he had managed to summon up enough strength to cry for help. Crunk and his buddies loaded the grateful Marine onto a poncho and carried him back.

They had just settled down when a machine gunner, set up on the right end of Sugar Loaf, yelled to Crunk, "Hey artillery, come here. I see something—a helmet moving out there—and I don't know whether it's a Jap or a Marine. Bring your binoculars up here and look."

Crunk scrambled up and peered through his binoculars. "Well, I can't tell," he said finally. "But I believe it is a Marine." As he gathered up another rescue party, he saw a Japanese soldier some 150 to 200 yards away running toward them across the open ground, a rifle in his hand. The man suddenly stopped and thrust the end of the rifle down into a hole. As he did, a foot shot up out of the hole and kicked him squarely in the crotch and someone reached up and twisted the rifle out of his grasp. The Japanese soldier turned and fled.

Realizing there were Americans in the hole, the Marines yelled for them to come out—they would cover them with fire. Three men emerged from the hole. All had been wounded, but all three made it to the safety of the Marine line. That left the man spotted earlier by the machine gunner. "Okay," Crunk told his rescue group. "Follow me. I'll take off and you all follow me."

The valley bottom was pocked with shell holes and littered with parachutes from flares fired during the night. The area had apparently been a vineyard at one time; now the grape vines were all sheared off about knee high. As he zig-zagged across at a dead run, Crunk became aware of shouts from behind him. He turned and looked and realized he had overrun the wounded Marine and was now on the skyline on part of the Horseshoe. "And I looked over that hill there and there were Japs everywhere," he observed. The artillery had stopped and the enemy soldiers had apparently emerged from their caves.

Crunk ran back down the slope and found the wounded man. It was a Marine and he had been hard hit through the body, but was still conscious. As the Marines rolled him onto a poncho and started back, the youngster croaked, "When we get back, don't let them give me morphine. I can't take morphine. It'll kill me." They got him back and Crunk talked the corpsman out of giving the wounded man morphine.[2]

Later in the day a major came up and asked to talk to the officer in charge of the men who had ventured out after the wounded. Crunk's lieutenant stepped forward. "Lieutenant," said the major, "I want you to know that that is not your job and your forward observer team's job to go out and get the wounded. That's the line company's job." He paused and added, "But I want you to know that I appreciate it."

Hours after Captain Mabie's D Company settled in on Sugar Loaf to stay, General Shepherd received a dispatch from his superiors at IIIAC: "Resistance and determination with which elements of your division attacked and finally captured Sugar Loaf is indicative of the fighting spirit of your men X My hearty congratulations to the officers and men concerned."

The IIIAC Periodic Report also betrayed a note of elation—or perhaps relief—behind its normally cool phrasing, observing, "The high point of the day's operation was the final seizure of this bitterly contested Sugar Loaf Hill in the Zone of the 6th Marine Division."

Colonel Robb was more blunt. "It was a hell of a price to pay," he told a news correspondent. "But we took the damn thing."

NOTES

1. Horvath kept the sword until he ended up in the naval hospital at Mare Island. There, broke, he sold it to a Seabee for $100 to raise beer money for his buddies.

2. Years later Crunk was working as county collector and treasurer in Kennett, Missouri, when an Air Force man came in and mentioned he had just returned from Okinawa. Crunk asked him if he'd ever heard of Sugar Loaf Hill. The man said he had; his former employer, a filling station operator in Oklahoma, had been shot through the spleen there. Interestingly enough, he continued, the wounded man couldn't take morphine and his life had been saved by the Marine who came out and got him and wouldn't let the corpsman inject him with morphine. As he continued with the story, Crunk realized the filling station operator was the same man he had rescued in the valley. The man survived his wounds, but had since died, said the former employee.

Chapter 11

Enter the 4th

Despite the sense of relief at IIIAC, the Japanese were not yet prepared to relinquish the Sugar Loaf anchor. Days before, when the 6th Marine Division had advanced to the Asato Gawa (Asato River), the Japanese had countered the threat of a breakthrough at Naha by bringing up four battalions of naval troops to the area south of the 44th Independent Mixed Brigade's front lines. The naval battalions were to back up the Sugar Loaf position, holding the hills northwest of the Kokuba River, guarding Shuri's western flank should the 44th IMB's defenses be penetrated.

Now, with Colonel Mita's 15th Regiment decimated, these troops were available to stiffen a new 44th IMB line between the Kokuba River and Shuri Heights or to counterattack to restore the Sugar Loaf position. Much depended on these men, for when that line collapsed, General Ushijima's flank would be open to a Marine thrust up the Kokuba River Valley behind the Shuri bastion.

Considered a motley group by regular army standards, the bulk of the new arrivals were inexperienced service troops, civilian workers and Okinawans attached to Admiral Ota's Naval Base Force built around a core of men trained in land combat. However, the battalions had a generous allotment of automatic weapons taken from supply depots on the Oroku Peninsula and from the wrecked planes that littered the peninsula's airfield.

Typically, the 3d Battalion of the so-called Iwao Force, a three-battalion group organized to reinforce the Thirty-second Army, had 415 men in two companies. Arms included 28 machine guns, 258 rifles, 27 grenade dischargers, 191 mines and 1,744 grenades. Now, even as U.S. commanders exchanged weary congratulations, new enemy troops were moving to retrieve their lost positions.

At daybreak, Companies K and L of the 3d Battalion, 4th Marines began relieving units of the 29th Marines on Sugar Loaf. Companies F and E of 2/4 took over the rest of the 29th Marines front.[1] As he moved forward, Private First Class Jack Brainerd saw an old friend coming back with the 29th Marines. The man seemed to be in a state of shock. Carrying a machine gun on one shoulder, he reached out and grabbed Brainerd with his other hand, croaking, "It's crazy up there! Absolutely nuts!"

The ground itself told some of the story. "Line after line of men had come in and occupied the same foxholes," recalled Major Phillips Carleton; "the ground along the approaches was covered with the grim detritus of battle, gear in the process of salvage, broken helmets, bits of personal possessions strewn from a wounded man's pack, broken rifles, the great piles of cardboard cases of mortar shells. The ground had become filthy with too much trampling, with occasional C ration cans. And there were always a few Japanese bodies strewn around in various stages of decay. Some had been buried, but many others lay swollen, with the greasy shine of putrefication over their exposed arms and faces."

Private First Class Paul Ulrich, a machine gunner with L Company, went with his outfit past the battered smokestack of the destroyed sugar refinery, to an open area just back of the front lines. There was a major there. He stopped them and told the L Company CO, Lieutenant Marvin D. Perskie, to go to a different hill than the one originally assigned. Word came back down the line, "Go to the same positions on the other hill." The "other hill," as it turned out, was Sugar Loaf.

Ulrich, a Pennsylvania farm boy whose last civilian job had been spraying lacquer on radio cabinets for Philco, headed toward Sugar Loaf in a crouching run. Japanese artillery was falling on the approaches. Ulrich passed a young private he knew; the man was married and had two little girls. Now he was dead. A shell had cleaved the whole top of his head off, leaving his body in the crouch he had assumed in his last instant of life. One ear hung down like a tattered rag near the chin, the other remained attached to the smashed skull. Ulrich would never have recognized him, but for some reason the dead man's pack was gone and his name was plainly visible stencilled across the back of his jacket.

Ulrich's machine-gun section made it onto the forward slope of Sugar Loaf. They scrambled to a cave or tunnel entrance and found a lone Marine from F Company, 29th Marines, tucked back just inside the doorway. Other Marines, all dead, lay scattered around an area of about 20 square feet or so. "Thank God," said the F Company survivor as Ulrich's outfit flopped down by the hole. The Marine had both arms and one leg bandaged, but had retained possession of his Browning Automatic Rifle (BAR). He had wormed his way back into the entranceway of the cave so he would be able to fire on any Japanese coming around the corner. Alone and surrounded by his dead buddies, he had been prepared to fight—now, with the arrival of L Company, it appeared he would also survive.

Also up on the hill was Lieutenant Danny Brewster. A veteran of the fighting on Guam, Brewster was something of a legend in his outfit. Heir to a Baltimore chemical company fortune, he had been commissioned at the age of 19, reportedly becoming the youngest officer in the Marine Corps. His father had fought with Lem Shepherd in World War I and Brewster, who dropped out of Princeton to join the Marines, could presumably have sat out the war in a safer berth. That was not his style. He insisted on a combat slot and ended up with L Company's 1st Platoon.

Now it seemed to Brewster that the elements of the 29th he had been sent to relieve were barely holding the hill. Heavy small arms, mortar and artillery fire was falling, and there were still Japanese in the tunnels down under the hill. Brewster found a noncommissioned officer (NCO) from the 29th who promptly extinguished whatever optimism Brewster had left when he blurted, "Thank God you're here! There's not many of us left!" Brewster called to his platoon sergeant, Philip "Paddy" Doyle, to tell him how he wanted to deploy the three squads in his platoon. As they were talking, a knee mortar shell blew Doyle's head off. Fragments also slammed into Brewster's legs, knocking him down. Ignoring his injuries, Brewster got his platoon settled in as fast as he could. As they were digging in, Japanese would emerge periodically from the caves and the Marines would pause to shoot at them.

A historian of the campaign noted that "the reliefs were effected smoothly despite the difficult terrain, steady bombardment, and opposition from small enemy groups which had infiltrated the lines during the night." That complacence was not echoed in the special action report of the 4th Marines, which noted, "the relief was a very difficult maneuver and was accomplished at a cost of over 70 casualties, due mostly to mortar and artillery fire. The 4th had to practically fight its way into the lines and the 29th to fight its way out."

Moving up with 2/4 to the forward slope of Half Moon, Private First Class Tom McKinney stumbled across the bodies of an officer, a radioman and another Marine sprawled in a little bowl in the ground. "They had been laying up there two or three days, judging by the condition of the bodies," he recalled. They still had their weapons. The dead radioman still had his radio strapped on. "But they were all shot to hell," observed McKinney. "Evidently, a nambu worked them over. They were full of bullet holes. It was terrible."

Among those leaving the line was Private Ken Long. A Marine from the relief unit tumbled into his foxhole, announcing, "Piss call." It was the first bit of humor Long had heard in two weeks, but he didn't waste any time on introductions. "I got the hell out of there," he remarked. As his company regrouped for the hike to the rear, Long noticed that everyone seemed to be in a daze, their eyes red and sunken, their personal equipment in disarray. There was no conversation and "definitely no smart remarks." Walking back in a stupor, his head down, Long stopped as his rifle butt smashed into something. He slowly raised his eyes and found he had inadvertently run into General Shepherd himself—the rifle butt had struck the division commander in the knee. "He didn't show any signs of discomfort, but it seemed to me he did have a look of compassion in his eyes," remembered Long. "Not a word was spoken and I moved around in front of the jeep and continued to walk. It was the only time that I had seen the man."

Even as Long walked back, his unit's old position was under attack. At about 1600 the enemy launched a counterattack against the left flank of the 4th Marines clinging to the small section of Half Moon Hill seized by the 29th the day before. The attack, supported by heavy mortar fire, was broken up. The Marines claimed 65 Japanese killed. Nevertheless, concerned about security, the Marine flank was withdrawn to more defensible ground 300 yards to the north, where they dug in for the night.

The morning of 20 May did not start well for Paul Ulrich, dug in on Sugar Loaf with his machine-gun section. As it got light, a fire team leader slid into their hole. He had a piece of paper in his hand with the assignments for the day. The man raised his head up over the edge of the foxhole and was surveying the points mentioned in the assignment sheet when a sniper shot him in the middle of the forehead. The fire team leader clapped a hand to his forehead and said, "Oh, mother," and slumped over dead.

Corporal Robert Powers, a former Raider and veteran of Bougainville and Guam, was told to take out a three-man patrol to reconnoiter the Horseshoe that morning. Powers and the three Marines made it to the top of the ridge and looked down on the reverse slope to what "must have been a couple of platoons of Nips . . . and there was some officer or NCO with a sword out and he was trying to incite them." Someone spotted the Marine patrol and the Japanese opened fire. "God, it must have been 20 or 30 of them that fired at us, automatic weapons," recalled Powers.

All three of the Marines in Powers's patrol were hit. Two were killed outright in the first sweep of bullets; one man, a fellow Minnesotan and good friend of Powers, died instantly as the top of his head disappeared. The other man took two bullets in the chest and also died on the spot. The third Marine, also shot in the chest, remained conscious. Powers scooped him up in a makeshift fireman's carry and scrambled down the hill as best he could. As he stumbled across an open area, a Japanese soldier popped up out of a spider hole. Powers hit the ground, dropping the wounded man and scratching for a grenade. "I had a WP [white phosphorus] grenade and a fragmentation grenade and I threw them both over there," he recalled. "I think we got him because when everything cleared, nothing happened. He didn't come out again." Powers picked up his wounded buddy and made it the rest of the way back to friendly lines.

Though there were plenty of Japanese in the area, both assault battalions of the 4th Marines made promising gains on 20 May. Jumping off at 0800 behind heavy artillery fire and tanks, the assault troops moved rapidly for 200 yards before running into fierce opposition from Horseshoe and Half Moon. The 22d Marines on the right provided fire support for 3/4 as that outfit attacked the high ground on the western end of the Horseshoe. Their method of attack was to send the tanks out ahead to methodically close or reduce all visible cave openings by fire from their 75 mm guns or by flame from the two flamethrowing "zippo" tanks supporting the attack. Infantry would then move in with portable flamethrowers and demolitions.

Lieutenant Marvin Perskie led Ulrich's machine gunners toward the Horseshoe. Perskie normally wore thick glasses, but he'd apparently lost or misplaced them because he wasn't wearing them and he seemed to be having trouble seeing. "Where is that damn railroad?" he asked a squad leader. The squad leader pointed out the railroad in front of them and some little brush covered knobs beyond. The lieutenant said they were supposed to go down across the railroad and occupy the knobs, which stood about 10 or 15 feet high.

The machine gunners set up a line behind the little knobs and started firing. Ulrich stopped to change a gun barrel. "I looked to my left," he recalled, "and saw three mortar rounds land, one-two-three, right in a row. It was just a perfectly straight line with where we were. And I said, 'Uh oh, here they come. Turn around.' "

Ulrich threw himself forward, simultaneously turning his helmet around to better protect the back of his neck. The fourth mortar round went off when he was still in the air. An ammo box by his left foot flew about 20 feet into the air. Ulrich was flipped over and metal drove into his left foot and leg. Nearby, Ulrich's buddy Corporal Cal Frost had dropped his head down toward his chest to protect his face, a reaction which may have saved his life. Metal fragments hit him in the arms and chest, but missed any vital organs.

Four other Marines had taken cover in a large hole, apparently the beginning of an unfinished Okinawan tomb. By some freak of ballistics, two had been hit badly, the other two weren't even touched by the blast. One of the severely wounded Marines was Private First Class George Stovall. A chunk of metal had driven into his chest, leaving a hole about three quarters of an inch long. He was in bad shape.

Ulrich was also hit worse than anyone knew. Superficially, it looked as though he had taken a peppering in the leg—serious enough to get him off the line, but not bad enough to cripple him. "Ohhh you lucky bastard!" his buddies kidded him. "You got hit in the foot. You can go home now."

Frost and Ulrich started back. "The foot was numb and I was walking on it and he was helping me," recalled Ulrich. "We got part way back up Sugar Loaf Hill, right out in the open, and I couldn't go any more. I was getting dizzy. And he saw my left trouser leg was full of all just red blood. He put his fingers in the hole and ripped the trouser leg open and I can still see the blood pumping out with every heartbeat. I severed the main artery in my left leg." He was bleeding to death.

Somewhere, Ulrich never knew where, Frost found a bit of rope and a stick. He tourniqueted the leg and gave Ulrich a shot of morphine. Some stretcher bearers suddenly appeared, loaded Ulrich onto a litter and lugged him back to the battalion aid station. Ulrich had a habit of checking his watch at the most curious times. When they had landed on Okinawa on 1 April he had looked at his watch and noted that they were three minutes behind schedule. He did the same thing when he was wounded. He had been hit at exactly 2:15 P.M., Sunday afternoon, 20 May.

To the east of L Company, the 2d Battalion's attack on the Half Moon was turning into the usual nightmare. Heavy and accurate flat trajectory fire from the direction of Shuri Heights shot up the battalion's flank. Mortars operating from defiladed positions on the reverse slopes of Half Moon covered the entire zone of advance. Japanese resistance continued to harden throughout the morning as the enemy fought to hold the dominating ground.

At 1130 with all three rifle companies in the assault and casualties rising, Lieutenant Colonel Reynolds H. Hayden decided to shift the attack from the front of Half Moon to the flanks. F Company held its lines in the center and supported an attack by E Company south down the division boundary. G Company was to drive past Sugar Loaf and then turn to attack the reverse slopes of Half Moon from the southwest. One company of tanks would provide overhead fire support, while a second tank company assisted Companies E and G in a double envelopment of the hill.

The details of the plan were in place by 1245 and the attack was renewed. The tanks with G Company picked their way through a mine field on the right flank of Half Moon. Stiffened with this support, the infantry was able to seize and hold the western end of the hill. The tanks with E Company were less successful. A tank bulldozer attempting to provide an approach route to the east of the hill broke down, and the tanks were unable to reach positions where they could bring fire on the reverse slopes. Torn by grenades and mortar fire from three sides as they advanced, the left wing of the envelopment took heavy casualties. E Company finally dug in on Half Moon's forward slopes. The night positions of the 2d Battalion and the Japanese defenders were close, but remained somewhat insulated by a swath of no man's land along the hill crest swept by continual mortar and artillery fire—both from Japanese and from friendly guns.

The 3d Battalion was having better luck. Cave positions honeycombing the forward slopes of the Horseshoe were blasted by the tanks, then burned out by flamethrowers and closed with demolitions. The extent of the underground defenses continued to surprise the Marines. Sometimes a charge or smoke shell would be placed in one cave entrance and smoke and dust would spew from five or six other entrances in the vicinity—or even from the other side of the hill.

Among the heroes of the day was Corporal Hugh Vogel, reconnaissance noncom of a 37 mm antitank platoon with Weapons Company. Vogel was assigned to observe enemy fire so he could direct the return fire of his platoon. To gain a better perspective, he ventured out past the front lines where he came upon an enemy dual-purpose 13 mm weapon. Materializing out of nowhere, he killed the crew, captured the gun and turned it on the Japanese, destroying a mortar position and killing all members of the mortar crew, according to his citation.

By 1600 when the regiment stopped the attack to go into night defenses, Companies K and L held the dominating ground overlooking the Japanese mortar emplacements in the Horseshoe bowl. Colonel Shapley anticipated a counterattack in the 3d Battalion area—specifically on Captain Marvin "Stormy" Sexton's K Company—and alerted the 1st Battalion to back up the Marines defending the Horseshoe. B Company drew the job. "It was getting dusk and we were told to place our gear where we could find it in the dark because it was possible that we may have to move out sometime that night," noted Private First Class C. Stuart Upchurch. "This seemed unusual for it was SOP [standard operating procedure] that at night we didn't leave our foxhole for anything. The only people who left their holes were corpsmen, telephone men and stretcher bearers. And plenty of them were shot by their own men."

Back at the 3d Battalion aid station, Paul Ulrich was still lying on the ground, his artery tied off by the surgeon, awaiting evacuation. It was going to be a while. Just after Ulrich came in, an amtrac loaded with wounded had taken a direct hit from a Japanese artillery shell. The explosion killed everyone aboard. Rather than risk another such occurrence, the aid station decided to keep everyone there until after dark.

Ulrich's friend, George Stovall, lay to his left; he was obviously dying from his chest wound. The irony was Stovall didn't even have to be there. His brother had been killed in Europe and his father had died since he'd been overseas. Back on Guadalcanal, before the division staged out for Okinawa, Colonel Shapley had called the young Michigan Marine in and told him he could go home since he was the last surviving male in the family. "No," said Stovall. "I'll stick this out. It'll probably be the last one." Now, he apparently realized he was dying, and he was not going easily. It took five men to hold him on the stretcher as he thrashed around. Finally he stopped fighting. He was dead.

After dark, some men with flashlights guided the amtracs forward and Ulrich was evacuated to a big army hospital. An army medic gave him a cup of coffee that tasted like he'd put about a pound of sugar in it. Later that night, as Ulrich was being taken by landing craft to the hospital ship USS *Relief*, he got sick. The crew lifted him to the rail and he lost all that wonderful sweet coffee over the side. A few days later, a corpsman called the nurse over to Ulrich's bed and said, "Look at this." He counted off spots where pieces of shrapnel, most about half the size of a match head, had hit the Pennsylvanian's leg. There were 64. That did not include the half-inch sized chunk that drove into the joint of the ankle.

Colonel Shapley's suspicion that the Japanese would counterattack his 3d Battalion became a reality at about 2200 when a battalion-sized enemy group hit the positions of K and L Companies, following a barrage of 90 mm mortar shells.

Private First Class Paolo DeMeis, a tough little Italian kid from Brooklyn, had seen two banzai attacks on Guam—he'd taken a bayonet in the guts during one of them—but this attack looked nothing like a banzai. "This one was synchronized," he recalled. "They weren't messing around. They meant business and they *really* meant it. They weren't hopped up. They weren't smashed and they weren't drunk. There was no banging the bottles. First the mortars and all that shit and all that artillery and smoke . . . and then they came."

Still a few hundred yards out, the Japanese looked like squat little green cartoon characters in the light of the flares. DeMeis could hear one of the Marines radioing for artillery support; "he was yelling his brains out" correcting the fire on the approaching Japanese infantry. Enemy mortar and artillery fire pounded the Marines as the Japanese sought to cover the assault.

Private First Class John Eason, the 19-year-old son of a Michigan dentist, was in a foxhole on the left of K Company. One by one, three foxholes to his left were knocked out by artillery rounds. Another shell struck directly in front of his own hole, but he escaped injury. As the Japanese closed on his position, Eason worked out a defense with an L Company Marine off to his left. The L Company Marine was in the curve of the hill and could see the area directly in front of Eason's hole without exposing his head. Similarly, Eason could see in front of the L Company man's hole without exposing his own head. "He'd yell at me to toss grenades at 10 o'clock or whatever," recalled Eason, and Eason would do the same for him. Between them, they kept the slope fairly clear of marauding Japanese.

But the Japanese had hit the company with at least a battalion—450 to 500 men—and there was no stopping them all. Soon they were in among the foxholes. One of the forward observers was calling for artillery and Eason heard him shout, "I know goddammit it's right on top of us—but so are the Japs!"

The Marine sharing the hole with DeMeis had found a Japanese knee mortar left there by a previous tenant. There were eight or nine shells for it and he fired them all off at the advancing enemy. It didn't seem to help much. "There was no let-up," recalled DeMeis. "They just kept coming. And you know how it is, it looked like they're all coming for *you*. For a while it was just like a Wild West shootout, people were running all over the place. Grenades coming from both ways." DeMeis went through every clip he had for a BAR he had picked up, then shot off the better part of two bandoliers of M1 ammo.

Enemy infantrymen ran through the position. "What was funny was, if they missed you in the foxhole, they kept right on going," noted Eason. "They had one goal—to get on through —and they figured somebody else coming behind would get you anyway. If you were a few steps one way or the other, they would keep on going."

Eason raised up to shoot a scuttling figure with his carbine. Just as he went to pull the trigger, a shell fragment took the stock off right behind the trigger guard. Somehow it missed his hand. He didn't have much ammunition left anyway, so he dropped back into the hole and started whittling the stub down with his K-bar. He was crouched down in the hole when a Japanese suddenly loomed up at the edge with a bayonetted rifle. "I think he thought he had me," observed Eason. The Japanese lunged forward with the bayonet and Eason instinctively raised his left arm to ward him off. By some miracle of miracles, the bayonet slipped harmlessly under his left armpit between his arm and his chest. Holding his K-bar in his left hand, Eason thrust the knife into the other man, at the same time jerking him forward and up on the blade. "I think he was one surprised Japanese," he recalled. It was perhaps a sign of his own state of mind that he then took the dead man and pitched him—knife and all—back down the slope.

K Company was holding, but for a while it was touch and go. "They kind of poured over," Corporal Robert Powers said of the Japanese. "It's such an eerie deal; you look out and there's nothing there, then a flare goes up and they're right next to you. There were guys running by me—Nips—and we were trying to take a swipe at them. It was just a mess."

A 1st Division Marine watching from the heights to the east later told Eason his outfit had been told three times to pull back and close off the right flank because the 4th Marines were being overrun. Each time the order was rescinded. All they could see down below, he told Eason, was an area of red—and it just kept getting bigger and bigger and bigger from all the artillery and mortars exploding on K Company battlefield.

Surrounded by chaos, John Eason did a strange thing. "During that fire fight, I'd run out of ammunition and everything—and I'd heard them call the artillery in on top of us," Eason recalled. "And I thought, what the hell. My knees were hurting, cramped from kneeling in that foxhole. And I thought, 'I'm going to get it anyway. I'm going to go out right.' So I sat on the edge of that foxhole with my feet down in it and lit a cigarette and sat there smoking it. . . . And one of the guys in the next foxhole yelled at me to get the hell down, so I did, but I can still remember sitting on the edge of that foxhole smoking a cigarette because my knees hurt so much. I didn't have anything left to fight with anyway. I figured, what the hell . . . I wasn't going to go out with sore knees. I can still remember looking up the line and seeing the machine gun and the barrel was a nice cherry red, but it was bent like you'd hold your finger up and bend it just a little bit. They'd been firing it so much up there that it was just cherry red. It was shot. Light machine gun. We laughed about how they were using it to shoot downhill without exposing themselves. Your sense of humor gets warped when you're up there."

The melee lasted for two hours in the garish light of the flares. "Anguished and fearful shouts filled the air," a Marine wrote later. "Men shouting to their comrades, Japs and Marines trying to identify movements, rebuild lines in the dark. 'Who's that?' 'Sound off or I'll shoot.' 'You okay?' 'There's a Nip, shoot the bastard!' 'Mac, look out, there's a Nip.' Shouts, curses, open prayers and flashes of grenades."

By midnight, the few Japanese who had penetrated the lines were either dead or trying to withdraw. "There was still some popping going on, not much, but you heard it," noted Paolo DeMeis. One survivor compared it to the last few kernels of popcorn popping off. The air was very wet; it was misting and John Eason saw a line of Marines emerge from the haze behind him. It was B Company. He thought they were about the prettiest thing he'd ever seen.

The new arrivals were from B Company, and they included Private First Class C. Stuart Upchurch. Upchurch and three other Marines were told to deploy on top of the rise to protect the mortar platoon. There they found the deepest foxholes Upchurch had ever seen. Apparently the holes had changed hands a few times, and each newcomer had dug a little deeper. Upchurch had to stand on a shelf to see over the parapet.

A forward observer (FO) from the navy cruiser was dug in nearby, and he was having some kind of trouble with his radio contact on the ship. Upchurch could hear the man yelling into the radio, "You tell that fucking captain that I want the flares *all night* long and I want one every 15 seconds or tomorrow I'll come back on board and kill the son of a bitch." The Marines couldn't believe a young officer would talk that way about his captain, but "we were told that the FO when he was directing fire sort of owns the ship," observed Upchurch. In any case, they got their flares. Gruesome light was also provided by an unfortunate Marine from the 1st Platoon. Sometime during the night the Marine was shot and the hit set off three white phosphorus grenades he was carrying. His body burned until morning.

Returning from the K Company command post (CP) where he had gone to get more grenades, Corporal Joe McNamara helped guide the B Company men into the front line. Now, returning to his foxhole, he saw his platoon sergeant, another sergeant and a B Company noncom all crowded into the hole adjacent to his. A corpsman was lying beside the hole. McNamara considered this gathering most unwise, but he was exhausted and the platoon sergeant was in charge, so he kept his mouth shut and ducked down in his foxhole to try to get some sleep. It seemed he had no sooner closed his eyes than a terrific explosion blew him partly out of the hole. "So I'm standing there in the hole and it felt like somebody'd hit me in the right side of the head with a baseball bat," he recalled. Another Marine came up to him and said, "Mac, lie down, you're wounded."

McNamara's right sleeve was wet with blood, but when he ran an exploratory hand under his jacket, he found no wound. "I'm not," he replied. Then he turned and looked at the adjacent foxhole. The B Company noncom was in precisely the same position McNamara last saw him in, except now he had no head. A mortar shell had sprayed the man's head all over McNamara's combat jacket. The corpsman who had been lying by the side of the foxhole was also dead, chopped up by shell fragments; he "looked like a pile of rags." The platoon sergeant was out of his head from concussion and had to be evacuated. The other sergeant stayed, but seemed unusually quiet. Soon afterward another mortar shell whispered in and badly wounded him, too. Corporal Joe McNamara suddenly found himself in charge of a platoon.

The morning light revealed an abattoir of dead Marines and Japanese and shattered body parts strewn through the K Company area. "Pieces of bodies were seen everywhere thrown into the oozy mud or splashed against boulders flanking the valley," noted a Marine. Men had been cut in half, severed arms, legs and detached heads were strewn about. When Frank Hepburn, a G Company Marine came through the area, he was awed to see he could reach down almost anywhere and pick up a piece of shrapnel, the shelling had been so heavy. "The drizzle had washed off the surface mud of both metal and flesh and these articles in the mud stood out startlingly real in the hazy light," he recalled.

Hepburn was careful to step in the footprints of the man ahead of him, lest he step onto a body. Lumps of mud with pieces of weapons, bandoliers of bullets and live grenades lay about among the flesh. Where flesh could not be identified positively, he assumed it was Japanese, but here and there he could see the black letters USMC printed on the blouse pockets of Marine dungaree jackets. The leather Marine boondockers were easy to identify. "No one walking through the area dared to disturb anything," he observed. "By moving a shoe, we might learn there was a body under it. A cartridge belt meant there was a torso under it. We dared not lift a helmet."

Among the survivors was Paolo DeMeis. He noticed almost in passing that a lot of the Marines were walking around "with those brown stars on the back of their pants. Shit plastered on the back of their pants." The man he had fought with all night was being carried out on a litter. An hour or two after midnight, the Marine, a former Raider, had told DeMeis he didn't feel right, he'd been hit. A corpsman took care of the wound, which looked like a small slice in the right shoulder area. The Marine was talking and seemed fine as they carried him out, but DeMeis later heard he died.

Morning found John Eason still intact and uninjured. Before the U.S. artillery had opened up that night he had looked down into the small enclave in front of him and seen Japanese bodies "stacked up like stacks of oats." They were everywhere. Now, in the morning, after all the U.S. artillery fire on the approaches, he looked over the edge of his little part of the hill "and it looked like a plowed field. There wasn't anything left."

Private First Class William Scott, a farmer-turned-Marine from Iowa, had gone through a whole box of grenades during the night. The embankment in front of him was fairly steep and he had heard the Japanese as they scrambled up. Now, peering over the edge, he found two dead Japanese sprawled in front of his foxhole. Each man carried a light machine gun. The first corpse was so close, Scott was able to reach out from his foxhole and pick the nambu out of his arms. The second Japanese was six or eight feet behind the leader. By the looks of him, one of Scott's grenades had gone off right under his chin.

But the thing that impressed Scott the most that morning, was the smell in the air. There was so much blood saturating K Company positions, he recalled, "it smelled like hamburger." Some of that blood was on him. During the early morning hours, he had helped two badly wounded Marines back to an aid station behind Sugar Loaf. Both had been bleeding hard, and their blood soaked Scott's dungarees. "I mean I was completely saturated," he recalled. "And in a couple of days I smelled like I was dead."

The enemy battalion-sized force involved in the attack had been destroyed. The 4th Marines counted 494 Japanese dead in front of their positions. A search of 16 bodies was completed before being interrupted by shell and small-arms fire. Forty more were searched in the 22d Marines area. "The enemy uniforms were relatively clean and fresh," noted a U.S. intelligence report. "Some articles of U.S. Marine Corps gear, such as helmet and cartridge belts, were worn."

The viciousness and size of the effort showed how seriously the enemy regarded the penetration of Shuri's western flank. The dead were Japanese troops, not Okinawan forces. One corpse carried identification indicating he was a 2d class seaman. Also found among the carnage was a 1st class seaman's insignia and a postal savings folder belonging to a member of a naval flight engineers unit. A later search turned up IDs from the 1st Independent Battalion and numerous naval IDs, indicating that many of the enemy had been naval service troops brought up from Naha. This was confirmed three days later when I Company, 4th Marines, captured a badly wounded prisoner from a naval unit who said he had participated in the counterattack. Before the man died, he told interrogators his 300–man unit had been ordered north from Oroku about 17 May and subsequently joined elements of the 15th Independent Mixed Regiment in the counterattack of 20 May. "POW believes his own unit was wiped out and said that it had been hit by a heavy concentration of all weapons," noted a U.S. intelligence report.

The 6th Marine Division attacked again on 21 May. Its objective was the upper reaches of the Asato River.

The 4th Marines made the main effort. The 22d conformed to the advance and delivered supporting fire. Under the command of Lieutenant Colonel George B. Bell, 1/4 (less C Company which was in regimental reserve) attacked in the center down the southern slope of Sugar Loaf toward the eastern end of the Horseshoe. Progress was slow and the fighting was bitter as Companies A and B struggled to reach the river. In his diary, machine gunner Melvin Heckt recorded what happened to his buddies after B Company passed through the K Company positions at about 0800:

"Donvito was the first to be hit. Shrapnel in the hip. Dunham was next. He received a concussion and possible broken collar bone. I couldn't believe he was hit. I just couldn't believe it. I just looked at him and didn't say a word. Next, Ward Bowers was killed by Nip artillery.

"[At] 9:30 we were held up in reserve of 2nd and 3rd platoons. We were in a couple of bomb craters. Cullen was passing by with a piece of shrapnel in his back. Andriola was helping him walk back when a Nambu opened up and wounded Andriola in [the] buttocks and Cullen in [the] leg. Hassell was close to them and ran out to drag them out of the fire lane and was hit in [the] nose, mouth and arm. McGee and Congdon ran out and drug Cullen, Hasell and Andriola to safe positions.

"The artillery and mortar fire became heavier and more intense, so I took my section and ran across the open field to [Lieutenant Richard] Baumhardt's 3rd platoon. It is lucky we moved out for Congdon was killed in [the] location from which we came and probably more of us would have been killed had we not moved. Maritato was hit in [the] buttocks and testicle. Acuna was hit. We tried to set up lines and contact A Company. A placed M.G.s in and had the men get in a ditch by the R.R. track. Supposedly this was the safest position anywhere. But the Nips lobbed a mortar shell right in the ditch and killed instantly three of my men. Jennings, Ablett and McGee.

"Simons was sitting with the other three and received shrapnel in [the] leg, arm and side. I patched him up while the corpsman administered plasma and albumen. Simons will be O.K. Well, that makes 6 men killed out of my squad. Too damn many to lose for any damn land. Poor Red McGee was blown all over the side of the hill. Only his red hair and scalp remained where he had been sitting. Jennings, a devout Catholic and one of the most religious among us, said before his death, 'It will be only by the grace of God for those who remain to walk today.' He never knew what hit him for it was concussion. I could hardly recognize his body for it was blown up twice the normal size."

Also hit early on was Corporal Joe McNamara, knocked sprawling by a shell fragment in the shoulder. Fortunately, it had hit flat, pushing instead of slicing. But when McNamara got up, he found his left arm hanging useless. Over his protests, a corpsman tagged him for evacuation. "Okay, but if nothing's wrong, I'll be back," insisted McNamara. But back at the battalion aid station he found a horrifying scene with doctors in bloody aprons working over badly wounded Marines. Men lay on stretchers, bottles of plasma hanging over them. It was, thought McNamara, "like something out of Dante's." They didn't even bother with McNamara. They put him on an amtrac and by the end of the day he found himself at the 6th Marine Division Hospital.[2]

Rain fell steadily throughout the morning and most of the afternoon. The shell-torn ground became muddy and slippery. Supply became difficult. The Marines managed an advance of some 200 yards, fighting both the weather and the many enemy pockets of resistance along the approaches to the river. The 3d Battalion attacked into the interior of the Horseshoe, which now no longer offered protection to the Japanese on the reverse side. Demolitions and flamethrowers were utilized to wipe out resistance in the nest of enemy mortar positions. Companies K and L halted their drive in midafternoon and set up a defense line about halfway between the Horseshoe and the Asato Gawa. The mortars in the interior of the Horseshoe had been neutralized. On the division left, 2/4 made negligible advances under the heavy fire brought to bear from Shuri.

By midnight on 21 May, heavy rains recommenced. Efforts to resupply the assault troops and replenish forward dumps bogged down in the thick mud. "The major obstacle to the success of the 6th Division's new plan of attack was not the fiercely resisting enemy defenders, but the unrelenting torrents of water that poured out of the heavens and rapidly turned southern Okinawa into a sea of mud," wrote a Marine historian of the campaign.

A good part of that rain seemed to be pouring into Stuart Upchurch's foxhole. Toward midnight, Upchurch had spotted two intruders in the light of a flare and gunned them both down with a long burst from his BAR.

Now, coming off watch, he drifted into sleep only to be jarred awake by an explosion. Cries came from an adjacent foxhole. "They weren't crying 'Mama' like those about to die cried," he observed. "These were asking for help and crying at the same time." As Upchurch tried to get out of his foxhole, something smashed into the top of his helmet, slamming it down around his ears. After a dazed instant, he realized that a Japanese soldier was hitting him over the head. Upchurch grabbed an M1 just as his attacker slipped in the mud by the edge of the hole. The Japanese, who appeared to have a saber in his hand, tried to regain his balance. Upchurch fired four fast rounds with the M1, hitting his attacker in the middle of the chest and dropping him like a wet rag. The "saber" turned out to be a four-foot stick of bamboo.

The Japanese had apparently tossed his last grenade into the adjoining foxhole before attacking Upchurch. The two men in the other hole were severely hurt. One Marine's legs had been mangled, the other man had been hit in the testicles. The man hit in the testicles was in terrible pain and hard to sooth. A corpsman gave him a shot of morphine and quieted him down, but he started keening again when Upchurch said he was going to throw two grenades out front. The corpsman hugged the wounded Marine and whispered assurance that everything was going to be all right. Upchurch threw the grenades and there was no more reaction from the front. It was daylight before the stretcher bearers came up and took the two wounded men out. One lost both legs, the other had to have his testicles removed.

In the gathering light, another Marine turned over the Japanese Upchurch had shot. "He's still alive!" the man shouted. "The son of a bitch is still alive! Damn!" And with that, he put two shots into the enemy soldier's head. Upchurch somewhat resented the other Marine shooting his victim again; in fact, he doubted the Japanese was alive at all. The enemy soldier looked to be about 15 years old. He had been wounded in one thigh and the injury had been crudely bandaged. Upchurch went through the man's pockets and found some photos and a small amount of money. Months later he spent the money in Japan—in a whorehouse.

By now, after five days of unfruitful combat in the Half Moon area, General Shepherd had become persuaded that the guns on the Shuri Heights would continue to prevent the seizure of Half Moon. Until the 1st Marine Division could seize Shuri, Half Moon would have to wait.

Unable to swing eastward for a close envelopment of Shuri, Shepherd changed the direction of the division's attack. He decided to establish a strong reverse slope defense on his left, on Half Moon, "making no further attempt to drive to the southeast in the face of the Shuri fire, and to concentrate the division's effort on a penetration to the south and southwest" toward Naha. He subsequently directed 3/22 to take up positions facing almost directly east, toward the Shuri Hill mass. The battalion was to maintain contact between the battalions of the 4th Marines on the right and the 1st Marine Division on the left. Shepherd believed this arrangement would partly relieve the menace to his left flank and support his division's effort to envelope Shuri from the west.

On 22 May, the Marines drove toward the bank of the Asato Gawa against sporadic and ineffective resistance. IIIAC intelligence reported, "Overrun strong points were found to contain enemy dead, but few weapons other than rifles, indicating automatic weapons and much used knee mortars were being carried to the rear as strong points became untenable." Patrols crossed the river and advanced 200 yards into the outskirts of Naha before drawing scattered enemy fire. Plans were laid for a crossing in force for 23 May. At 1030 Companies A and B of 1/4 and I and L of 3/4 began wading the river. By 1100, they had established a firm line on the opposite bank.

General Geiger shifted the boundary of the 1st Marine Division to the right so 2/4 could close up and better protect the left flank and rear of the 4th Marines' bridgehead. Meanwhile, heavy rains flooded the Asato Gawa, turning it into a chest-high torrent. Engineers struggled to get bridging material forward so the 4th Marines could expand their penetration.

As the rain beat down on the ruins of Shuri Castle the night of 22 May, General Ushijima called a conference. The Shuri Line was cracking. On the western flank, the 6th Marine Division had finally broken the Sugar Loaf triad. The Marines were now in a position to flank the Shuri Line. On the eastern coast, GIs of the U.S. 96th Infantry Division had forced a breakthrough at Conical Hill and XXIV Corps was pouring the U.S. 7th Infantry Division through the hole. The Japanese Thirty-second Army was in danger of being encircled in the Shuri fortress.

Interviewing Colonel Yahara after the war, U.S. interrogators reported the operations officer's view that, "The capture of Sugar Loaf Hill alone could have been solved by the withdrawal of the left flank to positions south of Naha and, in Colonel Yahara's opinion would not have seriously endangered the defense of Shuri. However, the loss of remaining positions on

Conical Hill in conjunction with the pressure in the west rendered the defense of Shuri extremely difficult."

Ushijima was faced with a choice: he could fight to the end from the Shuri Line; he could withdraw to the Chinen Peninsula; or he could retreat 11 miles south to a new line across the Yaeju Dake-Yuza Dake Escarpment with its many caves and stockpiles of ammunition and weapons left by the 24th Division when it moved north to the Shuri Line. More than 60,000 of his troops were dead. The 62d and 24th Divisions and the 44th Independent Mixed Brigade had been shattered. The Shuri Line was on the verge of collapse.

One major drawback to making a last stand at Shuri was the shrinking size of the position. Trying to cram the estimated 50,000 surviving officers and men into a final defense area less than a mile in diameter would be self-defeating. Once surrounded, noted the Japanese, these troops would become "easy prey" for superior American firepower. The best solution—and the best way to prolong the battle—Ushijima decided, was to withdraw his surviving troops to the escarpment. There, backs to the sea, they would fight to the death.

Withdrawal of the ammunition and wounded would begin immediately. Communications and service units would follow. Artillery units would come next, followed by the combat infantry on 29 May. A shell of a defense would be maintained to delude the Americans into believing the final stand would be at Shuri. Hopefully, the rains would help conceal the withdrawal from enemy observation. The shielding force, consisting of some 5,000 men, would hang on until 31 May.

Walking wounded started to leave their hospital caves on 24 May. Now the true horror and impossibility of the Japanese situation began to emerge for all to see. Noboru Kuriyama, a soldier with the Thirty-second Army, recalled seeing from 300 to 400 wounded, some of them double amputees, crawling along the road, pleading to be taken along. "They used shovels as crutches," he recalled. "We couldn't take them and it still bothers me." Those too seriously hurt to move were killed or abandoned. Many were given grenades or potassium of cyanide so they could end their own misery. The survivors headed south. Once the soldiers had treasured their weapons, guarding their rifles against the smallest scratch, observed an officer. Now their rusty weapons trailed in the mud as the exhausted men straggled away from the Shuri Line.

Among the survivors from Sugar Loaf was a farmer named Masatsugu Shinohara. He had originally been assigned to man mortar positions on the hill's southern slope. Subsisting mostly on dried biscuits, he and his comrades tried not to move during the daytime except when called on to fire their mortars. Still, American firepower exacted a steady toll. When Shinohara finally withdrew, he was one of only five survivors from his 60–man unit. Visions of glory were long gone. Wrote a Japanese soldier bitterly, "It was no longer a glorious man-to-man fight but a grotesquely one-sided process in which a gigantic iron organism crushed and pulverized human flesh."

NOTES

1. As the battalion prepared to move forward, a strange and tragic thing occurred. A plane flying overhead suddenly burst into flames, swerved and crashed among the assembled Marines. Nearly 30 were killed or injured.

2. The next day McNamara felt better, and he insisted on returning to his unit.

Chapter 12

Bitter Victory

The 6th Marine Division was in firm possession of Sugar Loaf. But there was little mood for celebration. There were too many dead Marines to bury.

A man from the 29th Marines recalled how his sergeant asked for volunteers to go up on Sugar Loaf and gather the dead. "He stated to us that Marines take care of their dead. And there are a lot of Marines on and around Sugar Loaf Hill that needed to be buried. And he said it was important that we get up there now at that time because some of them had been hit five days previously or so and were now disintegrating and some of them might be melting into the ground. I thought that was quite a statement."

Private First Class Robert Rooney volunteered to go up on Sugar Loaf and help collect the dead of the 29th Marines. They found bodies all over, not just from the 29th—identifiable by the circles painted on the backs of their helmet covers and jackets—but from the 4th Marines and 22d Marines as well. "We had to pick up a handful of machine gun belts and wrap them around their arm and try to slide them," recalled Rooney. "And if you did, you'd pull an arm off. Then you'd try to get them around both legs." The recovery party had some fold-up stretchers, and they tried to roll the corpses onto them. "You couldn't find dog tags on half of them," observed Rooney. "The ones that were wounded and died, they still had the bandages; some of them had made the attempt to put their own bandage on stomach wounds. [They were] bloated up."

The relatively whole bodies were picked up first, explained a Headquarters Company Marine. "And since most Marines carried ponchos with them onto the back side of their belt over their buttocks. . . . We picked up a poncho and tried to get a fellow onto the poncho. It was not that easy. We picked out the more recently killed that were still whole, but they had already started to turn green. And the skin of the hands was now coming off somewhere around the wrists and it looked as if they were wearing surgical gloves.

"We were stacking these fellows up as neatly as we could, which would be like lining heavy wood onto a pile, logs if you will. We laid down four Marines, then three on top of them, then two, then topped it off with another Marine. So they were pyramid style. And we started to build up quite a few of these piles.

"Then we were getting to where these Marines were not in whole body form. So it was suggested . . . that we put a body onto the litter or poncho that we were using and that it consist of a head, torso, two arms and two legs—and if they didn't match, we would [put them on] anyway and graves registration could sort out the pieces later. And this is what the process now was. We gathered the pieces together and brought them and stacked them up also."

Private First Class Charles Kneller of E Company, 29th Marines was assigned to help gather the dead. "I don't know why, but I seemed to get picked for these details," he recalled. "I was assigned to pick up the bodies of our Company E men, comrades from the front slope of Sugar Loaf Hill . . . It was raining like mad, mud knee deep. The Jap snipers were taking pot shots while we were working—even dropped a couple of mortar shells for excitement. I picked up one of our sergeants, ID unknown, on a stretcher. He had been hit in the neck. I was on the back of the stretcher going down the hill to the waiting amtrac. Due to dropping in the mud when these shells came in, it loosened up the sergeant's head and it came separated while on the stretcher. I dropped everything; the corpsman told me to quit and go back to the amtrac . . . As I climbed up in, [it] was full to the top with bodies. Guess I was too weak for that stuff. I jumped out and decided to walk for those muddy miles." Among the dead he found that day was his own platoon sergeant, still lying face down by the railroad tracks where Easy Company had been caught in its first attack on 17 May.

Ordered to find Major Courtney's remains, a team from H&S Company, 29th Marines located the major's decomposing body on the crest of the hill. They put him on a litter, but he hung over the edge; "he was too long, too tall," remembered one of those involved. "We made the decision to break his legs under him and compact his body so we could run through the enemy shell and machine-gun fire." The major was carried back to the north slope of the hill where they set him apart from the other dead. His remains were ultimately returned to his family in Duluth, Minnesota.

On the battered ground beyond Sugar Loaf sprawled hundreds—maybe thousands—of Japanese dead, the better part of the 15th Independent Mixed Regiment. Private First Class Malcolm Lear was astounded. He had never seen so many dead people in his life. They lay everywhere with no rhyme or reason, arms and legs askew "just like a child's ten pins." It was, he thought in his bitterness toward the enemy, "the prettiest sight in the world."

Other Japanese lay rotting in Sugar Loaf's caves and tunnels. A Marine who ventured inside one of the caves on the back side of Sugar Loaf found three of the enemy lying next to their machine guns. Their uniforms hung from the remains and their skin was "lying almost like a pool, still attached to the skeleton, but in a pool beneath the bodies." The stench in the confined space was beyond description.

"We buried them as best we could," said George Niland of the many dead. "Then it started to rain. Jesus, they'd pop up. You'd walk up and a head would come up and feet and all covered with maggots and the goddamn island stunk like garbage."

The Japanese were covered where they lay or left in the open to rot. The dead Marines were loaded into amtracs and removed to the 6th Marine Division Cemetery for burial. One member of a burial detail found himself riding in the back of an amtrac with 18 or 20 dead Marines. There was three or four inches of water in the bottom of the amtrac and as the vehicle roared up and down the various knolls, the bodies started to tumble back and forth in the slopping water. Clinging to a wire handle, the Marine's screams for help went unheard over the roar of the engine. A wall of corpses and water rolled toward him and he lost his footing. "And at that stage some of the heads were coming off, some of the arms coming off. I was on the bottom of all those guys and they all come on top of me," he recalled in horror. "And I was drowning, drinking into my system, water, maggots, bits of flesh . . . And I was hollering out, 'Enough! Enough! Enough!' And then I blacked out."

Sometime later, apparently recovered, the Marine sat down to eat. "So we had canned ham, canned sweet potatoes, a wonderful meal," he remembered. "But when they opened up the can of tomatoes, immediately I seen those seeds moving around like maggots. I couldn't eat." It would be years before he realized the emotional damage this and other horrors had inflicted on him.

The agony of the division's experience seeped through even the normally dispassionate militarese of IIIAC intelligence evaluation of 23 May. The report observed: "From the onset of the operation the enemy has shown a keen appreciation of terrain and the need for conserving his force. Never before has he had such a diversity of firepower and supporting arms, nor has he utilized his available firepower so effectively. His defense has been elastic and active; he has carefully coordinated his firepower to hold ground in lieu of mere physical occupation; he has organized strong points covering only key terrain features and avenues of approach, siting these strong points in mutually supporting positions; he has not hesitated to launch counterattacks to regain critical terrain and thus maintain the integrity of his defense."

The 22d and 29th Marine Regiments lost nearly 3,000 men killed or seriously wounded. Another 1,289 men were lost to sickness and combat fatigue. Some companies came out of the fighting with only a dozen or so survivors of the 240 men who entered the battle. In two companies, not a single officer or noncom remained.

Ralph Miller, a corpsman with a platoon from C Company, 29th Marines, chronicled the fate of his outfit in his little casualty notebook.

—Gunshot, left knee.

—Gunshot wound stomach (dead).

—Shrapnel in legs.

—Shrapnel in side.

—Shrapnel in head.

—Heat exhaustion.

—Deafness.

—Nuts & yellow.

—Gunshot, left side.

—Shrapnel right hand.

—Kidney trouble.

—Shrapnel in ass.

—Went blind.

—Gunshot dead.

—Gunshot in back.

—Shrapnel, right arm and leg.

—Concussion.

—Dead.

—Broken foot by dud.

—Fractured skull, wound arms, legs back.

—Dead.

The list went on and on. "There was 56 went up, the full platoon, went up Sugar Loaf . . . and eight of us walked off," recalled Miller.

"I lost a real good friend of mine [on Sugar Loaf]," recalled Paul Brennan, a forward observer with the 15th Marines. "He was a radioman, [Private Joseph T.] Cullen from Philadelphia. Tough Irish kid. He always had a cigar in his mouth. He said, 'Hey, they can't kill us Irish.' He thought he was immortal. Another guy, a friend of mine, when I met him down in Tucson years later, he was telling me that after he went in and we pulled out of there, he was standing on something and this other guy came up and says, 'Hey, get the hell off that guy's grave!' He was standing on Cullen's grave."

"We lost a lot of people—I won't say killed, but a lot wounded," noted Private First Class Chris Clemenson of Easy Company, 29th Marines. "After Sugar Loaf, we divided up what we had left and there was a corporal had one platoon, he had 18. I had 17."

Among the survivors in G Company, 29th Marines, was Ross Wilkerson. What remained of his platoon was pulled back to the seawall by the Asa Kawa to recoup. It was a Sunday morning. Wilkerson stood up. "Gosh, what a feeling," he recalled. "This is terrific. I had already forgotten what it felt like to stand straight up. The greatest feeling I ever had in my life was just standing straight up. And I said to the boys around me, 'Hey fellas, stand up! See how it feels.' Everybody got to getting up. I said, 'Boy this is something, isn't it?' We hadn't stood straight up for ten days."

Private First Class Warren Wanamaker, hit on the Horseshoe the night of 18–19 May, found himself aboard a ship bound for Guam. "They pumped me full of penicillin and I think I slept for about 48 hours," he recalled. "I don't remember a hell of a lot about the first couple of days on that ship." It seemed as if a corpsman or some navy personnel was assigned to each Marine casualty. The wounded men had hot showers and clean pajamas. "If you could walk, you could walk to the mess hall—and if you didn't want to, they'd bring the food," said Wanamaker. "I was hurting a little bit, but I still felt like I could walk. And somebody said something about food . . . well, I'd walk a mile for a hamburger. When we got into the mess hall there . . . God, they had roast beef and they had baked ham and they had potatoes and Jesus, I loaded up my tray. I could hardly carry it I had it so full. And I sat down and had about three bites and I couldn't eat any more."

All around him it was the same. The Marines had been living on cigarettes and D-bars so long, they simply couldn't stomach the very food they wanted so desperately to eat.

Easy Company of the 22d Marines had been withdrawn but was still considered in reserve. Of the 244 men they had started with, the company was now at about 25 percent or 30 percent strength.

The Marines were located in a little compound that was the centerpiece of an Okinawan shrine of some sort. They were still under harassing fire from mortars and snipers. Executive Officer John Fitzgerald observed, "it was still a precarious position and psychologically devastating to troops who were about ready to crack anyway." Some medical personnel arrived, recalled Fitzgerald, and they started interviewing survivors. Pretty soon they started tagging people for evacuation. "They had that thousand yard stare," Fitzgerald said of the evacuees. "There seemed to be quite a few, particularly the older men. They [the tags] went to the men who had been on Samoa, Kwajalein, Eniwetok and Guam."

Among those taken out was one of Fitzgerald's most experienced and gallant lieutenants—a man who, on Guam, had bludgeoned three Japanese to death with his rifle and who had been awarded the Silver Star for heroism. Fitzgerald was not completely surprised. Days earlier, clinging to one of the small hills near Sugar Loaf, he and the lieutenant had come under sniper fire. The sniper had put two or three rounds right in front of the lieutenant, who never moved. Fitzgerald kicked at him and tugged on him and urged him to roll over and get under better cover. "And he turned over and looked at me and he didn't know who the hell I was I don't think. At that time. He had that blank stare." Fitzgerald finally managed to grab him and roll him to a small bush and under some cover from the sniper. "He never remembered that or he didn't want to remember that," recalled Fitzgerald of the lieutenant. "He just had enough."

John Eason had also had enough, at least for the time being. He had vague memories of being blown out of a shell hole, but he had been blanking in and out and it was all very unclear. The next thing he knew he was sitting in the back of a halftrack and for some reason he was crying. "I remember I was crying and I was mad about something," he recalled. "That's all I remember. The next thing I knew they had me in the track and I was on my way back and I kept telling them I was okay, but I couldn't figure out what the hell I was crying about.

"I got back in the hospital and I went to bed and the next morning I woke up. There were three doctors standing there beside the bed and they said, 'What's the matter with you?' And I said, 'Nothing' and I sat up and just grabbed my head. I said, 'Oooooh.' It was just like getting kicked by a mule. They looked at my eyes and a couple of things and the next thing I knew I was stashed over in a locked ward." Eason stayed in the ward for a couple of weeks and was then ordered back to K Company.

John Eason, who was probably suffering from the effects of repeated concussion, was one of the lucky ones. Some men simply broke inside.

"You'd be surprised how you'd see some of these big strong husky guys up there on the line, they'd come back crying or something like that," recalled First Sergeant Peter C. Maresh. "I'd have to get them away from the rest of the company so they wouldn't see it. It would break their morale." Maresh kept a list of all the men in his company—G Company, 22d Marines—who had to be evacuated for combat fatigue. On 12 May, the date of G Company's first bloody encounter with Sugar Loaf, 18 men were sent back for combat fatigue; 4 more were sent back on 13 May; 7 on 14 May; and 12 on 17 May. The number then decreased until 1 June when 11 men were sent back. Most subsequently returned to duty.

G Company's experience was not unique. The fighting around Sugar Loaf produced a steady stream of combat fatigue cases in all units. The division psychiatrist approached the problem logically. The general course of action was to allow the patient to retain his self-respect, rest him physically and mentally and return him to his outfit. Rest areas were established behind the front lines where medical personnel could sort the true combat fatigue cases from the malingerers . . . and the salvageable from the unsalvageable. Cases were marked "physically exhausted" to allow the man to retain his dignity. Major Phillips Carleton observed, "The young men, particularly, who suffered from combat fatigue had a strong sense of guilt. The mental breakdown was usually precipitated by physical exhaustion which ended the conflict between fear and conscience."

A day or two of food and rest was often the solution, but not always. And as the fighting continued, the number of cases began to overwhelm the rest camps. By the end of the campaign the 6th Marine Division reported 4,489 "nonbattle" casualties, most of which were combat fatigue/neuropsychiatric disorders.

This was by no means the highest number among the divisions on Okinawa. In XXIV Corps, the 7th Infantry Division reported 4,825 cases; the 27th Infantry Division reported 1,969 cases; the 77th Infantry Division reported 2,100 cases; and the 96th Infantry Division reported 2,817 cases. The 1st Marine Division led with 5,101 reported cases. The high numbers among the Marines were due in large part to the lack of available replacement divisions. Unlike the army's XXIV Corps, the Marines had no divisions in reserve on Okinawa, so they had no way to rotate battle-weary divisions off the line. The constant strain inevitably took its toll.

Overall, Tenth Army reported about half of all combat fatigue cases were treated in divisional installations, the other, more serious cases were treated in field hospitals. Of the latter, 80 percent were returned to duty in ten days—but half of these had to be assigned to noncombat duties. Alarmed by the loss of manpower, the 6th Marine Division decided officers were being overly sympathetic. A new strictness was ordered in an effort to reduce the drain.

But some men would never fight again. A Marine officer recalled a visit to a hospital set up for battle fatigue cases near Chatan some ten miles behind the lines on Okinawa's western coast. The doctor in charge brought in a Marine who had cracked psychologically after a near miss by an enemy mortar shell. The Marine had been engaged in heavy fighting on the southern front, was presumably exhausted, hungry and generally run down, when a mortar shell burst on the edge of his foxhole. Though not hit, the Marine passed out and remained unconscious for some time. When he finally came to, he was completely out of his head and had to be taken to the rear. "Several days later he was still shaking," noted the visiting officer.

The doctors injected the man with "a solution" (probably phenobarbital) to free his inhibitions—almost putting him in a trance state—and the doctors began gently questioning him. When he had finally been brought to the point where the shell had landed, the doctor suddenly hit the wall with his fist and shouted, "Mortar!"

"No actor could have portrayed fear like this man did," recalled the visiting officer. The Marine started gurgling, "Mortar . . . mortar . . . mortar." The doctors asked him what he was going to do now. The Marine replied, "Dig deeper! Dig deeper!" He got on his knees and went through the motions of digging.

The doctor quieted the agitated Marine and put him on a bunk. He asked the Marine if he read the Bible. The Marine said he did. The doctor asked what the Bible said about killing. The Marine said it was forbidden. "What about Japs?" asked the doctor. The Marine gritted his teeth and muttered, "Kill 'em all." The doctor accused the Marine of being a coward. The Marine's hackles rose and he shouted, "I'm not yellow! I want to go back." He repeated this several times.

Recalled the visiting officer, "The patient was then quieted and allowed to leave. The doctor explained that, of course, what we had seen had nothing to do with effecting a cure. It would give the doctors some leads on the basis of which they could continue talking to the man without the benefit of drugs and probably bring him back to normal."

Some men recovered. Some never did. And still the fighting continued.

On Half Moon Hill Private First Class Eugene Sledge huddled in a muddy hole in the never-ending rain. His outfit, K Company of the 5th Marines, had taken position "in this stinking half-flooded garbage pit" on 23 May when the 1st Marine Division extended its right to cover the 6th Marine Division's concentration to the west.

Sledge had been in combat for nearly eight weeks and was suffering from nightmares, or perhaps they were hallucinations—he was never quite sure. The vision was always the same: the dead would rise slowly out of their water-logged craters and stagger aimlessly and desperately around the battlefield. Sledge felt they were asking for his help and was agonized at his own inability to comply.

The muddy cratered ground to the west, toward Sugar Loaf and the Horseshoe, seemed a no man's land. But there was no shortage of dead. Almost directly below Sledge's position on the hill was a partially flooded crater about three feet in diameter. A dead Marine sat in the hole with his back to the enemy. He still wore his helmet and what remained of his face looked directly at Sledge. He looked as if he had just sat down for a rest. His rusting BAR, still clutched in skeletal hands, lay across his knees. The toes of his boondockers stuck out of the muddy water. His helmet cover and gear looked new. Sledge was sure the man was a new replacement killed in the early attacks against Half Moon. He had made it to the hill and died there. Now rain splashed in the puddles around his rotting remains.

Eventually, graves registration teams found their way into the area. "They each were equipped with large rubber gloves and a long pole with a stiff flap attached to the end (like some huge spatula)," recalled Sledge. "They would lay a poncho next to a corpse, then place the poles under the body, and roll it over onto the poncho. It sometimes took several tries, and we winced when a corpse fell apart. The limbs or head had to be shoved onto the poncho like bits of garbage . . . With the corpses being moved, the stench of rotting flesh became worse (if possible) than ever before."

Out in the drizzling rain beyond Sledge's muddy hole, the Japanese were on the move. The 24th Transport Regiment, accustomed to night movement from their experience in Manchuria, used what was left of their wheeled transport to begin evacuation of supplies and the wounded as early as 22 May.

Survivors of the Japanese 62d Division left on 26 May. The remnants of the 44th Independent Mixed Brigade moved out on 28 May, replaced in the line by naval troops. The 24th Division held until the last moments, with some elements still in action on the Shuri Line as late as 30 and 31 May. Weather aided Ushijima. Twelve inches of rain fell during the last ten days of May. Heavy fog and low cloud cover limited both the American advance and American observation. "The result," wrote an historian of the campaign, "was that Buckner's Tenth Army missed a golden opportunity to turn Ushijima's tactical retreat into a rout."

Partial clearing on 26 May provided one of the first indications of a Japanese withdrawal. Observers from the 1st and 5th Marines spotted considerable enemy movement south of Shuri. Lieutenant Colonel John W. Scott, Jr., the 1st Division intelligence officer, requested immediate air observation at 1200. Braving rain and poor visibility, a spotter plane from the battleship *New York* got into the air and reported large numbers of enemy troops and vehicles jamming the roads south of Shuri. Within less than 13 minutes, the cruiser *New Orleans* had opened fire, followed by every artillery piece and mortar within range of the target area. Less than half an hour after the spotter plane's report, 50 Marine fighters took off to strafe and bomb the enemy concentrations—an estimated 3,000–4,000 Japanese with tanks, trucks and artillery pieces caught in the open.

During the night, artillery and naval support ships fired harassing and interdictory fire on the roads and junctions south of Shuri. On 27 May, General Buckner informed IIIAC and XXIV Corps:

Indications point to possible enemy retirement to new defensive position with possible counteroffensive against our forces threatening his flank. Initiate without delay strong and unrelenting pressure to ascertain probable intentions and keep him off balance. Enemy must not repeat not be permitted to establish himself securely on new position with only nominal interference.

Strong combat patrols were sent out all along the front. The patrols encountered stiff resistance, leading intelligence to believe the enemy still held the Shuri defenses in strength. Typical patrol reports noted "No indication of Japanese withdrawal" and "Does not appear that resistance has lessened." The weather closed in again on 29 and 30 May, completely grounding U.S. airpower. Ushijima's staff noted that withdrawal was "proceeding in good order without any signs of confusion due to slackened enemy pressure."

The retreat was not unscathed. Of the 50,000 troops at Shuri, only some 30,000 got out. With about 5,000 designated as the rear guard, this meant Ushijima had lost 15,000 men on the roads south, most to U.S. air and to naval gunfire. Nevertheless, by dawn of 30 May, the bulk of the Japanese Thirty-second Army had slipped away from the Shuri Line, eluding the flanking drives of IIIAC and XXIV Corps. Ushijima's headquarters was established in a cave in a hill outside Mabuni, 11 miles south of Shuri Castle.

The 6th Marine Division pushed into Naha on 27 May and found the city virtually abandoned. On 30 and 31 May, U.S. forces seized the Shuri Line against mixed resistance. Marines and GIs cautiously entered Shuri, finding it in ruins. Japanese corpses lay strewn about, but their equipment was gone. The stench of rotting flesh hung in the air. Shuri Castle, which had taken 10,000 laborers eight years to build, had been ravaged by naval gunfire, the huge stones knocked all atumble like an oversized set of toy blocks. Ushijima was gone.

Major General Lemuel Shepherd gave largest credit to his battered division. "Viewed in its analytical aspects . . . it appears probable that plans for evacuation of the compromised Shuri position were initiated by the enemy upon the loss of Sugar Loaf," he observed.

A jubilant General Buckner declared, "Ushijima missed the boat on his withdrawal from the Shuri Line. It's all over now but cleaning up pockets of resistance. This doesn't mean there won't be stiff fighting, but the Japanese won't be able to organize another line."

He was wrong, but one of the bloodiest encounters of the Pacific War—the battle for Sugar Loaf Hill—was finally over.

Chapter 13

Forgotten Warriors

The fall of the Shuri Line did not mark the end of combat for the 6th Marine Division. Three more weeks of fighting—and dying—remained before organized Japanese resistance finally ended on Okinawa.

On the evening of 21 June, as U.S. forces closed in on his headquarters cave, General Ushijima and his Chief of Staff, General Cho, prepared for death. Ushijima radioed a farewell message to Imperial headquarters. Cho wrote another. "Our strategy tactics and methods were all utilized to the utmost and we fought valiantly, but they had little effect against the superior material strength of the enemy," he wrote.

Shortly after sunrise, on 22 June, Ushijima sat for a last ritual haircut. By noon, the Americans had seized the upper entrance to the cave headquarters. Ushijima opened a can of pineapple—the last food in the cave—and shared it with anyone who passed by. Late in the afternoon, he and Cho kneeled side by side. Cho lowered his head to expose his neck. A fellow officer, a kendo expert, swung his sword to cut off the general's head, but muffed the job as the sword did not go deep enough. A sergeant seized the sword and severed Cho's spinal column. As Ushijima bared his abdomen and cut himself, the sword swung again, decapitating him. Seven of his staff, using their pistols, committed mass suicide.[1]

Only hours before, at Tenth Army Headquarters near Kadena Airfield, the band played the "Star Spangled Banner" and representatives of the U.S. corps and divisions stood at attention as the flag was raised formally signifying the capture of Okinawa. The campaign was declared officially ended on 2 July.

General Buckner did not survive to savor his victory. On 18 June, he had gone forward to watch a fresh unit of Marines from the 2d Marine Division enter the lines. As he watched from the high ground near Mezado Ridge, a Japanese shell exploded nearby, shattering a coral outcropping. A chunk of coral drove into the general's chest. Ten minutes later, he was dead.

He was survived by the controversy over his battle plan. The debate became public with a series of articles by Homer Bigart of the *New York Herald Tribune*, who was highly critical of Buckner for not agreeing to a second amphibious landing behind the Shuri Line. His reports sparked a heated battle in the American press in late May and through June. Editorial writers called Buckner's tactics "ultraconservative," a "fiasco," and "a worse example of military incompetence than Pearl Harbor." Others rose to his defense.

After the end of the campaign, even General Douglas MacArthur weighed in on the controversy. He argued there had been no need to seize southern Okinawa; having pushed Ushijima's divisions into the lower part of the island, U.S. forces had plenty of room for airfields and anchorages to stage for the invasion of Japan, he observed. Ushijima's force would have simply withered on the vine. Any raids they might have made would certainly have cost much less in U.S. casualties than Buckner's head-on approach. But by then, of course, no amount of hindsight was going to change what had already happened.

The Japanese lost approximately 110,000 troops in the Okinawan campaign. The 6th Marine Division claimed to have killed 20,582 Japanese. It also took 3,307 prisoners, most of the latter in the final days of the campaign. (As of 19 May, the 6th Division reported having taken only five regular military prisoners on southern Okinawa.)

By contrast, U.S. forces lost 12,520 GIs, Marines and sailors dead or missing—the highest losses of the Pacific war. Of the combat infantrymen who landed with the 6th Marine Division on 1 April, few remained by the end of the campaign. In the course of the fighting on Motobu, the Asa Kawa, Sugar Loaf Hill, and later on the Oroku Peninsula and Kuwanga Ridge, the division lost 1,656 officers and men killed, 7,429 wounded and 11 missing, not including casualties among Navy corpsmen. These were the highest casualties of any U.S. division at Okinawa.[2]

As was to be expected, the greater share of those losses was borne by the infantry regiments. The 4th Marines led the list with 3,106 casualties from all causes (500 killed, 2,411 wounded, 161 combat fatigue and 4 missing and presumed dead); the 22d Marines took 2,971 casualties (489 killed, 1,975 wounded and 507 combat fatigue cases); and the 29th Marines suffered 2,821 total casualties (551 killed, 2,099 wounded, 166 combat fatigue cases and 5 missing in action).[3]

Among the dead was Lieutenant Colonel Horatio Woodhouse, shot in the head by a sniper on 30 May east of Naha near a nondescript hump in the ground known as Hill 27. The colonel was such a slight man, the corpsman couldn't find a vein in his arm to start the IV. It probably wouldn't have mattered. Grievously wounded, Woodhouse died within moments, mourned by all who knew him.

Also killed was Colonel Harold Roberts, who had replaced Merlin Schneider as commanding officer of the 22d Marines at Sugar Loaf. He was killed in action at Hill 69 on 18 June. Roberts had been up forward watching the advance of the 2d Battalion with his executive officer, Lieutenant Colonel August Larson, and one of his men, Private First Class Nicholas Woloschuk, when a sniper opened fire on them. "Colonel Roberts was the only one hit," recalled Woloschuk, "and at first we thought he'd got it in the left shoulder. He clutched it and said, 'I've been killed.' Colonel Larson and a corpsman helped to move him back a few yards and I ran behind a rock to see if I could spot the sniper. I did, and when he raised his head I fired a few bursts with my tommy gun and got the Jap who hit the Colonel. When I got back to where Colonel Roberts was, he was dying."

Private Declan Klingenhagen was wounded by mortar fragments on 1 June near Naha. He was evacuated to Guam, recovered and rejoined the division on Guam before leaving for officer's training in the United States. Lieutenant Francis X. Smith was badly wounded on 1 June, shot in the abdomen. Dale Bertoli, who with Corporal James Day had defended the shell hole on Sugar Loaf for four days, was shot in the back of the neck on 8 June. He died aboard the USS *Relief* four days later.

When the end finally came, G Company, 22d Marines, the first unit to bloody itself against Sugar Loaf, had 24 of its original complement left. On 21 June, the company was chosen to raise the flag above Okinawa's rugged southern cliffs, officially marking the U.S. victory. Among the four victory flag raisers was Corporal Dan Dereschuk.

Major Henry A. Courtney was posthumously awarded the Medal of Honor for his exploits on Sugar Loaf during the night attack of 14–15 May. He received one of five Medals of Honor awarded the 6th Marine Division men—and the only one presented for the Sugar Loaf action.[4] As might be expected, Courtney's parents took the news of his death hard. That distress may have been deepened by the seeming futility of their son's effort to hold Sugar Loaf. But when they worried that his life may have been wasted, one of Courtney's friends, Major A. B. Overstreet, hastened to reassure them.

"It is certainly a horrible thing to lose so fine a son or in my case a friend as Bob, but I feel that Bob would be the last one to say he had been wastefully expended," he wrote to Major Courtney's mother. "There have been many fine officers and men killed on Okinawa," he added, "and to say that any of them was expended is to say that the goal was not worth while."

In later years, many officers and men would speculate on what prompted Courtney to take charge and to launch his "own banzai attack"—and how much Lieutenant Colonel Woodhouse really knew about what Courtney was doing that night. A career noncom said bluntly, "he should have been back squaring the troops away instead of leading the charge." Others were less cynical. Referring to the great stress of combat, one 2d Battalion Marine later observed, "Oh, I think he might have gone a little wacky, but, you know, that happens. It seems like you'd spend an eternity trying to take a place like Sugar Loaf, watching so many of your buddies getting shot up so badly. Then you think the hell with it and you do something you wouldn't normally do."

Lieutenant John Fitzgerald, who knew Courtney and served in the same battalion, noted that he and many of his colleagues believed Courtney felt "the troops would benefit from seeing a senior officer up forward." This was perhaps especially true after the 2d Battalion took such a beating and lost so many officers on 12 May. "Not showboating," noted Fitzgerald, "but leading and there to help."

General Shepherd offered his own professional assessment of Courtney's action after reviewing the manuscript for the official Marine Corps monograph on Okinawa in the early 1950s. The authors suggested that Courtney led his men up the hill simply to avoid annihilation. Shepherd strongly disagreed. He wrote that Courtney realized that the seizure of the hill "demanded action of individuals rather than the delivery of heavy fires. Courtney, it is clear in retrospect, recognized fully the significance of the hilltop and decided to launch the attack without further directive or instruction from higher authority in order to bring that hill into our possession at a time when it looked like the enemy's hold on it might be wavering. His attack, in other words, was not for the purpose of escaping annihilation—as the manuscript states—but in order to carry out the mission of his command."

Other men were also recognized for their valor in the fight for Sugar Loaf. Jim Chaisson received the Navy Cross for his heroism rescuing wounded Marines on 12 May. Lieutenant Dale Bair, severely wounded in the same action, also received the Navy Cross. Lieutenant Ed Ruess's Navy Cross was awarded posthumously. James Day received a Bronze Star for his shell hole stand with MacDonald and Bertoli from 12–16 May. He couldn't help but notice that his buddy Private First Class Dale Bertoli, now dead, hadn't received an award of any kind.

Sixteen-year-old Donald Kelly received the Navy Cross for sticking to his machine gun despite his wounds the night of 14–15 May. Kelly, who received four Purple Hearts before the campaign was over, received his Navy Cross in a ceremony at Washington, D.C. shortly after a five-day stint in the brig for punching a sergeant. "Then when I got out of the brig I was told to report to the mess hall at 100 hours in full dress," he recalled. "And everybody was looking at me and I was wondering what the hell are they looking at? I did my five days. When I got there, everybody was dressed and there was some officers there, colonels and such. So I went around and got in one of the aisles; they called my name front and center, they read off the citation. Hell, I was as shocked as anybody."

Lieutenant Colonel William G. Robb, commanding officer of the 2d Battalion, 29th Marines, also received a Navy Cross for his "inspiring leadership, perseverance and personal courage" in the final capture of Sugar Loaf on 17–18 May. An enlisted man in his battalion remembered standing at attention as Robb was presented his decoration. "If he was any kind of man, he would have handed it to Mabie," remarked a Marine, still partisan 50 years later. Captain Mabie, the D Company commander who came up with and executed the final flanking movement on Sugar Loaf, received the Silver Star. Lieutenant Francis "Bobby Sox" Smith was also awarded the Silver Star.

There were others—equally deserving or more so—who received no recognition. Perhaps Corporal James White put it best when he remarked, "The Marine Corps didn't give out many medals in World War II (except for Purple Hearts, and we all seemed to get one of those); but every time you climbed out of your foxhole and went forward when the man said, 'Let's go,' you deserved a medal."

The 6th Marine Division was later honored with a Presidential Unit Citation, the highest unit award conferred by the United States, for its actions on Okinawa. All three infantry regiments and certain supporting units were also recognized. The 22d Marines was cited for the drive across the Asa Estuary from 10 May through 1 June, a drive that included the initial fighting for Sugar Loaf Hill. The 29th Marines was cited for their capture of Sugar Loaf Hill on 14–19 May. The 4th Marines was cited for the assault on Oroku Peninsula from 4–16 June, following the battle for Sugar Loaf.

Marine infantry won the day at Sugar Loaf. More specifically, it was the small units, the depleted platoons, the squads, the fire teams. As officers and senior noncoms became casualties, the burden fell on the small unit leaders to keep the remnants together and continue to carry the fight to the enemy.

Statistical studies of Marine operations in the Pacific during World War II indicate that the proportion of officers wounded was almost exactly equal to the proportion of enlisted men wounded. The proportion of officers killed was slightly higher. The average loss of officers in the fighting around Sugar Loaf averaged 60 to 75 percent. Three battalion commanders were wounded or killed; 11 out of 18 company commanders in the 22d and 29th Marines were killed or wounded. Of the original lieutenants, only a handful remained. Years later, James Day, by then a Marine Corps major general, observed, "I think if you took a classical situation and took a real good look at it and said, 'Hey, our NCOs have to take over when the officers fall,' then Sugar Loaf would be that classical situation. I give these young men more credit than probably any other single phase or single factor in the battle."

It was true. But it was hard to feel much elation or even satisfaction at the time. Homer Noble remembered how a colonel walked down the thin line of survivors after the battle shaking hands with the exhausted men. One Marine failed to extend his hand. "I don't deserve any commendation," the youngster mumbled bitterly. "I took the worst licking of my life and never even got one of them in my sights."

Weeks after Sugar Loaf receded to the backwaters of the war, the litter of battle remained strewn on the torn and battered hill. Knocked-out amtracs still dotted the approaches to the Japanese strong point; helmets, discarded ammunition, papers and other assorted rubbish littered the ground.

Marine combat correspondent Corporal T. Vincent Mullahy accompanied a small group of men from the 22d Marines on a visit to the deserted hill. "The hill was deafening in its stillness," he recalled. "Dust rose into the hot sun for a brief moment, spiraled above empty foxholes and settled gently to earth again. . . . A helmet, torn by bullets and shrapnel, rocked in the breeze, a pathetic thing lying beside a shattered rifle and an open ammunition box."

A Marine bent to examine the relic and noticed something white. It was a greeting card, tucked into the helmet liner. The gay, colorful letters proclaimed "Happy Easter to My Dear Son." The visitors picked their way past broken weapons, grenades half buried in the dirt, ration cans and discarded utensils, looking into empty foxholes. Here and there lay the rotted bodies of Japanese, some still clutching grenades in skeletal hands. Another hole contained a dirty old poncho and a ripped leather bag spilling its contents: a shaving brush, razor, toothbrush, letters stained and streaked by rain but still legible.

The place looked like nothing so much as a garbage dump. But to the Marines, observed Mullahy, this "was hallowed ground."

Okinawa, July 4—(Associated Press)—The Sixth Marine Division dedicated a cemetery on Okinawa today near where they stormed ashore Easter Sunday.

There are 1697 graves in it—including 91 Navy men, 11 Army and 55 unidentified who fell in the Marine sector.

The men, regardless of their service, were buried side by side and each grave is marked by a newly painted white cross.

The Red Cross received a shipment of American flags in time to place one on each American grave on Okinawa.

One hundred and one days after the landing on Okinawa, the bulk of the 6th Marine Division boarded ships at Naha for the return to Guam. There, located in a newly built camp on the high ground overlooking Pago Bay in the southeast corner of the island, the division began to relax and refit.

There were lessons to be learned from their experiences on Okinawa. Suggestions from various units included less delay between the request for air support and its delivery; more emphasis on the principal of fire and movement and the selection of covered routes of approach; better training in map reading; and better fire discipline. One battalion noted bluntly, "Insufficient men are trained as flame thrower operators, bazooka men, rifle anti-tank grenadiers and in the use of demolitions."

There were other reminders of Sugar Loaf as well. One morning Private First Class Bill Pierce's outfit was driven out to a group of long quonset huts in the pier area. The Marines were told to load seabags—the Marine equivalent of duffle bags—onto the trucks and then get back on the trucks with the bags. "We thought we were going to some ship, but the convoy of trucks was heading up the winding coast road to the interior jungles," recalled Pierce. "We came to a clearing and the trucks were backed into a huge fire burning in the center of the clearing. Sea bags had been thrown or piled in the clearing and had been set on fire!"

The Marines were told to throw the locked bags onto the fire. They watched as Guamanians, some draped only in wet sheets, used long sticks to try to salvage a blanket, shoes or whatever they could get. "We headed back, went to the mess hall for lunch, and then got an idea," said Pierce. "We hit our tents and grabbed our K-bar knives and hid them under our clothing. The next load we slit the bags open while on the truck. We poured over letters, pictures, clothing, shoes, you name it! I grabbed a good pair of cordovan shoes, my size, and stuffed them in a corner. Some found watches, money, jewelry."

Later they found out the hundreds and hundreds of sea bags belonged to Marines killed on Okinawa.

The 6th Marine Division was still on Guam preparing for the invasion of Japan when the atomic bombs were dropped on Hiroshima and Nagasaki and the war suddenly ended. The 4th Marine Regiment went to Japan. The rest of the division was sent to North China. On April 1, 1946, the 6th Marine Division was inactivated—the only Marine division to be formed overseas and demobilized overseas, never seeing duty in the United States during the 19 months of its existence.

For the most part, its men returned home to find that few people knew much—or seemed to care—about what had happened at Sugar Loaf. One notable exception was Lieutenant Frank Smith, whose Woodside, New York, neighborhood greeted him with a huge block party complete with homemade confetti and a banner proclaiming, "Welcome Home, Bobby Sox Smith, Hero of Sugar Loaf, Okinawa."

Sadly, the experience of most returning Marines was more like that of Sergeant William Manchester, who served with the 29th Marines. Manchester, who survived serious wounds and went on to become a famous author, later mused, "It was rather diminishing to return in 1945 and discover that your own parents couldn't even pronounce the names of the islands you had conquered."

Under other circumstances, Sugar Loaf Hill might have become as famous a name as Tarawa or Iwo Jima. Instead, circumstances conspired to relegate it almost to the footnotes of World War II. The fighting there—and at other bloody hills and ridges on Okinawa—was consistently pushed to the back pages by other events: the death of President Franklin D. Roosevelt on 12 April; the surrender of Germany on 8 May; the incredible news of the atomic bomb; and finally, the end of the war itself.

America wanted to forget about the war. It was time to enjoy the peace. And so, the men who fought at Sugar Loaf hung up their uniforms and got on with their lives. But they would never be the same. In later years, at division reunions, a survey of the hotel pool would show hardly a one who did not have a scar or a piece missing from his back or a missing arm or a leg. Some carried so much metal in their bodies, as aging men they set off metal detectors at airports. All carried the memories of Sugar Loaf, though often those memories remained intensely private. "I'm really at a loss for words," observed former rifleman James Miller when asked about the battle nearly 50 years later. "You know, nobody ever asked me this question before and I never tried to answer it. I've thought about it a million times, but it didn't seem very important to anybody else but me, anyway."

Some were almost physically unable to talk about what they had seen and endured. "For years after that I could not talk to anybody about my experiences without taking the shakes," admitted Charles Pugh. "It was almost as if I had taken a chill." Another veteran, a senior noncom who fought bravely throughout the campaign, suffered a nervous breakdown after leaving the service. "It lasted five years," he recalled. "I used to do a lot of funny things at night." One night he woke up and found he was strangling his wife. He obtained medical help and finally pulled himself together, but subsequently found he remembered very little about the war.

He was not alone. Many other veterans remained troubled by their experiences. One Marine, who spent the years after the war fighting alcoholism and severe depression, did not realize until he entered therapy some 40 years later that his combat experiences were the root of his problems. Through all these years, he conceded later, "I've always had the feeling. . . . I could sit on a park bench by myself and eventually cause chaos." A former Marine lieutenant, observing an interview of some Sugar Loaf veterans almost 50 years later, noticed that time still had not entirely dulled the horror of their experience; "there was almost a bent of hysteria that was seeping into their question and answer thing," he remarked.

Others found their experiences seemed unreal, much like a bad dream only half remembered. "You know you just wonder how you got through all that, but we did . . . some of us," observed a survivor. There was also fierce pride. Floyd Enman, who spent a night alone behind a machine gun on top of Sugar Loaf, observed, "There's one thing about the Marine Corps . . . I mean, regardless of life or anything . . . we got what we went after."

Some have become philosophical, even forgiving. In 1987 a group of veterans returned to Okinawa to dedicate a monument to all who fell, both Japanese and Americans. Edward L. Fox spearheaded the Okinawa Memorial Shrine Committee and campaigned avidly for the memorial. Those who supported the memorial dedicated to both sides felt it was time to put the bitterness of the war behind them.

Others took a less rosy view and support for Fox's project was far from unanimous. "To this day I haven't had a Japanese car in my garage," observed one Marine survivor of Sugar Loaf. "They say you're supposed to forgive and forget? I can't do it. I still hate them as much today as I did then. They were vicious. The only regret they have is that they didn't win."

"If I could go back *free* I wouldn't go," added Irv Gehret of the old battlefield. "There's nothing there I want to see. Even my buddies' graves aren't there any more."

The remote spots men died for 50 years ago are now—preposterously—covered with McDonald's hamburger franchises, Dairy Queens, Kentucky Fried Chicken outlets, pawn shops and used car lots. Naha was rebuilt on the ruins; today swarms of Toyotas and Hondas crowd its streets. Shuri Castle is the site of the University of the Ryukyus. To the south, General Ushijima's last command post has become a popular tourist attraction among the Japanese. The Okinawans themselves refer to the Japanese and themselves as "we." The Americans are more coolly dismissed as "them." Those of "them" who fought on the island in 1945 mostly stare in slack-jawed wonder at the place it has become today.

Urban sprawl from a growing Naha has engulfed the Horseshoe to the south of Sugar Loaf and Half Moon to the east. The narrow gauge railroad that once ran north-south between Sugar Loaf and Naha was torn out long ago and replaced with a very busy four-lane highway, which follows the old rail line almost exactly. Sometime after the war the top of Sugar Loaf was bulldozed flat to accommodate a water tank serving a large U.S. military neighborhood of cinder block homes. In the mid-1980s this development was abandoned, torn down and the land returned to the city of Naha. More bulldozing of the hill was done to facilitate removal of the water tank. Nevertheless, relic hunters going over the site with metal detectors continued to find thousands of pieces of shell fragments in every conceivable shape and size, from jagged pieces a foot long to pieces the size of slivers. Spent 30–06 slugs, fuse assemblies from shells, dud grenades, and an occasional clip of bullets for Marine M1 rifles were turned up, along with metal squares from exploded U.S. grenades.

In 1993 the Okinawans began work to develop the area. Bulldozers working around Sugar Loaf unearthed human remains, old canteens, rusted ordnance and other bits and pieces of equipment. Plans were made by the Okinawan prefectural government to erect another water tank on Sugar Loaf and considerable excavation was done. At that point an Okinawan artist, Seicho Gushiken, came forward with a suggestion for a park-like setting for a peace monument and history display at Sugar Loaf Hill. He founded the Sugar Loaf Peace Memorial Park/Water Pond Friendship Association to persuade the prefectural government that the memorial park would be an asset to the city. "There is no peace monument in the city of Naha," he said. Every people must know their own history—Okinawans must know what happened here." The 6th Marine Division Association supported Gushiken's efforts and in 1994, the idea for the park was approved by the city.

It is an acknowledgement somewhat late in coming to the men who survived the fighting at Sugar Loaf. Time and age have thinned their ranks.

The stubborn young Marines who refused to quit and took the best the Japanese could throw at them are now senior citizens. Many of them gather each year for the 6th Marine Division Association reunion. Every division newsletter contains a roster of men who have passed on in previous months—not in the maelstrom of battle, but peacefully in bed. The lists have grown longer in recent years. But neither time—nor even death itself—can sever the blood bonds between the men who fought at Sugar Loaf.

A simple, almost innocuous story: One rainy day during the fighting near Sugar Loaf, a visiting officer gave a mud-covered Corporal James Day a lemon pie. Day took this unimaginable treasure and carefully divided it among his squad, a tiny fragment for each man. It is a small thing, perhaps, but in it, for those who understand, lies the heart and soul of the combat Marine.

Semper Fidelis.

> We few, we happy few, we band of brothers;
> For he to-day that sheds his blood with me
> Shall be my brother.
> —Shakespeare, *Henry V*

NOTES

1. There are differing versions of Ushijima's death. This account is based on John Toland's research.

2. The 1st Marine Division suffered 1,254 killed and 6,405 wounded. The U.S. Army official history of the campaign lists the following casualties among Army divisions: 7th Division, 1,122 killed, 4,943 wounded and 3 missing; 27th Division, 711 killed, 2,520 wounded and 24 missing; 77th Division, 1,018 killed, 3,968 wounded and 40 missing; 96th Division, 1,506 killed, 5,912 wounded and 12 missing. By way of comparison, on Iwo Jima the 5th Marine Division suffered 9,925 casualties, including 2,884 killed, and the 4th Marine Division lost 8,157, including 2,006 killed.

3. It has been widely reported that the 29th Marines suffered the highest rate of casualties of any Marine Corps regiment in one battle, losing 2,821 out of its formally authorized strength of 3,512 over 82 days at Okinawa. A study of final casualty figures compiled by Statistics Unit, Personnel Accounting Section, Personnel Department, Headquarters Marine Corps, indicates that this claim is incorrect. However, the regiment's number of dead—551—does appear to be the highest of any single battle.

4. Other winners were: Private Robert M. McTureous, 29th Marines, posthumously for actions on 7 June; Corporal Richard E. Bush, 4th Marines, for actions on 16 April; Private First Class Harold Gonsalves, 15th Marines, posthumously, for actions on 15 April; Hospital Apprentice First Class Fred F. Lester, 22d Marines, posthumously for actions on 8 June.

Sources

INTERVIEWS

The following provided interviews, written memoirs or other material for this book.

Lt. Howard Berrian—K Company, 4th Marines

Cpl. Arthur Bishop—L Company, 22d Marines

Cpl. Paul Brennan—D Battery, 15th Marines

Cpl. David C. Butler—Headquarters Company, 29th Marines

1st Lt. Joseph Bystry, Jr.—F Company, 22d Marines

Pfc. Joseph L. Campanella—G Company, 22d Marines

Pfc. James Chaisson—G Company, 22d Marines

Pfc. Angelo D. Cifarelli—G Company, 22d Marines

Pfc. Chris Clemenson—E Company, 29th Marines

Lt. Arthur Cofer—I Company, 22d Marines

Cpl. Lail Conner—B Company, 6th Tank Battalion

Pfc. Joseph Cormier—D Company, 29th Marines

Pfc. Daniel F. Creedon—A Company, 29th Marines

Pvt. Frederick Cross—A Company, 29th Marines

Cpl. Tom Crunk—K Battery, 15th Marines

Cpl. Earl H. Curnutte—D Company, 29th Marines

Sgt. Arthur Davis—E Company, 22d Marines

Cpl. James Day—Weapons Company, 22d Marines

Platoon Sgt. Ed DeMar—G Company, 22d Marines

Pfc. Paolo DeMeis—K Company, 4th Marines

Pfc. Jim Denny—E Company, 29th Marines

Cpl. Dan Dereschuk—G Company, 22d Marines

Pfc. John Eason—K Company, 4th Marines

Pfc. Floyd Enman—K Company, 22d Marines

Cpl. Robert E. Everett—A Company, 29th Marines

Sgt. Robert E. Fair—A Company, 29th Marines

Lt. John P. Fitzgerald—E Company, 22d Marines

Lt. Eugene Folks—2d Battalion, 29th Marines

Pvt. Edward L. Fox—G Company, 22d Marines

Pfc. Irv Gehret—D Company, 29th Marines

Sgt. Ray Gillespie—K Company, 22d Marines

Lt. Frank E. Gunter—E Company, 22d Marines

Platoon Sgt. Frank Habern—G Company, 22d Marines

Pfc. James Hart—H&S Company, 22d Marines

Cpl. Melvin Heckt—B Company, 4th Marines

Pvt. Donald Honis—I Company, 29th Marines

Cpl. Charles Horvath—D Company, 29th Marines

Pfc. Jack Houston—G Company, 22d Marines

Lt. Walter R. Jamieson—F Company, 22d Marines

Pvt. Donald J. Kelly—F Company, 22d Marines

Pvt. Declan Klingenhagen—D Company, 29th Marines

Lt. Col. Victor H. Krulak—6th Marine Division

Pfc. Malcolm Lear—L Company, 22d Marines

Pfc. W. R. Lightfoot—D Company, 29th Marines

Pvt. Ken Long—I Company, 29th Marines

Pvt. Donald R. Mahoney—G Company, 29th Marines

Pvt. Wendell K. Majors—G Company, 22d Marines

Pfc. Ronald A. Manson—C Company, 29th Marines

First Sgt. Peter C. Maresh—G Company, 22d Marines

Pfc. Frederick McGowan—F Company, 22d Marines

Pfc. Thomas McKinney—F Company, 4th Marines

Cpl. Joe McNamara—K Company, 4th Marines

Cpl. Al Meade—A Company, 29th Marines

Sgt. Al Merritt—G Company, 22d Marines

Pfc. Cliff Mezo—G Company, 22d Marines

Pfc. James G. Miller—K Company, 4th Marines

Phm. 3/C Ralph Miller—29th Marines

Pfc. Glenn F. Moore—2d Battalion, 29th Marines

Capt. Phil Morell—A Company, 6th Tank Battalion

Lt. Hugh R. Morris—A Company, 29th Marines

Pfc. George Niland—L Company, 22d Marines

Pfc. Homer Noble—E Company, 29th Marines

Pfc. Jack Nuckols—K Company, 22d Marines

Pfc. Landon E. Oakes—Weapons Company, 22d Marines

Sgt. Irving Ortel—G Company, 22d Marines

Cpl. John D. Oudsteyn, Sr.—B Company, 29th Marines

Pfc. Leon Paice—F Company, 22d Marines

Lt. Edward Pesely—F Company, 22d Marines

S/Sgt. James D. Phillips—A Company, 29th Marines

Cpl. William T. Pierce—Weapons Company, 29th Marines

Cpl. Robert A. Powers—K Company, 4th Marines

Pfc. Ben H. Prophitt—H Company, 29th Marines

Pfc. Charles Pugh—K Company, 22d Marines

Pvt. J. A. Ranne, Jr.—A Company, 29th Marines

Pfc. D. C. Rigby—H&S Company, 22d Marines

Pfc. Robert Rooney—H&S Company, 29th Marines

Cpl. Walter B. Rutkowski—G Company, 22d Marines

Pfc. Ray Schlinder—K Company, 22d Marines

Pfc. William N. Scott—K Company, 4th Marines

Capt. Martin Sexton—K Company, 4th Marines

Lt. Francis X. Smith—D Company, 29th Marines

Pvt. Edward J. Soja—G Company, 29th Marines

Capt. Owen Stebbins—G Company, 22d Marines

1st Sgt. Robert E. Stevens—I Company, 22d Marines

Pfc. Harold Tayler—C Company, 29th Marines

Cpl. Charles E. Trofka—K Company, 22d Marines

Pfc. Paul Ulrich—L Company, 4th Marines

Pfc. Stuart Upchurch—B Company, 4th Marines

Lt/jg. Charles A. Veatch—3d Battalion, 4th Marines

Pfc. Warren R. Wanamaker—F Company, 29th Marines

Cpl. James S. White—G Company, 29th Marines

Pvt. H. Ross Wilkerson—G Company, 29th Marines

Lt. Buenos A. W. Young—3d Battalion, 22d Marines

Lt. Perry Zemlicka—G Company, 29th Marines

Mrs. J. L. Courtney Bean

Mr. David Davenport—Battle of Okinawa Historical Society

UNPUBLISHED

Beans, Fred D., Brig. Gen. USMC (Ret.), interview, 1971 (Oral History Collection, Marine Corps Historical Center, Washington, D.C.).

Heckt, Melvin. *Pacific Diary*. Diary of Heckt's experiences with B Company, 4th Marines.

Larson, August, Maj. Gen. USMC (Ret.), interview, 1970 (Oral History Collection, Marine Corps Historical Center, Washington, D.C.).

Loomis, Francis Butler, Jr., Maj. Gen. USMC (Ret.), interview, 1970 (Oral History Collection, Marine Corps Historical Center, Washington, D.C.).

Luckey, Robert B., Lt. Gen. USMC (Ret.), interview, 1969 (Oral History Collection, Marine Corps Historical Center, Washington, D.C.).

McQueen, John Crawford, Lt. Gen. USMC (Ret.), interview, 1969 (Oral History Collection, Marine Corps Historical Center, Washington, D.C.).

Pierce, William. "Brotherhood and Semper Fi! . . . Discipline and Duty." Typescript account of experiences with Weapons Company, 22d Marines.

Shapley, Alan, Lt. Gen. USMC (Ret.), interview, 1971 (Oral History Collection, Marine Corps Historical Center, Washington, D.C.).

Shepherd, Lemuel Cornick, Jr., Gen. USMC (Ret.), interview, 1967 (Oral History Collection, Marine Corps Historical Center, Washington, D.C.).

Shilling, Alan I., and Ben Price. *The Sixth Marine Division on Okinawa*. National Archives. Record Group 127, Box 39, 65–A-5188.

Silverthorne, Merwin H., Lt. Gen. USMC (Ret.), interview, 1969 (Oral History Collection, Marine Corps Historical Center, Washington, D.C.).

Smith, Oliver P., Gen. USMC (Ret.), interview, 1969 (Oral History Collection, Marine Corps Historical Center, Washington, D.C.).

Thomas, Gerald C., Gen. USMC (Ret.), interview, 1969 (Oral History Collection, Marine Corps Historical Center, Washington, D.C.).

Thompson, George, Lt. "82 Days of Hell and Glory." (Author's experiences with the 6th Marine Division.)

White, James S. "On the Point of the Spear." (Author's experiences with G Co., 29th Marines).

DOCUMENTS

Note on documents: Special action reports, unit logs and other material on IIIAC and the 6th Marine Division are on file at National Archives in Suitland, Maryland. The 6th Marine Division material, which is housed in a variety of cardboard boxes, is poorly organized and some reports appear to be missing or misfiled. Nevertheless, there is much of interest to the researcher patient enough to look. The comment and letter file compiled during the writing of the Marine Corps monograph on the campaign contains some interesting observations by 6th Marine Division officers. Unit logs and war diaries were also illuminating, particularly sections pertaining to 2/22's attack on 14 May and D/2/29's actions on 15 May. Space precludes a listing of all the documents examined. Some of the more important material consulted appears below:

Tenth Army Action Report, Ryukyus Campaign, 26 March–30 June 1945.

III Amphibious Corps Action Report, Ryukyus Operations, 1 July 1945.

III Amphibious Corps G-2 Periodic Reports, 1 April–30 June 1945.

6th Marine Division Special Action Report, Okinawa Operation, Phase III (including separate annexes for regiments and most battalions).

6th Marine Division Unit Journal, Okinawa Operation, Phase III, 23 April–30 June 1945.

6th Marine Division G-2 Summary, Okinawa Shima, 1 August 1945.

6th Marine Division G-2 Periodic Reports, 28 April–31 May 1945.

BOOKS

Appleman, Roy E., James M. Burns, Russell A. Gugler, and John Stevens. *Okinawa: The Last Battle*. Historical Division, U.S. Department of the Army, *The United States Army in World War II: The War in the Pacific*, Vol. I. Washington, D.C.: Government Printing Office, 1948.

Asprey, Robert B. *Once A Marine*. New York: W. W. Norton & Co., 1964.

Belote, James H. and William M. Belote. *Typhoon of Steel*. New York: Harper & Row, 1970.

Berry, Henry. *Semper Fi, Mac*. New York: Arbor House, 1982.

Blakeney, Jane. *Heroes, U.S. Marine Corps 1861–1955*. Washington, D.C.: privately published, 1957.

Bradley, John H., and Jack W. Dice. *The Second World War: Asia and the Pacific*. West Point, N.Y.: Department of History, U.S. Military Academy, 1979.

Carleton, Phillips D. *The Conquest of Okinawa: An Account of the Sixth Marine Division*. Washington, D.C.: Headquarters, U.S. Marine Corps, 1946.

Cass, Bevan G. *History of the Sixth Marine Division*. Washington, D.C.: Infantry Journal Press, 1948.

Condit, Kenneth W., and Edwin T. Turnbladh. *Hold High the Torch: A History of the 4th Marines*. Nashville, Tenn.: The Battery Press, 1989.

Davidson, Orlando R. *The Deadeyes: The Story of the 96th Infantry Division*. Washington, D.C.: Infantry Journal Press, 1947.

Dyer, Vice Admiral George C. *The Amphibians Came to Conquer*. Washington, D.C.: GPO, 1969.

Feifer, George. *Tennozan*. New York: Ticknor & Fields, 1992.

Frank, Benis M. *Okinawa: The Great Island Battle*. New York: Elsevier-Dutton, 1978.

Frank, Benis M. *Okinawa: Touchstone to Victory*. New York: Ballantine Books, 1969.

Frank, Benis M., and Henry I. Shaw, Jr. *Victory and Occupation: History of Marine Corps Operations in World War II*. Vol. V. Historical Branch, G-3 Division, Headquarters, U.S. Marine Corps. Washington, D.C.: U.S. GPO, 1968.

Gillespie, Raymond. *The K Company Marines: 3rd Battalion—22d Regiment*. Privately printed, 1992.

Gow, Ian. *Okinawa 1945 Gateway to Japan*. Garden City, N.Y.: Doubleday and Co., Inc., 1985.

Hough, Frank O. *The Island War*. Philadelphia: J. P. Lippincott Company, 1947.

Isely, Jeter A., and Philip A. Crowl. *The U.S. Marines and Amphibious War*. Princeton, N.J.: Princeton University Press, 1951.

Karig, Walter. *Battle Report: Victory in the Pacific*. New York: Rinehart & Co., 1949.

Leckie, Robert. *Strong Men Armed: The United States Marines Against Japan*. New York: Random House, 1962.

Long, Kenneth J., ed., *Okinawa 1945*. 4 vols. n.d. privately printed by author.

Love, Edmund G. *The 27th Infantry Division in World War II*. Washington, D.C.: Infantry Journal Press, 1949.

Manchester, William. *Goodbye Darkness*. Boston: Little, Brown & Co., 1979.

McMillan, George. *The Old Breed: A History of the First Marine Division in World War II*. Washington, D.C.: Infantry Journal Press, 1949.

Morrison, Samuel Eliot. *Victory in the Pacific*. Boston: Little, Brown & Co., 1960.

Myers, Max, ed. *Ours to Hold High: The History of the 77th Infantry Division in World War II*. Washington, D.C.: Infantry Journal Press, 1947.

Nichols, Charles S., Jr., and Henry I. Shaw, Jr. *Okinawa: Victory in the Pacific*. Washington, D.C.: Historical Branch, U.S. Marine Corps, 1955.

O'Sheel, P. *Semper Fidelis: The U.S. Marines in the Pacific, 1942–1945*. New York: William Sloane Associates, 1947.

Potter, E. B. *Nimitz*. Annapolis, Md.: Naval Institute Press, 1976.

Pratt, Fletcher. *The Marines' War*. New York: William Sloane Associates, 1948.

Schuon, Karl. *The Leathernecks*. New York: Franklin Watts, Inc., 1963.

———. *U.S. Marine Corps Biographical Dictionary*. New York: Franklin Watts, Inc., 1963.

Sherrod, Robert. *On to the Westward*. New York: Duell, Sloan and Pearce, 1945.

Sixth Marine Division Association. *Sixth Marine Division: The Striking Sixth*. Paducah, Ky.: 1987.

Sledge, E. B. *With the Old Breed at Peleliu and Okinawa*. Novato, Calif.: Presidio, 1980.

Smith, S. E., ed. *The United States Marine Corps in World War II*. New York: Random House, 1969.

Toland, John. *The Rising Sun*. New York: Random House, 1970.

Wheeler, Keith. *The Road to Tokyo*. Alexandria, Va.: Time Life Books, 1979.

Wheeler, Richard. *A Special Valor: The U.S. Marines and the Pacific War*. New York: Harper & Row, 1983.

Willock, Roger. *Unaccustomed to Fear: A Biography of the Late General Roy S. Geiger, USMC*. Princeton, N.J.: Privately printed, 1968.

———. *Uncommon Valor: Marine Divisions in Action*. Washington, D.C.: Infantry Journal Press, 1946.

PERIODICALS

Bartlett, Tom. "The Striking 6th." *Leatherneck*, December 1976.

———. "Giants of the Corps." *Leatherneck*, December 1976.

———. "The Overseas Sixth." *Leatherneck*, December 1976.

Luedke, Sgt. Charles H. "WWII Veterans Tour Former Battlegrounds." *Okinawa Marine*, April 13, 1990.

Manchester, William. "The Bloodiest Battle of All." *New York Times Magazine*, June 14, 1987.

Myers, Ralph. "Key to the Castle." *Leatherneck*, December 1945.

Pound, Kate. "Return to Okinawa." *Pacific Stars & Stripes*, April 29, 1990.

Sixth Marine Division Association. *Striking Sixth Newsletter*, (various).

Stebbins, Lt. Col. Owen T. "A Maneuver That Might Have . . ." *Marine Corps Gazette*, June 1995.

———. "Must Seize at Any Cost." *World War II*, September 1995.

———. "Rifle Company vs Fortress." *Marine Corps Gazette*, April 1973.

Stockman, Capt. James R. "The Sixth Division." *Leatherneck*, December 1945.

Taylor, Blaine. "Final Island Assault." *Military History, June 1987.*

Upchurch, C. Stuart. "Two Days on Okinawa, 1945." *Military*, May, June, July 1993.

Index

About the Author

JAMES H. HALLAS is publisher of the *Glastonbury Citizen*, a newspaper in Glastonbury, Connecticut. He has published articles in *American History Illustrated* and *Yankee Magazine*. He has written two books, *Squandered Victory: The American First Army at St. Mihiel* (Praeger, 1995) and *Devil's Anvil: The Assault on Peleliu* (Praeger, 1994).